Software Quality Assurance

A practical approach

Ernest Wallmüller

Translated by Helga Tallon and John Hopkinson

Carl Hanser Verlag

Prentice Hall

Software-Qualitätssicherung was first published in German
by Carl Hanser Verlag München Wien
© 1990 Carl Hanser Verlag

First published in English in 1994 by
Prentice Hall International (UK) Ltd
Campus 400, Maylands Avenue
Hemel Hempstead
Hertfordshire, HP2 7EZ
A division of
Simon & Schuster International Group

© Prentice Hall International (UK) Ltd, 1994

Typeset in 10/12 pt Times
by MHL Typesetting Ltd., Coventry

Printed and bound in Great Britain by
T.J. Press (Padstow) Ltd, Padstow, Cornwall.

Library of Congress Cataloging-in-Publication Data

Wallmüller, Ernest.
   [Software-Qualitätssicherung in der Praxis. English]
   Software quality assurance: a practical approach / Ernest
Wallmüller.
      p. cm. — (BCS practitioner series)
   Translation of: Software-Qualitätssicherung in der Praxis
   Includes bibliographical references and index.
   ISBN 0-13-819780-6
   1. Computer software—Quality control. I. Title. II. Series.
QA76.76.Q35W3513 1994
005.1′068′5—dc20

                                     94-1831
                                      CIP

British Library Cataloguing in Publication Data

A catalogue record for this book is available from
the British Library

ISBN 0-13-819780-6

1 2 3 4 5   98 97 96 95 94

Contents

Editorial preface

The aim of the BCS Practitioner Series is to produce books which are relevant for practising computer professionals across the whole spectrum of Information Technology activities. We want to encourage practitioners to share their practical experience of methods and applications with fellow professionals. We also seek to disseminate information in a form which is suitable for the practitioner who often has only limited time to read widely within a new subject area or to assimilate research findings.

The role of the BCS is to provide advice on the suitability of books for the Series, via the Editorial Panel, and to provide a pool of potential authors upon which we can draw. Our objective is that this Series will reinforce the drive within the BCS to increase professional standards in IT. The other partners in this venture, Prentice Hall, provide the publishing expertise and international marketing capabilities of a leading publisher in the computing field.

The response when we set up the Series was extremely encouraging. However, the success of the Series depends on there being practitioners who want to learn as well as those who feel they have something to offer! The Series is under continual development and we are always looking for ideas for new topics and feedback on how to further improve the usefulness of the Series. If you are interested in writing for the Series then please contact us.

Software quality assurance is an important topic for all professional software developers. This book contains an authoritative summary of a wide range of techniques and methods for managing and improving software quality. The author uses his extensive experience in the field to provide insights into the practical problems of improving software quality. If you are concerned about software quality then this book should find a place on your bookshelf.

Ray Welland
Computing Science Department, University of Glasgow

Editorial Panel Members
Frank Bott (UCW, Aberystwyth), Dermot Browne (KPMG Management Consulting), Nic Holt (ICL), Trevor King (Praxis Systems plc), Tom Lake (GLOSSA), Kathy Spurr (Analysis and Design Consultants), Mario Wolczko (University of Manchester)

Preface

In the past, the concept of quality was closely related to the work of an individual or a small group. Excavations by archaeologists brought utensils as well as works of art to the surface which bear witness to the quality of the work by artists and craftsmen of thousands of years ago. The craftsmen's guilds of the Middle Ages show us how quality of a product was achieved. The master craftsman of the Middle Ages was able to instruct others to produce quality work and to judge what was good or bad quality having served a long apprenticeship and having passed his master's examination. In this context, quality constitutes an assessment not of the existence of an object, but of the way in which it can be distinguished from other objects. This concept can be traced back to Aristotle's theory of categories.

The manufacture of mass-produced goods during the industrial revolution created the necessity for control of the production process, in particular in the car and engineering industries. The transition from manual to industrial production was accompanied by the introduction of testing in the production process.

The quality of industrial products has wide economic consequences. Deviation by a small percentage from the prescribed quality features can cause losses in the range of millions in a competitive market. Production-orientated quality assurance involves the use of a wide variety of equipment and specific management measures ('quality management'). Philip Crosby, an internationally recognised expert in the field of quality assurance, argues that quality assurance is primarily the responsibility of top management. This must be reflected in a quality policy which regulates the scope and the guidelines of quality assurance at all levels of the enterprise.

At the present time there are a number of reasons why quality assurance demands attention in the economy and in industry:

1. Growing customer demands with respect to quality. The customer expects to receive first-class service. Furthermore, customers are aware of their own influence on the market and feel that they can demand a satisfactory response to their requirements. Through international mergers and uniformity of the markets, enterprises are compelled to guarantee compensation for defective goods or for faulty services. Substantial claims for damages from the producer of faulty goods or services are awarded via the courts.

2. Intensive international market competition. Enterprises have to compete in an international market which is segmented into specialisms. Product quality plays an increasingly important part in such a competitive situation.
3. Products are parts or components of systems which become increasingly complex. The requirements for reliability have grown enormously since, for example, the deficiencies of a computer in a flight control system can cause extensive damage.
4. Considerable cost savings through better quality management. As an example, after improvements in the field of quality management, a large computer manufacturer has been able to reduce stocks by 66 per cent and the manufacturing area by 25 per cent.

All these reasons explain the degree of importance which is now given to quality and services.

In this book we are concerned with the quality of software products and the processes which are required for the production and maintenance of these products. We are also interested in examining which production technology would be most suitable for achieving a good product quality. Besides purely technical factors we will also attempt to show organisational and psychological factors which influence the quality of products and processes.

In Chapter 1 we are concerned with the role of software quality assurance in the field of software engineering. At the centre are the different types of quality assurance method. A quality assurance plan serves as an operational aid. Furthermore, the role of testing, measuring and evaluating software is examined more closely and the most important measurements and metrics are discussed. Finally, quality models are introduced as major aids for quality planning and evaluation.

In Chapter 2 the connection between quality and productivity is shown in more detail. Apart from explanatory models, influences on productivity are discussed. The chapter closes with procedures for productivity improvement.

Chapter 3 reinforces the issue of constructive quality assurance, beginning with principles, methods and tools. These constructive elements are integrated with process models. Process models offer a number of possibilities for the inclusion of quality assurance procedures. Of particular importance for quality assurance is project documentation. The supporting procedures, influences and quality features for documentation, are explained, and the chapter closes with a commentary on the subject of software configuration management and psychological influences which can affect quality.

Chapter 4 describes the procedures of analytical quality assurance. The focus is on reviews and the systematisation of the test process.

Chapter 5 deals with problems of maintenance — the loss of structure and quality of software products through permanent changes. Quality assurance procedures for maintenance are discussed with regard to the reduction of maintenance cost and the improvement of maintaining and structuring processes. The chapter goes into detail with regard to standards, reviews/audits, metrics, software information systems, tools for analysis and education/training.

In Chapter 6 organisational procedures are described which may be implemented and run in an enterprise. Further discussion points are reports on quality control and considerations of cost and application.

The aim of this book lies in the integrated exposition of four aspects of quality assurance (planning administration, construction, analysis and psychological orientation) which form the framework for all kinds of quality assurance procedures. Quality assurance is seen primarily as a way of adhering to standards or of testing requirements. In particular the section on constructive and psychology-orientated procedures describes how quality software is developed. The recommendations in this book will probably not resolve all quality assurance problems. Rather, it sets out to offer an extensive and systematic synthesis of well-known procedures.

The book is mainly intended for

- computing experts who have to pay attention to quality assurance when developing software products;
- quality assurance specialists who want to extend their expertise; and
- teachers/students who are dealing with quality assurance issues within software engineering.

It is assumed that the reader of this book has basic knowledge of computing and especially of software engineering.

E. Wallmüller
Zürich, Spring 1990

Acknowledgements

A number of people have directly or indirectly contributed to the creation of this book, from the first preliminary tasks in 1986 until its completion. I would like to take the opportunity of thanking them for their help and advice.

During my consultancy appointment for SPARDAT Vienna, I gathered valuable experience in the construction of a quality assurance system.

Through my activities at ETH Zürich, I have familiarised myself with many modern software engineering concepts which are necessary for the development of good software. I would like to thank all those who have made this opportunity possible for me.

While working for the Schweizerische Bankgesellschaft, I gained valuable insight into and a realistic assessment of quality assurance problems in practical situations. I would like to express special thanks to Mr Fuchs and Mr Schärli for their expert contributions to our discussions.

During my time spent with SAQ (Schweizerische Arbeitsgemeinschaft für Qualitätsförderung, the Swiss Society for the Promotion of Quality), I gathered advice, ideas and valuable experience. I would like to thank in particular Messrs Frühauf, Burton-Smith, Mühlemann, Jäggin, Kiml, Schweizer, Brändle and Rudin, and Mrs Tomica, who contributed to the clarification of issues in a number of discussions.

I would like to thank my long-standing collaborator in matters of software quality assurance, Mr Wintersteiger of Softwaretest Österreich, for his untiring efforts and his initiative in Austria in the field of software quality.

I would like express special thanks to my dear wife Agathe who made the writing of this book possible by typing the manuscript and proofreading.

1 Software quality and software quality assurance

We live today in a society in which the computer plays an ever increasing role. One of the major elements contributing to the success of the computer is software. Due to the use of microprocessors, software is becoming increasingly important in industrial products and machinery. Business administration can no longer be imagined without software; neither can banks, insurance companies, commercial enterprises or other sectors manage without it. Everyone is becoming more and more dependent on software systems. In areas such as transport systems, flight security and energy systems, software can assume a critical safety role. Software systems are particularly important in the military world. The North American Air Defense Control System, NORAD, of the United States serves as an example. In this system the warning time is 20 minutes. Within 20 minutes unidentified flying objects have to be registered and identified, and possible measures taken.

In addition to the growing importance of software systems, there have been an increasing number of reports about faults in systems applications. Examples of the most spectacular cases of software faults have included:

- The first Venus probe missed its target in 1979 because a full stop was used in place of a comma in a Fortran program. The result was the loss of several hundred million dollars worth of effort.
- In 1983 type F18 fighter-bombers practised with new on-board software. On test flights across the equator the aircraft turned upside down. This was caused by the wrong 'marker' in a program.
- In 1984 there was a flood in the southern French Tarn Valley because the computer of an automatic lock system at Requista did not recognise a faulty flood danger message and opened two gates.

This list of software errors is not exhaustive. The more computers appear on the market, the more software is used. This increases the dependence on software systems which have a controlling and regulating function. On the other hand, we recognise that there is too little healthy mistrust and constructive criticism of the use of software systems, probably due to a general belief that software means progress. One of the reasons for this may be found in the fact that there are far too few reports about unsuccessful computing projects. Computing specialists avoid speaking about failures in their work. The use of software in business, industry and public administration is still unsatisfactory from the point of view of software engineering. Evidence for this is the absence of a systematic development process supported by methods and tools. There are still many instances where the development of software is carried out by word of mouth.

Because of these factors it is advisable to pay attention to software quality and to use appropriate principles, methods and tools. All sections of our society look towards software producers with high expectations. On the one hand, they are expected to produce high quality; on the other hand, there are stringent demands on cost and time in the development of projects. Adequate product quality is an implied demand which only comes to light when it is not met.

Nenz noted the following problems regarding the three factors of time, cost and product quality [Nenz83].

Time factors

- Only 5 per cent of all projects are completed on time.
- More than 60 per cent of all projects have at least a 20 per cent time overrun.
- Many projects are terminated altogether because of delays.

Many software projects are not completed on time, and completion problems often lead to the failure of the entire project or to its scrapping.

Cost factors

- Development cost increases exponentially with the complexity of software. The high degree of integration of modern software systems, complex interfaces between components, and the demand for adequate user friendliness and reliability (particularly in interactive systems) also cause higher development costs.
- In many instances, 60 per cent more of the entire software cost of a product is spent on maintenance.
- Delays can reduce market opportunities for a product and render investment unprofitable.

The problems of cost estimation and the absence of adequate mathematically based models are widely known. Attempts are being made to improve cost estimation by extrapolation of results from earlier projects and by estimating metrics such as lines of code (LOC) and person-months.

Product quality factors

- Errors are often found too late, frequently not until the customer tries to put the system into operation.
- The software product documentation is missing, incomplete or not up to date.
- Because of product faults more than 50 per cent of development time and effort is spent on error detection and correction.
- Quality as a development aim can often not be proved because of lack of quality planning.

The causes of the present problems in software development are on several levels. In many instances, the complexity of the software to be created is underestimated not only by management, but also by the developers of software products. Further reasons lie in the software production, process itself. In many cases of software production, there is too little planning and too much improvisation. The management of software projects, in particular of project organisation, does not meet with the requirements. Software product requirements are not adequately specified. When requirements are stated in the form of ideals or concepts, the requirement definitions are vague, confusing or contradictory. The developers often try to improve the quality by testing instead of developing the quality step by step. There is a general lack of accompanying project quality assurance measures. The only 'measure' is often the method of unsystematic testing. The documentation, one of the most important foundations for quality testing, is often missing or of poor quality.

The factors mentioned here lead to the realisation that planning and production of software must be systematic and carried out by professional engineers, and that quality must be a development goal.

1.1 Software engineering and software quality assurance

The development and maintenance of medium and larger applications require extensive resources of time, staff and finance. These resources must be used economically when working to predetermined targets and plans. Bauer postulated software engineering as a discipline which would help the developer to produce and maintain high-quality software by the use of engineering skills and economic practices [Naur69].

Software systems are in use for ten to fifteen years before they are completely replaced. We talk of the life cycle of a software system in this context. In order to perform construction and maintenance in ordered phases, models and aids have been developed which are called phase models. One of the first phase models stems from Royce [Royc70]. Over the years these have been improved and extended to process models (see section 3.2). Since software systems are, as a rule, embedded in hardware, each development or maintenance process can also be seen from its system theory angle, which is described by means of systems engineering [Daen78]. Life-cycle models are therefore based on the observations from systems engineering and take into account the systems engineering tasks in an individual phase (see Figure 1.1).

In a classical life cycle, the following activities are carried out:

- *Systems engineering*. Since software systems are always part of a bigger system, the cycle begins with the analysis of the system requirements and with a feasibility study at the system level. Of particular importance is the interfacing of the software system with the hardware (e.g. in integrated systems), with the view of business organisations (e.g. large commercial interactive information systems) and with databases.

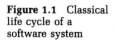

Figure 1.1 Classical life cycle of a software system

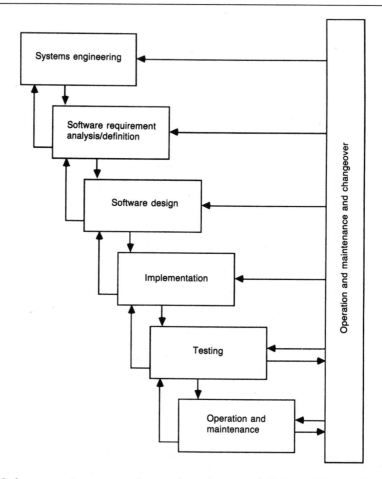

- *Software requirements analysis and requirements definitions*. The actual cycle for software development begins with the collection, analysis and definition of requirements of the software system. In order to understand the aims and objectives of the system, the developer needs exact knowledge of the requirements, which, in turn, are classified into functional and non-functional requirements. Documentation of these requirements and checking by the customer are important prerequisites for securing good-quality software and system development. Good specialist knowledge of the application contributes considerably to better understanding of the users and of their requirements.
- *Software design*. The design is the bridge between requirements and the implemented solution. Important tasks are the design of data structures, of the software architecture and of the interfaces of modules. A good design can be achieved only through creativity and discipline. A good design makes testing of quality and maintenance of software easier.
- *Implementation*. The design must be transformed into machine readable form. It is in this activity that the highest level of mechanisation can be achieved,

and it can be assumed that in the future this phase will be automated by the use of generators and transformation tools.

*   *Testing*. Through testing one can check that the implemented software system meets the requirements and that the system is reliable enough for installation and user operation.
*   *Operation and maintenance*. One of the earliest activities in the operation and maintenance phase is the introductory training of the user. This phase is influenced not only by the alterations necessary for the user and by the operational environment, but also by poor initial quality. The current state in computing is marked by an increasing amount of software requiring permanent maintenance.

Software engineering departments have, until recently, ignored maintenance. Problems with the classical life cycle have been known for some time:

1. Repeated use of this model often shows up considerable quality shortcomings (e.g. delayed documentation).
2. There is a limit in the extent to which requirements can be captured and specified. In some situations, applications and users allow only a vague specification of requirements. This leads to a high degree of uncertainty during project development and often results in quality problems.
3. The longer it takes for the customer, i.e. the user, to receive a working version (a prototype) of an application for trying out, the greater is the risk of not reaching the targets.

Software quality assurance is part of a discipline within software engineering which tries to take into account quality through particular aids and through planned and systematic application of software engineering within a life cycle.

1.2 Foundations of software quality assurance

In this chapter, different aspects of quality are examined in order to achieve a distinct and comprehensive idea of software quality. In principle, there is a distinction between the quality of a product and the quality of the development process. Masing [Masi88] refers to the entire range of activities related to the manufacture of a product as the 'production process'. (In software production we speak of the 'development process'.) Each individual activity has to meet specific requirements, which take the form of instructions or task specifications. The degree to which requirements and their implementation agree determines the quality. In this way the quality of a process becomes measurable and analysable. Masing excludes any extrapolation of this evaluation process to the market as a whole.

We use the following as a basic premise. The quality goals for the software product determine the quality goals of the development process. The quality of the former is based on the quality of the development processes. These have a

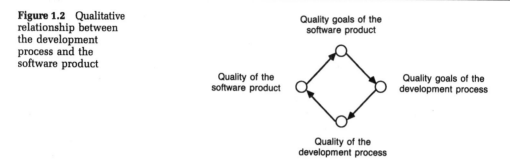

decisive influence on the quality of the product. This interaction takes place frequently during the development of projects (see Figure 1.2).

Software development is a very complex process which requires the use of many different disciplines for the development of a product to satisfy its requirements. The necessary disciplines are:

- project management;
- quality assurance;
- configuration management; and
- software engineering for the implementation process.

Apart from the application of the above-named disciplines, effective management and development practices are necessary according to the situation.

1.2.1   What is software quality?

Some fundamental observations on this question have been made by D. A. Garvin from Harvard University [Garv84]. He distinguishes between five approaches to obtaining a quality concept.

The 'transcendental' approach

According to this, quality is universally recognisable and is a synonym for a consistently high standard of functionality of a product. The advocates of this approach, however, believe that quality in this sense cannot be precisely defined or measured. They also postulate that quality can be evaluated only on the basis of experience. The concept of quality cannot be defined by implication, just as the concept of 'beauty' cannot be defined by implication.

The production-related approach

Advocates of this approach believe that quality is precisely measurable. According to this definition, quality differences mirror differences in the existing observable quantities of specific characteristics in a product. This approach allows the ranking of different products of the same category.

The user-related approach

This view holds that quality is determined by the product user rather than by the product itself. According to this, different product users have differing requirements and wishes, and those products which satisfy these needs best are seen as representing high quality.

The process-related approach

This approach relates quality to the reliable execution of specifications, and holds the ideal view that an activity in the manufacture of a product should be carried out right first time. This idea of quality is held with today's economy and industry in mind. In the centre is the production process, which is checked in order to reduce faults and revision cost. In this process, the level of automation plays an important part. The use of robots and automation in particular should guarantee that production processes are as far as possible fault free and consistent.

The price/user-related approach

This approach involves a relationship between price and quality. In this context, a quality product is a product which is designed for a specific use at an acceptable price, or which conforms to specification at an acceptable cost.

Apart from these approaches which try to clarify the concept of quality, there have also been a number of attempts to define the concept of quality. The emphasis depends on preference and individual interpretation. In the following, different quality ideas are discussed and their application for software products examined.
German Industry Standard DIN 55350 Part 11 states:

> Quality comprises all characteristics and significant features of a product or an activity which relate to the satisfying of given requirements.

Although this definition characterises the general concept of quality, it is not precise enough as a basis for checking the quality of a software product. However, two important conclusions can be drawn from this definition:

- The suitability of one thing can be different for different usages. For example, the text formatting system TROFF [Geha86] is suitable, by all accounts, for occasional use if it is important to use the minimum number of formatting commands. However, for professional word processing we need a display of the text as it currently is during manipulation (WYSIWYG = What You See Is What You Get).
- The requirements result from the purpose of the application of the software product. In order to produce professional programs, for example, a multi-document editor with full page displays for each document is needed. For alteration of a Basic program on a PC, a line editor such as EDLIN is sufficient.

A product or an activity (i.e. a service) has different characteristics not all of which constitute quality. Characteristics which constitute quality are those which are relevant for the product user or the service user, i.e. those which meet the predestined requirements. For example, for the user of a car the relevant characteristic might be how economical it is to use.

A 'feature' is, according to DIN 55350 part 12, that property which allows a quantitative or qualitative distinction of a product or activity from its whole. In our car example, economical petrol consumption would be such a quantitative feature. Naturally, we are interested in measuring the petrol consumption and for this we need a defined measure, a measuring process and a measuring instrument. The values of the measures — for example, the number of litres of petrol used per 100 driven kilometres — appear on a scale, which provides a comparison in the form of absolute values. In section 1.3 we look more closely at the problems of measuring software features.

The ANSI standard (ANSI/ASQC A3/1978) defines quality in a similar way to the DIN standard:

> Quality is the totality of features and characteristics of a product or a service that bears on its ability to satisfy the given needs.

The IEEE Standard for Software Quality (IEEE Std 729−1983) is based on the ANSI Standard and improves it with regard to satisfying customer expectations. It defines software quality as follows:

1. The totality of features and characteristics of a software product that bear on its ability to satisfy given needs: for example, conform to specifications.
2. The degree to which software possesses a desired combination of attributes.
3. The degree to which a customer or user perceives that software meets his or her composite expectations.
4. The composite characteristics of software that determine the degree to which the software in use will meet the expectations of the customer.

If we are not satisfied with the evaluation of finished software products but want to realise quality constructively, we must create a starting point for the evaluation of the development and maintenance process. This means that we need features and assessment standards for intermediate and end deliverables and for the development activities in all phases of the development. The concept of process quality is missing in the DIN definition.

At the same time we must be conscious of the fact that quality is not absolute but is always relative to given requirements. From this we deduce that quality evaluation is always subject to comparison between quality prerequisites derived from given requirements and the product actually created.

Boehm lists the following three patterns of defining software quality characteristics [Boeh78]:

1. *Problem of definition of software quality.* Is it at all possible to create a definition of characteristics and features of a software product which are measurable and not overlapping?

2. *Problem of quality testing.* How well can the quality of a software product be measured, or the characteristics and features which determine the quality of a software product?

3. *Problem of quality control.* How can information about the quality of the product be used for the improvement of the product in the life cycle?

Boehm's principal questions show clearly the contemporary weak points of software quality assurance. First of all, he addresses the problem of clarity and relevance of quality features. Nowadays we all define and interpret quality features differently. An explanation or standardisation of the concepts would be helpful. In some standards committees (ISO, IEEE) preliminary work on this process has begun.

The second question highlights the problem of the completeness and conciseness of quality features. In other words, we examine here how well individual requirements can be formulated with a given collection of tools, whether gaps are caused, and whether certain requirements are covered by several quality features.

The third question implies that quality is a control factor for the development process. Of importance is the feedback of the results of quality testing to process control.

One prerequisite when considering quality in software is that software is seen as a product: in other words, that up-to-date and adequate documentation exists in which not only programs but also data are described, so that one can speak of a product.

A software product (see IEEE Std 729-1983, Glossary of the Software Engineering Terminology) consists of the following parts:

- source code;
- object code; and
- documentation.

The documentation is divided into development documentation and operations documentation. In development documentation we include the documents which are produced at the end of each phase and all documents which contain agreements, contracts, guidelines, concepts and the like for the project. Operations documentation combines user documentation with installation, operation and maintenance documentation. User documentation constitutes all documents which make working with the software product possible for the defined user with the defined user profile and without the aid of further documents.

Quality models determine the scope of quality adapted to the refinements and requirements of software products. The best-known models are those of McCall [McCa77], Boehm [Boeh76a], Willmer [Will85], NEC [Azum85] and Siemens [Asam86, Zopf88]. Within the framework of a project, I have also created a quality model with a quality assurance system [Wall87a], which henceforth will be referred to as the SPARDAT model. Quality models contribute considerably to the standardisation of different ideas about quality of software. By means of their structured decomposition, the opaque concept of software quality is made real.

The models which are most developed, such as those of McCall and NEC, make quality planning and quality evaluation possible. We shall discuss quality models in more detail in section 1.4.

1.2.2.   Where are software quality and software defects created?

The quality of a software product is determined by its development process and by the features it possesses. The development process can be structured in time by the introduction of phases, in which case we speak of a phase or process model (see section 3.2). Quality must be achieved in each of these phases. It is important that there are requirements (related not only to the results of each phase but also to activities) and that these are checked for their completeness at the end of the phase. The achieving of milestones is an important process requirement for management. For example, the creation of a document (e.g. of a report) is a milestone at the end of a phase. The overall quality of a product is based on a number of steps, on the quality of phase results and on meeting the process requirements.

As mentioned before, the development process, and in particular its quality, plays an important part in the creation of product quality. In this context we also speak of process quality. Prerequisites for good process quality are the extent of systematic, methodical development (for example, observing development standards), careful project management, qualifications and training of staff, and the quality of aids used.

How and when are errors and faults created in the process? According to Mizumo [Mizu83] the creation of errors and faults is due to an accumulation effect (see Figure 1.3). The project normally begins with the collection, analysis and definition of requirements. These requirements are recorded in the form of a requirements specification. Experience has shown that part of this specification is correct, while the other part contains errors.

In the next phase the design is created. The result is a design document. Part of the design is correct, but another part contains errors which were created during the design phase, and a third part of the design is based on faulty specifications.

The next step is programming. Part of the program is correct, but another part contains errors. A further part of the program is based on faulty design, faulty specifications or faulty requirements.

In the following integration and test phase, the situation is as follows. Part of the program functions correctly. Another part of the program contains errors which can be corrected and which are being corrected. A further part contains errors which cannot be corrected. Yet another part contains hidden errors. Overall, the software product is not perfect. This imperfection is due to the cumulative effect of errors and faults and the overall effect can only be observed at the end of the project.

This effect also occurs in other technical product developments. In these areas, however, integrated intermediate checks have been carried out for quite some time.

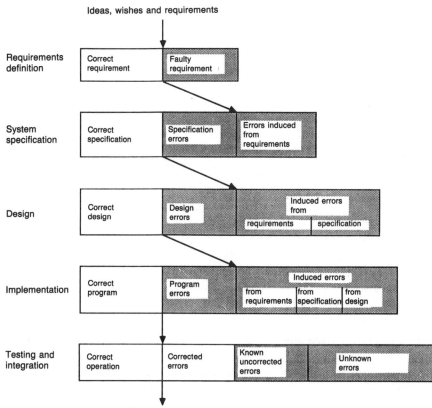

Ideas, wishes and requirements

Software with known and unknown errors and faults

Figure 1.3 Accumulative effect of errors and faults

The cumulative effect of errors and faults can be reduced by suitable quality assurance principles. One of the most important principles is to apply tests at the beginning of the life cycle (i.e. of the requirement specifications) as well as to test all process results. If this is not done, the correction of quality faults can become very expensive [Boeh81] (see Figure 1.4), since the cost of correcting errors increases exponentially with the time that an error remains in the product. Principles of quality assurance are discussed in detail in section 1.2.3.

A major source of faults and errors lies in planning: that is, in the planning of the project as a whole and in the planning of the development process in particular. An examination of problems in management of software projects by Thayer *et al.* [Thay81] found that 60 per cent of problems are due to project planning and 20 per cent to project control. The rest are varying management problems as well as problems in the understanding of technical project tasks. From this we can see how important planning is for the achievement of a successful project [Hein76, Hein88].

We start the software development process with specific requirements, such as the requirement of a given product quality, or the requirement to complete

Figure 1.4 Relative
cost of error
correction [Boehm]

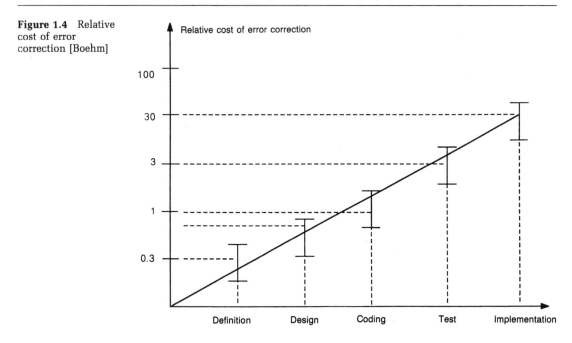

the project by a given time within a certain budget. How can we carry out the
development process in a way which allows us to meet these requirements? We
are dealing here with the planning component in project management, and the
interrelationship of project management, quality assurance and configuration
management (see Figure 1.5).

One of the most important aids for quality-orientated project planning is the
project plan itself, which consists of different parts [Metz77, Früh87a]. The most
important aspects of this plan are:

- project organisation (the setting up of an organisation chart, determining
  responsibilities);
- project description (size of task and delivery, testing process, requirements
  of project environment):

Figure 1.5 Elements
of a software project

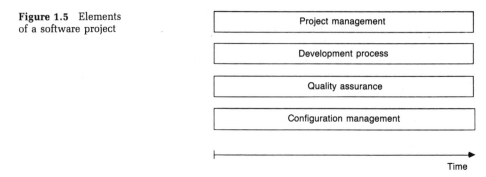

- development process in the form of a development plan (division of development work into manageable parts, deadlines, budget and a list of risk factors);
- quality assurance in the form of a quality assurance plan;
- configuration management with a configuration management plan; and
- project-specific training.

At this point we can draw the following conclusions:

- Project management can be a source of problems and errors in connection with quality assurance and configuration management.
- Quality assurance is, among other things, a management issue.
- Quality assurance is both a project-internal and also a project-external task (see Chapter 6).

An overview of and approaches to this topic can be found in [Früh87a], [Diek83], [DeMa82] and [Kupp81].

1.2.3   Quality assurance principles

The creation of software, as with every other industrial production and development process, is subject to the demand for high productivity. This, in turn, involves the goals of timescales, minimum cost and satisfactory product quality. If these goals are met, we speak of economical software development. To achieve goals like high productivity and the meeting of budgets, timescales and product quality requirements, certain general principles of software engineering as well as software quality assurance must be observed. These principles are derived from the aforementioned phenomena of the development process and experiences of software crises [DGQ86].

The following principles concerning assurance of quality are at present acknowledged.

Practical quality features

Of paramount importance to quality is the observation of customer and user quality requirements from the beginning of project planning. It is important that quality features are concrete and if possible quantifiable. This makes distinguishing between different project categories easier in standard projects and special projects with specific requirements. It is equally important to find concrete quality features for individual phases. These features can be process as well as product orientated. For example, when creating a project log, it makes sense to determine certain quality features from the start [SAQ88a]. From the view of processing quality it is important to make sufficient testing time and test resources available. In general, early availability and sufficient resources are an indicator of good process quality.

Product and project-dependent quality planning

These days insufficient attention is often given to examining the real application process of the software product to be planned and developed, such as the lifetime of the product and who the potential user will be. All these factors influence the style of quality requirements of a project considerably. Depending on these quality requirements, the appropriate software engineering methods and tools can be applied and suitable quality assurance measures taken. For example, important quality characteristics for a Customer Information System in a bank are easy handling, accessibility and reliability.

In quality planning, project uncertainties must also be taken into account. Experience has shown that quality assurance plans are useless if project uncertainties, such as complexity and degree of novelty of a product, are not taken into account. The following risk factors influence product and quality assurance planning:

- size of project (number of staff, cost person-years);
- qualifications of staff;
- technical product risk analysis:
  complexity
  degree of novelty
  number of requirements;
- degree of uncertainty of requirements;
- division of labour among in-house staff and external developers; and
- economic risk, e.g. time constraints for product release on to the market.

These risk factors are different in each project. Factors which involve a potential risk for project and quality assurance planning must be identified first of all. In the case of a risk, the respective quality assurance measures must be chosen and project planning (planning scope, resources) must be modified or made more precise.

Checking of results of quality tests

This checking process is an important part of successful quality control. Discrepancies from the planned quality level will be revealed. The aim is to arrive at suitable correction methods in the development process on the basis of findings in quality reviews. Reviews (inspections and walkthroughs) and audits (for inspection of the development process or the management process) provide the necessary information for correction of the development process.

Multiple quality reviews

The cognitive capabilities of individuals are better utilised in group work — as, for example, in the joint analysis of a document. It is a known fact that people are liable to make errors. It is therefore also feasible to use the intellectual abilities of people as a positive influence on quality. Apart from the test methods already described, we are here dealing with informal tests. This occurs, for example, when the developer of an intermediate or end deliverable of a phase asks his or her colleague to look at the documents and proofread them.

Maximum constructive quality assurance

While quality testing involves determining the existence or non-existence of quality, the aim of constructive quality assurance is to avoid errors in the development process. The maxim is: 'To make no mistakes is better than having to discover mistakes and correct them.' By the use of suitable preventive measures in the development process, the product quality will be directly improved. Experience has also shown that preventive measures can considerably reduce the number of quality tests. A further positive aspect of this principle is that only through constructive quality assurance measures will quality testing be made possible. For example, a suitable interface specification for modules which contains pre-operational and post-operational conditions, stating the effect of the module and error conditions, will make specification-orientated testing considerably easier. Constructive quality assurance measures and quality tests complement each other and result in real benefits.

Early discovery and correction of errors and faults

As Boehm [Boeh81] shows (see Figure 1.4), the cost of the discovery and correction of an error is exponential to the time between the error's creation and discovery. An error in a requirement definition which is not discovered until the product is put into operation by the end user costs about one hundred times more than an early discovery in the requirement phase. Therefore the strategy must be to recognise and eliminate an error as early as possible. This principle also guarantees improved quality control, and moreover the spreading effect of errors is reduced (see Figure 1.3).

Integrated quality assurance

Quality assurance should be integrated into the entire development process. This leads to quality assurance measures being planned and organised with other development measures. The basic principle is that each development activity consists of a constructive and an analytical/testing part. Both parts are reflected in the respective documentation. For example, requirements are listed and structured by means of a suitable requirements definition method. By means of an informal or formal requirements review, faults in the requirements are subsequently removed. The test is facilitated through use of a method for requirements definition which creates documentation (requirements specification) at the same time. This principle also makes the level of quality visible at each point in time, and is particularly important for the earlier phases. It is a prerequisite for realistic evaluation of project progress and for checking whether quality goals have been reached.

Independent quality testing

Many software development measures are of a constructive and productive nature, which means that the developer is the author of many components. With quality testing the situation is different because the central issue is the discovery of errors and faults. In fact, the opinion which states that quality tests must be carried out with a very critical if not destructive attitude is quite common. For instance, if a developer has to test his or her own working results, it often leads to tension and psychological problems. This basic conflict of interests can be resolved only through independent quality testing. The aim is to show the current actual quality and to deal with error elimination at a later stage. By applying this important principle, the consequences of operational blindness or lack of objectivity can be avoided. One disadvantage can occur if it is thought that it is the person who is being judged rather than the product, since this can lead to the boycotting of further quality testing.

Evaluation of applied quality assurance measures

At certain time intervals it is necessary to check the applied quality assurance organisation and its measures. In this instance we speak of internal or external quality audits. External audits are carried out by external advisers who check the current quality assurance system and the applied quality assurance measures. These audits usually result in corrections of the quality assurance system and of the applied quality assurance measures. This method also increases the viability of the investment in a quality assurance system. A further reason for quality audits is the opportunity to include up-to-date software in the project. Consequently, quality assurance measures have to be adjusted to this new technology.

In order to carry out these examinations, a relevant quality data collection and report system is necessary (see Chapter 6). This includes the recording of quality assurance cost items (costs which occurred through not keeping to the plan, e.g. not employing methods or standards).

1.2.4   Concepts and definitions

First of all, it is useful to define some concepts in connection with quality assurance. It is important to recognise that quality is as important in the end product as it is during its development. The concept of product includes intermediate and final results during different phases of the development process, such as during the module design phase.

Quality assurance (QA)

D. Reifer defines quality assurance as a complex system [Reif85]:

> Quality assurance is a system consisting of method and processing which interact in such a way that software products meet the requirements demanded. The system includes planning, estimating and supervision of development activities which are performed independently by the developers.

This definition is process related and determines at the same time the extent of the task as well as quality assurance.

Bersoff emphasises in his definition [Bers84] the meaning of standards:[1]

> Quality assurance consists of those procedures, techniques and tools applied by professionals to ensure that a product meets or exceeds prespecified standards during a product's development cycle; and without specific prescribed standards QA entails ensuring that a product meets or exceeds a minimum industrial and/or commercially accepted level of excellence.

The definition of quality assurance within the context of IEEE Std 729 can be summarised as follows:

> Quality assurance is a planned and systematic pattern of all actions necessary to provide adequate confidence that the item or product conforms to established technical requirements.

At strategic level, organisations employ the concept of quality policy in addition to these procedures and aids.

Quality policy

By quality policy we mean the basic aims and objectives of an organisation regarding quality, as stipulated by management. Examples are customer orientation, fast reactions to market conditions through the introduction of new products, manufacturing of products with high value, and comprehensive and efficient customer service.

Quality policy is a central task for top and middle management. Because of this allocation of responsibility, there is a danger that the daily routine might not be carried out with the highest degree of efficiency.

Quality policy in connection with software means, among other things, that the three project elements of time, cost and product requirements are equally important.

Quality assurance system (QAS)

This includes the organisation of construction and release procedures, the allocation

---

1 Standards may be seen as an internationally recognised and accepted network of regulations. A standard is the model of a commodity or service recognised as acceptable within a company.

of responsibilities and the selection of tools for the implementation of quality assurance.

Quality assurance systems provide the framework for all quality-assuring measures and strategies. There are different levels of quality assurance systems. The first level is company specific, where projects may be overlapping. The second level is project specific, i.e. each project has its own quality assurance organisation. The third level of quality assurance systems is phase related.

What are the main tasks of quality assurance? We can distinguish between quality planning, quality control and quality testing. In principle we assume that the planning and supervising of software quality assurance are management tasks. Software quality assurance as such affects the planning, controlling and testing of the quality of a software project. The task of the developer within the framework of a software project, in turn, comprises the planning, implementing and testing of the software product.

Quality planning

Quality planning is a process of assessing the requirements of the procedure and of the product, and the context in which these must be observed. For this, quality features must be selected, classified and weighted. Quantification of the features plays an important part, since it provides the evidence for compliance with the plan. If quantification is possible, the goals must be determined. In parallel with this, aids for measuring and evaluating (e.g. quality metrics) must be provided so that examination of the intended quality will be possible. Quality planning is product and process dependent and must be agreed with the client or user.

Quality control

By this we mean the control, supervision and correction of the implementation of work with the goal of meeting the given requirements.

Important aids to supervision are quality tests. The results of these make it possible to recommend developer-related and product-related correction measures. Recommended control mechanisms are constructive measures such as software engineering methods and tools, and also training. Quality control is closely linked with project management.

Quality testing

Quality testing is the assessment of the extent to which a test object meets the given requirements.

We can distinguish between static and dynamic testing. Examples of static testing are reviews (inspections, walkthroughs) and audits. To the category of dynamic testing belong, among other things, tests and counts of test features through the use of tools (for example, static analysers). In Chapter 4 we shall discuss both categories in detail. Another kind of quality testing is fault and error analysis, which is based on catalogues of faults and problem reports. We can use this to give answers to the following questions. In which phase do which types of error occur most frequently? How many errors in the product have not yet been dealt with? These form the basis for further improvements to the development process.

Quality assurance plan

The quality assurance plan is the central aid for planning and checking QA. It contains all deliberately chosen quality assurance measures for a software project, and consequently it is the written proof of quality control. In section 1.2.5 we shall look more closely at the quality assurance plan.

1.2.5   The quality assurance plan (QA plan)

In this section we introduce IEEE Std 730–1984, an internationally accepted standard which provides the basis of quality assurance plans.

The IEEE Standard for a Software Quality Assurance Plan contains the following points.

Purpose

In this section of the plan, the following questions are dealt with:

- Which software products are covered by the QA plan?
- What is this software used for?
- How critical is the application of this software?
- Why is a software quality assurance plan produced?
- Are there external or internal demands for this?
- What is the basis for the quality assurance plan (for example, the IEEE standard, an internal or an external document)?
- What are the reasons for possible deviations from the basis and where are these deviations described?

Reference documents

This part of the plan contains a complete list of all documents which are referenced elsewhere in the text of the plan. It must also be stated where these documents can be obtained and who is responsible for them.

Management

This part of the plan describes the organisation, tasks and responsibilities of the development process. The organisation created is shown by means of an organisational structure diagram with additional written annotations. These should contain the following:

- a description of each group of the created organisation which carries out quality assurance tasks;
- responsibilities which can be delegated;
- responsibilities for reports;
- identification of those groups which are responsible for the product release;
- identification of those groups which check the QA plan;
- all procedures which may be invoked for solving conflict between organisational groups;
- the size and magnitude of the quality assurance organisation; and
- all deviations from quality policy formerly stipulated by the organisation, or deviations from measures and standards for quality assurance.

All elements in this organisation should be described in full detail, so that the tasks which are listed in the QA plan can be allocated directly to the elements of the organisation.

The description of tasks in quality assurance, in particular the sequence of the tasks, must cover the entire software life cycle. This must include the names of the people publishing the QA plan and distributing, maintaining and releasing it. For each quality assurance task, the start and finish must be specified.

The description of responsibilities identifies which quality assurance groups are responsible for which quality assurance tasks.

Software documentation

Here all documents for the development and maintenance processes are described. Furthermore, all reviews and audits are noted which comment on the suitability and quality of the documentation. The minimum amount of documentation comprises:

- software requirements specification;
- software design description;
- software test plan;
- software test report; and
- user documentation.

The test plan contains the method and means by which it is proved that the design conforms to the requirements and the source code conforms to the design and the requirements (see Figure 1.6).

Figure 1.6 Goals of a test plan

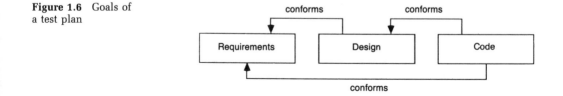

The test report describes the result of the execution of the test plan. In particular, results of all reviews, audits and tests of the test plan are described. Apart from this minimal amount of documentation, the point 'further documentation' describes the correspondence with the software development plan, the software configuration management plan and method, and the operations manual.

Standards, practices and conventions

Here all standards, practices and conventions to be applied are identified. In addition, organisational elements must be specified, indicating relevance to the monitoring and maintenance of standards, practices and conventions.

A minimum of standards, practices and conventions must exist for:

- requirements specification;
- design;
- implementation (special coding and comment);
- testing; and
- documentation.

Reviews and audits

Here technical and management-orientated reviews and audits are listed with the date of execution. Some attention should be given to how they are deemed to be completed.

The following test elements are a minimum requirement:

- software requirements review;
- high-level design review;
- detailed design review;
- review of test plan (appropriateness and completeness of chosen test methods);
- audit of system functions (code to be tested against requirements);
- functional audit (testing for consistency of software and documentation);
- physical audits (of the development procedure);
- management review for evaluation of the execution of the QA plan; and
- review of user documentation.

Software configuration management

This describes which methods and aids are applied to the identification of software product elements for control and implementation of alterations, and also lists and reports the enhancements.

Problem reports and corrective actions

This part of the plan describes which practices and procedures are to be followed for reporting, tracking and resolving software problems. It also specifies who in the organisation is responsible for the execution of these procedures.

Software engineering

This section describes which software engineering, and in particular which constructive software engineering measures (methods, techniques and tools) are to be used and why. For this it is advisable to provide references to methods and to the development manual. The appropriate section must be listed.

Code control

This part of the plan defines the procedures and tools to be used for the maintenance and storing of already validated versions of identified software. This can be done with the use of a program library.

Other features

Any feature not covered under the previous headings is described in this section. For example:

- *Media control.* In this section the procedures and tools are specified in order to protect the physical program media from unauthorised access or inadvertent corruption or degradation.
- *Supplier control.* In this section those preventive measures are listed which guarantee that any externally developed software conforms with the specified technical requirements. As a rule, those QA measures are listed which have to be met by the supplier of external services.
- *Collection, maintenance and retention of documents.* Archiving methods and installations are stipulated for the assembling, protection, maintenance and retention period of documentation. Organisational units responsible for the above measures must be named.

Critical examination of the IEEE Standard draws attention to the following points. No comment is made about personnel requirements and other resources for the execution of the plan. Comments on management risk evaluation in a project or product are also missing, as well as project results relating to aids and tools for product development. Equally, comments relating to quality cost, which invariably result in quality assurance measures, are not listed. Nevertheless, an increasing international trend towards the use of the Standard can be observed. An interesting comparison of this Standard with other international and national standards can be found in [Schu87].

1.2.6   Classification of quality assurance measures

Four categories of quality assurance measures can be distinguished:

- planning and administrative;
- constructive;
- analytic; and
- psychology orientated.

It makes sense to distinguish on which level these measures are defined. The following levels can be perceived: project overlap (global, company scope), project specific and phase specific.

Planning and administrative quality assurance measures

We are dealing here with the construction, introduction and maintenance of a quality assurance system. This system becomes effective on three levels, i.e. project overlap, project specific and phase specific (see Chapter 6).

Constructive quality assurance measures

Constructive quality assurance measures are all those which serve the creation of quality. They are preventive and should avoid the creation of errors and quality faults from the start by stipulating suitable principles, methods, formalisms and tools. They also include all measures for error correction. In Chapter 3 we shall discuss constructive quality assurance measures in more detail.

Psychological quality assurance measures

This category of measures concerns the person as a developer, project leader or project manager. We can distinguish between measures which concern the work of the individual and those which concern team work.

In software projects there is always the danger that technical aspects are overemphasised. Investigations have shown that the abilities of those involved in the software development process are very varied. Examples include the ability to collect and analyse data and the ability to code. It was noted that discrepancies in ability occurred in a range of 1 to 5, and coding showed a range of 1 to 30, which means that some developers are up to thirty times more productive than others. Contrary to other technical disciplines, the effects of the discrepancies in ability are not immediately noticeable in the development process. Therefore we have to look closely at the environment of software development and maintenance processes, and remove possible impediments. Examples of human aspects to be taken into account are:

- utilising the individual abilities and experiences of the developers;
- completing a whole and identifiable part of a task;
- emphasising the importance of the work;
- the possibility of giving the developers some degree of freedom;
- planning in areas of job satisfaction; and

- developing a style of leadership which is ability as well as staff related.

Taking into account the above-mentioned aspects leads to the following results. The staff are highly motivated and satisfied with their work. Better quality in their work can be observed, and there is less absenteeism and a lower turnover of staff.

Many computing projects can now be handled only by teams. The quality of the results from team work is influenced by a number of factors, such as company culture, style of communication and management attitudes. Prerequisites for effective team work are as follows:

- Each person knows the functional role of his or her work.
- Each has a desire to present the work. The team must make this possible.
- Each team member expects a reward (feedback) and is entitled to it.
- Teamwork is only be carried out in small groups with a maximum of five people.
- A project has a time limit (maximum of two calendar years).
- The workplace is be equipped in such a way that informal as well as formal communication is possible.
- The working climate is free of repression.

The area of psychology-orientated quality assurance measures has been little examined in computing. Computer experts are as a rule so convinced of the importance of their technical work that experts from other disciplines such as labour psychology are not thought of as suitable partners, and their disciplines are not seen as scientific. This is a fact which can unfortunately be seen in many places of research today, and which hinders progress in this field considerably (see section 3.7).

1.3   Counts and measures in software engineering

In this section we shall give an overview of the current state of software engineering with regard to software measurements and metrics. The meaning of counts, measures and evaluation is examined here.

1.3.1   Significance of measures in natural sciences and engineering

In each engineering discipline, counting and measuring play an important part. In order to express the significance and problems of measuring in the natural sciences and in engineering, we shall quote from some prominent practitioners in these fields:

> When you can measure what you are speaking about and express it in numbers, you know something about it, but when you cannot measure it, when you cannot express it in numbers, your knowledge is of a meagre and unsatisfactory kind.
> Lord Kelvin

To measure is to know.

J.C. Maxwell

Without measuring, any understanding of natural laws or the setting up of models which describe the structural connection between physical and technical values would be unthinkable. An important element in proving theories is provided by experiments. Without measuring, experiments would be useless as an aid to natural scientists and engineers.

After these considerations on the significance of measurement, it should be noted that there are fundamental difficulties when measuring software. If we look more closely at the concept of quality, and design quality in particular, we discover that human creativity and originality are closely linked with it. These aspects of quality can hardly be measured.

Pirsig sees the situation as follows [Pirs74]:

> What I mean by the word 'quality' cannot be broken down into subjects and predicates. This is not because quality is so mysterious but because quality is so simple, immediate and direct.

Pirsig notes the often intuitive view that quality is recognised less often by logical argument than by direct perception and observation. This view of quality is widespread among programmers. They see their work as a piece of art rather than as a commercial product. At first sight it appears that this is a contrary view of software engineering. On closer scrutiny of the situation, however, we find, that the creative part of human work in the entire software development process (especially in software design) is remarkable. We must reach a dual understanding of the concept of quality in software engineering. On the one hand, software products must go through a solid engineering development process on the basis of a logical/rational assessment of quality; on the other hand, good software products, such as an integrated software package for PCs, must be the result of the creative ability of the developer. This is reflected in a software design which is marked by originality, simplicity and strength.

1.3.2 Software measuring techniques

The engineering trait of observing, counting and measuring in the field of software development has so far been neglected. There are many reasons for this. One important psychological reason lies in the fact that no one likes to have the result of his or her work assessed. People believe that not their work but they themselves are being assessed.

A further reason can be seen in the lack of salient metrics for the development process: that is, the lack of technical values which help to evaluate the software product. Despite recognition of these characteristics of the software development process, it can nevertheless be said that software measuring is essential for efficient engineering-style planning, guidance and control of quality goals.

Large hardware and software producers have already recognised the importance of testing and evaluating quality levels. Siemens differentiates between the categories of observing, assessing and predicting [Asam86].

At Siemens observing is seen as a process which shows the value of features of a product during actual use. For example, response time of on-line programs is observed. The purpose of this concrete measure is to evaluate the suitability of design aspects.

By means of assessment, reporting on an expected type of feature takes place, using a product which is either in the development phase or completed and in a simulated application. For example, the reliability of a program in the target environment can be tried out.

Estimation leads to the critical assessment of an anticipated form of a feature. This is reached with the help of a model-like description of the product or of its application context. For example, response times in a large information system can be estimated using predictions on a simulated model.

The disadvantage of using observation lies in the fact that product development is already finished by this stage. Damage may already have occurred. Estimating partly avoids these disadvantages, since we are talking here of an early 'hypothetical' observing of types of feature in parts of the system. The important difference between predicting or estimating and observing lies in the fact that the conditions of product implementation or product application (the stipulated functionality, amount of data, structure of work units) are only partially known. A further difference is that with prediction no part of the system needs to exist or to be working. Model ideas are applied to an analytical, abstract product model.

For the software development process, we can apply Galileo's postulate, 'Count what is countable, measure what is measurable, and if something is not measurable, try to make it measurable!' We must begin modestly by counting relevant phenomena such as the number of errors or the number of code lines of a module.

In comparison to measuring techniques in physics, the measuring techniques in software engineering are taking only their first steps.

By measurement we understand the collection of values of a metric of the development process, the maintenance process or software products by means of tools (e.g. static analysers, project data collection and project evaluation systems). Examples of measuring are finding out how much time will be used for a sort program with the help of a software monitor, and determining a nesting depth of loops in a procedure by means of a source code analyser. Measurement is one of several empirical methods for finding the magnitude of a feature. Apart from measurements there are tests, sampling and the simulation of software.

When we classify these processes on an objective–subjective scale, measuring lies in the area of objective testing and sampling in the area of subjective testing. The finished software product is tested in the actual application environment with previously specified test cases. During this process, observations are evaluated. A possible process of measuring is as follows:

1. Defining measurement aims.
2. Deriving measurement tasks from measurement aims.
3. Determining measurement objects.
4. Fixing measurement metrics and measurement scales.

5. Allocating of measurement methods and measurement tools to measurement objects and metrics.
6. Finding measurement values.
7. Interpreting metrics.

As an example of measurement we shall look at ascertaining the frequency of literals in a procedure.

Measurement aim:	Determine the frequency of literals.
Measurement task:	Count the literals in the source code.
Measurement object:	Choose a special procedure, e.g. procedure x.
Metrics:	Number of literals/non-commented lines of code (NCLOC).
Measuring unit:	Literals/1000 NCLOC.
Measuring methods/ tools	LEX/YACC (UNIX environment).
Interpretation:	A large number of literals in the code means greater maintenance cost, e.g. higher probability of errors.

In this example, we can already recognise some questions and problems which the person responsible for this measuring task will have to answer or to solve. The first question is why we measure at all. The interpretation of measurement values shows us that there is a hypothesis which creates a link between error probability, maintenance cost and the existence of literals in the code. Measuring is probably done to guarantee quality and to improve maintenance.

A further problem is connected with the interpretation of measurement values. There should be a clear evaluation scale for measurements which makes it possible to distinguish between good and bad. In our example, it makes sense to show a scale with the two values 0 and 1. 0 means poor quality (the code contains a positive number of literals) and 1 means good quality (the code does not contain literals).

In section 1.3.7 we shall discuss rules and processes which make realistic ascertaining and utilisation of metrics possible.

1.3.3 Quality criteria for software quality metrics

The concept of quality measurement is widespread in specialist discussion and in the literature. It has spread further since the word 'metric' has come to be used interchangeably with measurement without any critical examination. I am reluctant to use the word 'measurement' for various reasons. First of all, in natural sciences and technological engineering there exists a measurement theory which was developed during the last hundred years. It defines 'measurement' exactly (see section 1.3.4). Second, in the last fifty years, in empirical social science research the concepts of measuring and measurement have also been discovered and defined [Hüls75, Hell74]. Third, the concept of measurement has also been exactly defined in mathematics. Attempts at applying these mathematical concepts in software engineering have failed [Schm87].

Since the concept of measure is preconceived, there is no general recognised theory which is suitable as a concept for software engineering. Nevertheless, for the purposes of measuring in software engineering, we shall examine quality criteria for quality metrics that will lead us towards software measures.

Most of the presently published metrics do not fulfil the following quality criteria for software measures and are falsely described as 'measures'.

According to Itzfeld, Schmidt and Timm [Itzf84] the following quality criteria must be met before we can speak of a software quality measure:

Objectivity

A measurement is objective if no subjective influence on measuring by the tester is possible.

Reliability

A measurement is reliable (i.e. stable and precise) if, on repeated measuring, under the same conditions, the same results are obtained.

Validity (measuring suitability)

A measurement is valid when the measurement results allow a clear conclusion on quality characteristics.

Normalisation

For normalisation it is necessary to have a scale on which the results of measuring can be clearly represented. A measurement is normalised when a comparative scale exists.

Comparability

A measurement is comparable when it can be set in relation to other measurements.

Economy

A measurement is economical when it can be carried out at low cost. The economy of a measurement depends on the degree of automation of the measuring process and on the number of measurement values. It is usually improved by the use of tools.

Usefulness

The criterion which is most difficult to prove is validity. Measurements for which no statements about validity exist are useless for objective quality evaluation.

Summarising, we can say that for measuring quality we need simple measurements which are expressive and relevant. They should be calibrated against each other so that derived statements complement each other.

1.3.4 Principles for measurement theory

In this section we shall consider the preconditions, requirements and principles for measuring software from the perspective of measurement theory [Zuse85]. Measurement theory starts from the premise that there are two aspects: an empirical area and, through mathematical aids, a definable range of numbers. Measuring in the sense of measurement theory means that there is a homomorphism between the empirical field and the range of numbers. This statement can be clarified with the example of two pieces of wire of the lengths a and b. The two pieces of wire form the empirical field, which may be examined more closely by physical measuring instruments. In the number range we define a 'greater than' relation based on real numbers. We can now say that, in the empirical system, b is longer than a when there is a measuring value $\mu(b)$ which is greater than $\mu(a)$ on the axis of the real numbers.

The same applies when placing pieces of wire in a row, which is sensibly presented in the numerical area by adding. If we generalise, this means that operations from both areas have the same characteristics. If wire a is longer than wire b, for example, and this in turn is longer than wire c, this means that a is longer than c. Analogues apply to the numerical area.

A further important consequence of measurement theory is that an expression involving measured values is meaningful when its true value is invariable under transformations. This means, for example, for longitudinal measures that we can do a longitudinal calculation in miles, kilometres, yards or metres at any time.

What are the problems in connection with measuring software? One of the main difficulties is that we first need to clarify what we want to measure, i.e. determine the volume and the object to be measured.

The statement that there is a homomorphism, i.e. a function from the real world into a formal numerical world, means at the same time that there is also a scale. The problem is to decide which scale. The solution to this problem depends on the empirical system. If we can determine definitely that there is a relationship between the real world and a set of numeric values, then we can also determine the form of the scale to be used. The number of scales is determined by which permissible transformations we can carry out on the scales. Coombs, Raiffa and Thrall (see [Zuse85]) differentiate between a hierarchy of scales built up in layers (Figure 1.7). Each hierarchically higher scale always has the characteristics of a hierarchically lower scale.

We shall now pay more detailed attention to the different scales and their characteristics.

The nominal scale is used for purely qualitative features. It shows equality or inequality of the features. With a nominal scale it is also possible to determine whether or not an object clearly belongs to a class. Examples of nominal scales

Figure 1.7 Scale
hierarchy according
to Coombs, Raiffa and
Thrall

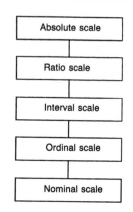

are the registration numbers on student identity cards and the ranking numbers
of leagues of football teams.

The distinguishing feature of an ordinal scale is that each monotonically
increasing function provides a permitted transformation. 'Greater than', 'less than',
or 'equal to' relations are possible. Ordinal scales permit the generation of median,
rank and rank correlation coefficients. Examples of ordinal scales are grades in
school reports, the classification of engine capacity in cars and the Beaufort scale
for wind forces.

An interval scale allows any positive linear transformation. It is significant that
on this scale not only the ranking but also the differences between intervals remain
invariant. Arithmetic means and standard deviations can be computed
meaningfully. Examples of interval scales are temperature scales (Celsuis,
Fahrenheit, Reaumur).

A ratio scale is noted for its permitted transformation of each similar function
($f' = u.f$, u real, $u > 0$). Meaningful units may be used on this scale and an
absolute or natural zero point is possible. The permissible operations on this scale
include the generation of quotients, percentage calculations, mean values and
standard deviations. Examples of the application of ratio scales are length, mass,
time, angle, volume, temperature (Kelvin) and price.

The absolute scale is noted for the permitted transformation of each identity
function ($f' = f$). This type of scale represents the most unequivocal scale. Because
only identity transformations are permissible, everything remains invariant.
Examples are frequency and probability.

The basic task of counting and measuring in software engineering consists of
the fixing of types of scale for values to be observed. For many of the values
known today, justification for the type of scale is missing. In my opinion, this
leads to invalid actions, for example, the generation of mean values from the
values of observations which do not justify numeric interpretations.

1.3.5 *Overview of quality measurement and metrics*

The history of software measurements is already relatively long. Rubey and Hartwick [Rube68] published a text on the 'Quantitative measurement of program quality' in 1968. Since that time a large number of measures, especially with regard to complexity, have been published or suggested. Complexity is often used in different contexts, however, so that it makes sense to look at different aspects a little more closely.

In theoretical computing, it is common to define a type of complexity which provides classification of algorithms and estimation of their efficiency. The principal questions which have to be asked with the aid of theory about calculable complexity are:

- How many steps of calculation does an algorithm need?
- How much storage space does an algorithm require?

Software complexity is a frequently used concept. It deals among other things with confusing relationships between software elements (i.e. different classes of instructions, data structures, interfaces of different kinds). The concepts of structure complexity and software technology complexity are used interchangeably.

A different view of software complexity places the activity of the software developer at centre stage. The situation becomes complex when the software developer needs to understand, alter or create software.

Specific measures of this kind of complexity occur again and again in the form of problem complexity and design complexity, but also as program or product complexity. Hidden behind this is the desire to estimate the amount of work involved in the software development with the aid of complexity measures.

Software measures are frequently divided into process and product measures. A process measure is a quantifiable attribute of the development (and maintenance) process or of the development (and maintenance) environment. Examples of this are measures which describe the experience of the developer (i.e. number of years of programming experience) and the cost of the development process. A product measure is a quantifiable attribute of the product which is measured. Product measures do not state anything about the creation of the product or the reason for the product being in its present actual state.

According to Conte, Dunsmore and Shen [Cont86] product metrics comprise the size of the product (e.g. the number of lines of code or the number of terminal symbols in a program), the structure complexity (e.g. control flow, depth of nesting, depth of recursion), the data structure complexity (e.g. the number of variables used or data files) and the product application area (e.g. payroll), or combinations of these.

In recent years, product or process measures have been increasingly used in connection with models for the explanation of the development or maintenance process. These models mostly serve for estimation of the productivity or the cost of processes.

We now return to the concept of complexity measures and try to create a system of metrics. Basili [Basi83] offers an interesting starting position. He enumerates:

1. Static measures which measure the quality of the product at a given time. They are divided into:

    (a) Measurements which embrace the size of the product: for example, number of instructions (LOC, ELOC), number of operators and operands (see section 1.3.6), number of functions (a function is activated by the user of the product) and number of modules (a module is an independently translatable program unit).

    (b) Measurements which measure the program control structure of a product: for example, the nesting levels or the number of binary branches. In this process, the program control structure is presented as a graph.

    (c) Measures which concern the data structures. We are here concerned with the use of data in the program: for example, the number of variable entries in the data map, the number of operands, the average scope of variables expressed in the number of lines of code from the first to the last reference or data, and the coupling metrics which describe the degree of utilisation of variables between modules.

2. Development measures (historical measures) which measure the quality of a product over a given time: for example, the number of alterations of the program text up to release.

At this moment in time about 100 metrics exist in the literature which can be consulted for evaluating static program complexity. Each of these 100 metrics represents a different view of complexity.

A small example [Blas85] shows the difficulty of comparing metrics. All metrics belong to the classification of static program complexity.

Figure 1.8 shows how difficult the interpretation of the different complexity metrics is. Each metric number has three control flow graphs: G_1 with three sequential if-then-else instructions, G_2 with three nested if-then-else instructions and G_3 with two nested if-then-else instructions and one do-while loop.

If we look at the values of the individual metrics, very different metric results can be noted. The conclusion from this example is that the chosen metrics measure different features and are therefore not comparable. The classification concept 'static program complexity' is too rough for an objective base of comparison.

In [GMD84] another system for metrics is suggested. Fifty metrics were divided into the following aspects:

*   analysability;
*   static complexity on the level of a module;
*   error predictability/frequency;
*   modifiability;
*   modularity;
*   system independence (from hardware or operation system);

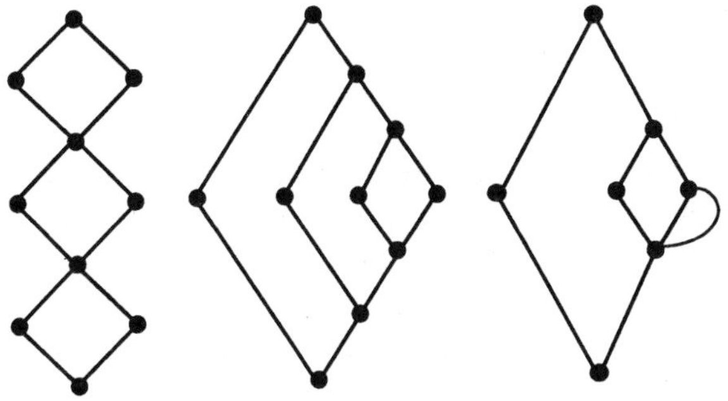

Figure 1.8 Examples of static complexity metrics

	G_1	G_2	G_3
McCabe	4	4	4
Belady	15	25	14
Chen	2	4	4
Withworth	18.44	15.8	12.3
Dunsmore	3	6	6
Harrison (Scope)	15	24	18
Oviedo	12	10	7
Schmidt	4	4.39	4.56
Blaschek H(T)	1.6	2.42	2.27
W(T)	9	8	7
Wr(T)	2.81	1.65	1.26

- testability;
- understandability of program text; and
- any other.

The study examined which qualification characteristic can be allocated to each metric. The following different characteristics were noted:

- utilisability;
- correctness;
- reliability;
- efficiency;
- security;
- maintainability;
- adaptability;
- extendibility;
- linkability;
- recyclability; and
- transferability.

Most metrics exist for the characteristics relating to maintenance and reliability.

Summarising, we can say that to this day no generally recognised system for measurements and metrics exists. A system which offers detailed representation in the area of process and product metrics, and which divides product metrics into the sub-areas of module-related and system-related metrics/measures, would be desirable.

Validation of most metrics can be considered as unsatisfactory. This may also be the reason for their reluctant acceptance. It must be admitted that many treatments in this study are lacking concrete statements about their validity: that is, the random samples chosen for validating metrics were too small.

1.3.6   Classical software metrics

After this overview we will now discuss some known metrics in more detail and note problems in the handling of software metrics. The most frequently used metrics are those of McCabe [McCa76] and of Halstead [Hals77]. Both are unsatisfactory because they simplify program features too much [Rech86] and overemphasise the source code as the central measured object.

McCabe's metric

McCabe started by presenting a program as a directed graph. The nodes on this graph are the instructions, and the edges are the control flow between the nodes. McCabe takes the view that program complexity is dependent on the number of main paths of this program graph. By main paths (linearly independent program paths) he means the minimum number of edge paths, V, which are necessary without overlapping in order to cover combinations of all the edges. The formula for this is:

$$V(g) = e - n + 2p$$

where e is the number of edges in the program graph; n is the number of nodes in the program graph; p is the number of components (disconnected components of graphs, e.g. procedures).

Figure 1.9 is an example of the application of McCabe metrics where $V(g) = 6$.

McCabe uses his metric in order to find a minimum number of test cases via the number of linearly independent program paths. He suggests that a good qualitative upper limit for his metric, $V(g)$, is 10.

McCabe notes further that the program graph (the graph of the flow of execution) is a very good means of recognising the program style involved. McCabe even says that through this control graph the programmer of a code component would be clearly identifiable.

McCabe's metric is none other than the number of decisions, ands, ors and nots + 1. The IBM Laboratory in LaGaude (France) has carried out tests on the metric of McCabe and has produced the following rules:

1. A module must be designed in such a way that $V(g) \leq 15$.
2. Modules with $V(g) \leq 9$ are to be ignored on inspection.

The main criticism of McCabe's metric is that only one program skeleton (flow

```
PROCEDURE StEval2__3 (VAR Evalarray      : Eval2__3;
                          Formarray      : Part2__4;
                          Limit          : INTEGER);
VAR NoCom : BOOLEAN;
        i,j : INTEGER;
BEGIN
    FOR i := 1 TO Limit DO
        NoCom := FALSE;
        FOR J := 1 TO 3 DO
            CASE Formarray [i,j] OF
                2 : INC (Evalarray [i,j] ) |
                9 : NoCom := TRUE |
                ELSE NoCom := NoCom;
            END (*case*)
        END; (*for*)
        IF NoCom THEN INC (Evalarray [i,4] ) END;
        END (*for*)
END StEval2__3;
```

Figure 1.9(a) Source code 'StEval2__3'

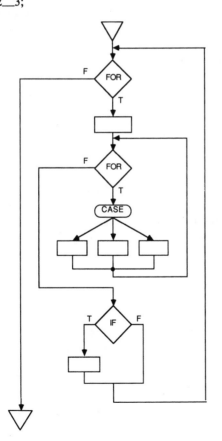

Figure 1.9(b) Program run 'StEval2__3'

Figure 1.9(c) Control flow graph of 'StEval2__3'

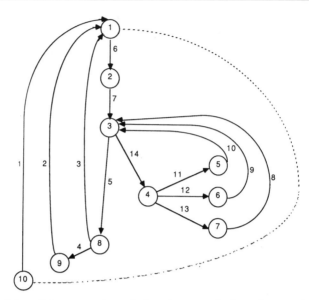

graph) is taken into account, and that the complexity of not only individual instructions (in particular those of expressions), but also of nested instructions is not taken into account. The wide use of McCabe's metric is due to the simple way in which it can be calculated. It relies on the fact that the program has only one entrance and one exit: $V(g) = 1 +$ number of binary branches in the program.

McCabe's metric was improved by several authors on the basis of the above criticism and has served as a departure point for further metrics development. A good overview of this can be found in [Rech86].

McCabe's viewpoint is one of many. There are examples of program graphs (see Figure 1.10) where $V(g)$ does not express inherent complexity.

As we can see from Figure 1.10, all three control flow graphs contain a $V(g)$ = 4. We note intuitively, however, that graph G1 appears more complex than G_2, and G_2 more complex than G_3. As a basis for our complexity observations we can look at the aspect of nesting. For this we use the metric by Monika Schmidt [Schm85]. The nested metric is defined as follows:

$$\epsilon = \sum_{n=1}^{N} \frac{1 - \dfrac{1}{d_n}}{N}$$

Where:

N is the number of branches in the program graph

d_n is the number of further branch points determined by the nth point + 1.

Consequently, $0 \leq \epsilon < 1$.

If we now compare the ϵ values ($\epsilon(G_1) = 0$; $\epsilon(G_2) = 0.22$; $\epsilon(G_3) = 0.39$) of the three control flow graphs, the complexity of the nesting becomes clear. However, on closer analysis we can see that normalising by using N gives invalid results (see [Roth87]).

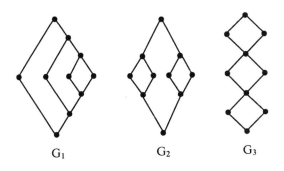

Figure 1.10 Example of three control flow graphs

G_1 G_2 G_3

This example illustrates the problem of definition and validation of metrics. On the one hand, there are different aspects of complexity which are in each case best expressed by their appropriate metric. On the other hand, from the economical and pragmatic view we want one and only one metric which expresses all complexity aspects. Rechenberg tries this in [Rech86] with his compound complexity metric (CC). His complexity metric takes into account readability, understandability and alterability of programs. But metric theory shows clearly the limits and dangers of this metric. Differing complexity aspects are linked by relational operators without the proof of whether this is at all possible on the underlying mathematical structures.

Halstead's metric

The approach of Halstead (see [Hals77]) rests on the premise that a program consists only of operands and operators. Each symbol or keyword which marks an action is called an operator (e.g. arithmetic operators like +, -, *, /; keywords like WHILE, FOR, READ, etc.; special symbols like =, brackets, etc.; functions like EOF, etc.). All symbols which represent data are called operands (variables, constants and labels). The classification of the operands and operators is language dependent and was not clearly noted by Halstead. The following are defined as basic metrics:

n_1 ... number of distinct operators in the program
n_2 ... number of distinct operands in the program
N_1 ... total number of all operator occurrences
N_2 ... total of all operand occurrences
$n = n_1 + n_2$ ... number of different symbols in the program
$N = N_1 + N_2$ ... total number of all symbols in the program

We also call n the vocabulary of the program and N the program length. The latter is an intuitive metric for program size.

The program volume (also program capacity) is defined as:

$$V = N \log_2 n$$

This formula was created by Halstead as an extension of information theory. It describes the length of a sentence in optimal binary coding under the condition that there is an equal distribution of words. Research work by Smith [Smit80] from the IBM Laboratory in Santa Teresa has shown that there is a strong correlation between executable lines of code (ELOC), program length and program volume, i.e. that all three metrics give a good estimation for the module size. The difference between the three metrics lies in the fact that the volume and the length are language independent, while ELOC is language dependent.

Halstead characterises the difficulty of understanding or writing a program thus:

$$D = \frac{n_1 \cdot N_2}{2 \cdot n_2}$$

where D is a function of the vocabulary and the number of operands. The quotient N_2/n_2 is an indicator of the average use of operands. From the formula for D (in particular because of $n_1/2$) one could derive that languages with a large number of operators (for example, assembler languages) lead to large D values. This conclusion does not take into account the semantics of operators (compare the semantics of operators in APL and in assembler languages). D describes the effort of coding from algorithms, the effort of code reviews (reading of code) and the understanding of code at maintenance time.

Halstead presents the programming effort E as a function of the volume V and the degree of difficulty D.

$$E = D.V$$

The metric units are elementary mental discriminations. Halstead sees E as a mental effort in the course of a programming task, and states that the programmer has to go through logical mental steps when formulating such a task. He referred to works by the psychologist, Stroud, who examined the rate of brain work and in particular the structure of elementary brain operations. According to his study, the brain of a programmer carries out between 5 and 18 elementary operations per second. This statement permits the conversion of metrics into time expenditure.

Sheppard [Arth85] noted in experiments in 1980 that there is a strong correlation between the programming effort, E, and the programming cost, which is calculated in person-days or person-months.

Halstead also considered the number of errors which occur in programming. He evaluates the number of expected programming errors by the following formula:

$$\beta = \frac{V}{3000}$$

Halstead noted in experiments that, after 3000 elementary operations in the brain, a programming error occurs in the product.

If we now summarise Halstead's approach critically, we note the following:

- Halstead only looks at one part of the development process, namely at translation of the detailed design in the source code (the so-called coding). He leaves many issues of complexity untouched (e.g. depth of nesting, scope of names, etc.).

- Halstead's metrics are to be viewed carefully, since multiple meaning in the fundamental measuring (classification rules for operands and operators) or errors in the measuring tool can falsify the results. Furthermore, he does not take into account the calibration of measuring tools.

However, Halstead's method surely points the right way towards measuring within the framework of software creation. It would be desirable if similar measuring approaches were created for earlier phases (e.g. the rough design or the detailed design), and if all relevant complexity causes were taken into account.

1.3.7   Experiences of the use of quality metrics

Itzfeld examined (see [Itzf87]) the use of quality metrics in practical computing in Germany. Regarding the interpretation of metrics for the evaluation of quality characteristics, the following ranking order was noted:

67%   maintainability (the ability to maintain easily, look after, test, alter, adapt, extend)

65%   user-friendliness (usability, ease of handling, operation, application and, documentation, transparency)

60%   reliability (availability, robustness, resilience, stability, maintainability, ability to react in error situations, reproducibility)

40%   correctness (function reliable, error free, correct, usable, complete)

19%   efficiency (performance, durability, economic use of resources, timings)

15%   portability (transferability, compatibility)

17%   other (modularity, structure, system conformity, use of standards)

An important outcome of these statistics is the realisation that maintainability is of great importance in commercial computing. Characteristics such as correctness and efficiency, which played a big part in the past, are now of less importance.

It is also interesting to note which metrics in practical computing are used for the evaluation of certain characteristics. The study leads to the following classes of characteristics and metrics:

- *Efficiency*: transaction times, implementation, number of entries and exit operations.
- *Correctness*: McCabe's complexity metrics, test cover metrics, number of errors per time unit, Biwowarsky complexity metrics, Moses metric, MTBF statistics.
- *Reliability*: test coverage metrics, down times or rates, remaining error rate, NDBF statistics.
- *Maintainability*: McCabe's complexity metric, number and size of modules, size of procedures, depth of nesting, number of errors per unit time in relation

to the number of altered lines of code, number of alterations per unit time, level of documentation for the program.

The random sample of the study comprises 285 users with a return rate of 20 per cent.

From this study it is clear that quality problems lie in maintenance. A collection of tools for a few salient metrics are required. The necessity for measurement of quality for objective control of software quality is no longer queried on competitive and legal grounds. The practitioner expects better tool support for measuring and proof of their suitability as instruments for measuring quality.

Arthur reports on the use of metrics in program tests [Arth85]. In a Cobol development environment, programs should be examined in more detail if the following levels of magnitude are exceeded:

- $ELOC > 100$
- $V(g) > 10$
- difficulty > 50
- effort $> 100,000$
- decision density $> 20\%$
- function density $< 10\%$
- comment density $< 10\%$

Note:
Decision density = (Total count of all decisions/$ELOC$) $\times$ 100
Function density = (Total count of all functions/$ELOC$) $\times$ 100
Comment density = (Number of all comments/LOC) $\times$ 100
ELOC = executable lines of code

A few thoughts on the practical use of metrics are offered in conclusion. Metrics are not the only solution to the software crisis. Many companies have more pressing problems than the use of metrics and quality measures. Nevertheless metrics are an important aid to making the qualitative creation and care of working results transparent. Beyond this they promote an engineering style and therefore a systematic process not only in the development, but also in the maintenance process.

It is important to remember that only the processes and the resulting products are to be evaluated with metrics and measurements, never the staff involved. Moreover, metrics can be misused. For example, isolated and strict prescription of quality goals in the form of measured values of quality can lead to deliberate adjustment of prescribed values of metrics by the software developer in fear of criticism of the modules being developed. This would prevent an optimal solution to the problem.

Like many other aids in software engineering, measurements and metrics must be used carefully and under control, and must only be applied together with comprehensive quality assurance measures. They are only ever indicators for certain points of observation within a quality expression.

Here we can pose a number of questions which facilitate the application of metrics:

Why do I measure at all?

The reason for measuring, and possibly the context of the situation to be measured, must be determined. The reason for measuring can be not only problems, but also goals which concern the development process or product (intermediate and final outputs of phases).

What do I measure?

Having established reasons, features are searched for which describe the problems or goals convincingly. In connection with this, the object measured must be determined. For each feature we need a metric which is simple to determine and to measure. The magnitude must be defined exactly, i.e. a calculation formula must be stated. All elements of this formula must be tested for ease of understanding, clarity and consistency. The metric of the dimension and the type of scale on which the measured values are to be registered need careful thought. Quality models (see Appendices A1 and A2) constitute a good aid for the determining of features and metrics.

The hypothesis between the metric and the feature/characteristic to be estimated must be stated. By this we mean the influence of measured value alterations on the feature or characteristic. In concrete terms this shows whether, for example, an increasing metric value causes the quality to improve or deteriorate. In addition, a possible connection between the metric size of one feature and those of other features can be observed.

How do we measure?

An algorithm or a tool must be prescribed with which the measuring is to be carried out. Appropriate organisational or staff preconditions must be seen to make measuring possible. Moreover, the question of how complete and up-to-date the metric data are must be asked.

What do the metric values tell us?

An interpretation or a guideline for evaluation of the metric values must be stated, i.e. it must be determined what a qualitative good or a qualitative bad metric value is.

Can I carry out measuring with changed trial conditions and parameters?

This leads us to the problem of the validation of metrics. With this line of questioning we want to indicate that the stability of measuring (i.e. the validity of measuring results) must be examined in the form of suitable trial planning when carrying out the experiment.

How viable is measuring?

In order to answer this question the information gain of the measuring activity must be examined. For example, through measuring relevant quantities the basis for decisions can be extended and arguments for improved measures of the development process can be gained. We must answer the question of whether, through the determination of metrics, technical or organisational changes are necessary. Either can increase the effort of a measuring activity considerably. When evaluating the cost—benefit relationship, the value of improved quality management must be included.

Summarising, the following measures are recommended to establish the measuring of magnitudes:

- First of all, convince management of the use of measuring. Without this, quality assurance cannot be carried out sensibly.
- Automate the finding and evaluation of metrics wherever possible. Construct the necessary measuring infrastructure (measuring tools, measurements database) for your requirements. This improves the potential use and acceptance considerably.
- Consult the programmers and analysts when developing and improving measurements. This improves the acceptance of measuring tools and results.
- Collect and store the obtained values of metrics over a long time (at least three years).
- Analyse the collected measured values and observe trends, regularities and irregularities in the measured values.
- Examine and research the causes of these analysed results. Consult the project leader and management on this activity.

With these measures, a simple metrics system can be established. Regular workshops help to reinforce comprehension and retention of such a system.

Research will have to make a concerted effort in validating measurements. Only proven metrics suitable for measuring can overcome existing acceptance barriers. Without co-operation between research and computing practitioners, we might have to wait a long time for safe and practicable quality measures.

1.4   Quality models

According to DIN standards, the quality of a software product is the totality of characteristics and features which relate to the suitability of this product to meet the prescribed requirements. This definition is a general statement for the concept of quality, but for concrete planning and evaluation tasks it is still not exact enough.

Not only for specification but also for testing the target levels of quality requirements, we therefore need aids which are related on the one hand to the development process and on the other to the product. Quality models make specifications possible which take into account the requirements of the software product as well as the process. In the past, different quality models have been developed: for example, by Boehm [Boeh76a], McCall [McCa77] (see Appendix A1), Murine [Muri84], NEC [Azum85], Schweiggert [Schw84] and Wallmüller [Wall87a] (see Appendix A2).

1.4.1 Structure and contents of quality models

With the aid of a quality model, the general quality concept is made operational by its derivation from sub-concepts (see Figure 1.11). The individual sub-concepts can be measured and evaluated through the determining of indicators, which are either product or process measures. We call these measures 'quality metrics'.

An important aspect of these quality models is the systematic partitioning of quality characteristics which has metrics as its lowest level. Boehm was the first to suggest and show 21 characteristics and about 60 quality metrics in his model for evaluation of software in 1976.

Depending on the prescribed quality model and the specific product requirements, a specific number of characteristics, features and metrics is determined for each project. The number of these can vary considerably. For example, when dealing with a product with high maintenance requirements, added attention will have to be given to the modularity of software architecture, readability and easy understanding of the code in design and coding. These features can have an inverse relationship with the efficiency of the executable code, i.e. a program with a clear modular structure and a clear code can be slower in its execution than an unstructured, complex solution. We can now see that there can be goal conflicts in the definition of different features.

On the whole, in many projects only functional requirements, performance requirements and requirements of the user interface are specified. Requirements regarding ease of maintenance, portability or similar characteristics are mostly

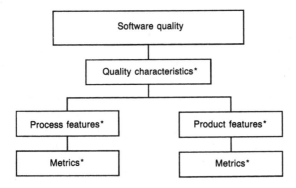

Figure 1.11 Structure of a quality model

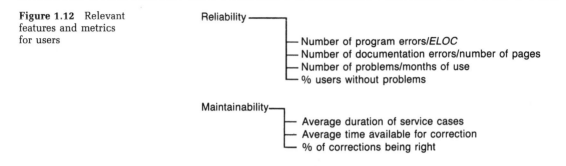

Figure 1.12 Relevant features and metrics for users

forgotten or ignored. The reason for this is that the people responsible for the specification do not have any aids for formulating these quality requirements. Quality models and, thus, quality metrics now provide the opportunity for specifying these requirements.

The application of these models must also be supported by the customer and contractor, and must be included in the project. Interesting features and metrics from the user's perspective are shown in Figure 1.12.

Examples of simple metrics from the perspective of the developer which can be obtained directly are the maximum number of instructions of a module, the nesting level of control structures and the percentage of the comments lines of a module. These metrics are suitable for estimating or evaluating the comprehensibility of a module.

The following objectives are attained through the application of quality models [Wall87a]:

- The different ideas of software quality are made consistent.
- There is uniform communication.
- Quality becomes concrete, i.e. it is definable and can be planned.

One disadvantage is that the conjectures and the connection between metrics, features and characteristics have not yet been proved theoretically, and thus are only at the stage of hypothesis. The development and validation of quality models is a current area of research in software engineering.

In Figure 1.13 the application of a quality model is demonstrated. The SPARDAT quality model, which is described in Appendix A2, serves as a basis. Operational effectiveness is important for a special project and can be further improved through different quality characteristics. As an example, one important characteristic is correctness. For the evaluation of correctness we use the features of achieved testing levels and complexity of a module. A number of modules which have been subjected to a code inspection and test cover for commands, branching and functions are suitable as metrics for the obtained levels of testing. The complexity of a module is estimated using McCabe's metric and depends on the maximum nesting depth of the control commands and the number of interface elements in the module.

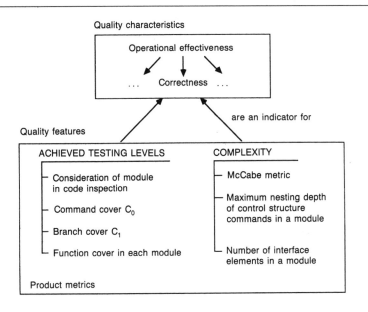

Figure 1.13 Detail from the SPARDAT quality model

For quality planning of a particular module, the following strategy is of interest. On the one hand, maximisation of the different test coverages is to be reached and verified where certain prescribed values are defined. On the other hand, the complexity of a module is limited by the prescribed values of certain bounds. On the basis of McCabe and IBM, a limit of 10 for $V(g)$ and of 4 for the nesting depth of procedures is sensible.

Quality models help to improve process quality. Typical process problems are, for example, unsatisfactory project planning and control, underestimation of development cost at the beginning of the project, and delayed delivery of the product. By choosing suitable metrics for specific process factors such as project planning and leadership, or through standardised procedures within the project, product or process problems can be more easily handled. For adherence to deadlines, the following metric could be introduced: deferred milestones/number of milestones per month and project.

Quality models can also help us to a better understanding and demonstration of the relationships between characteristics. We know of three classes of relationship between characteristics:

* unconnected;
* competing; and
* reinforcing.

Two quality characteristics are unconnected if there is no visible effective interaction between them, i.e. if there is no effective interaction between manifestations of quality features of these characteristics. For example, portability and correctness are unconnected.

Two characteristics are competing if the improvement of one characteristic results in the deterioration of the other. For example, increased reliability does, as a rule, lead to deterioration in performance.

Two characteristics are reinforcing if the improvement of the quality of one characteristic affects the improvement of the quality of the other. For example, correctness and reliability are reinforcing characteristics.

Quality models are also a very good aid for improving the influence of independent quality assurance staff. The problem when employing independent quality assurance staff lies in the fact that these people are distant from the actual project activity, and often do not have a direct relationship with the actual problems and difficulties in the project. Through a well-defined network of metrics in all phases and tailoring to the peculiarities of the project, independent staff can also discover faults in the development process or in intermediate and end products somewhat earlier. Hence, quality models can be used as early warning systems for quality assurance teams. In this way, weak points in the development process are recorded early and suitable constructive aids can be applied.

One important aspect of quality planning and evaluation is a set of ideas on quality. As already discussed, quality is not absolute but relative, and is always based on predetermined requirements. These predetermined requirements are, of course, very strongly dependent on the person who prescribes them. People from different environments dealing with the development of a software product have different ideas of quality. Dissmann and Zurwehn [Diss86] have tried to take this into account when constructing quality models. They define four groups of people who see the situation from different views. These are:

- users;
- managers;
- designers; and
- programmers.

For each of the various groups of people different quality views can be stated. Quality views comprise a large number of communicating quality characteristics which are relevant for planning and evaluation of quality for the group. In Figure 1.14(a)—(d) the relevant characteristics from the perspective of a user, a manager, a designer and a programmer are represented.

The first group are the users of a software product. Users of a software product can be people or technical systems which make use of the performance of a software system. Quality requirements of this group usually affect the interfaces of the product (user interfaces, system interfaces) and are activity related.

The second category of people with a distinctive quality view are managers of a software product. As distinct from the users, managers are those who provide software products in their area of influence i.e. they make the product available to the users, organise utilisation and determine the life cycle. The requirements of this group are, as a rule, application orientated and concerned with the future of the product.

The third group of people are the designers. They determine the technical structure of the product as the combination of components and the functions of components. The quality goals of this group affect, as a rule, the structuring of architecture, and aim at satisfaction of user and management requirements and control in the direction of development and/or further development of the product.

The fourth group of people are the programmers. They create the actual components of the system according to the prescribed functions in the form of programs and modules. Their quality goals usually concern the detailed programming structure, the programming style and the particular algorithms.

Evans and Marciniak [Evan87] hold the opinion that the different quality views determine the planning of the quality level of a product, and provide for a better understanding of the development process. They differentiate among customer, project manager and developer views. The customer view is, on the one hand, determined by the degree to which the delivered product meets the operational application conditions and the promised usefulness.

On the other hand, the customer is interested to know to what extent the quality and application of the product are affected by cost, time constraints and technical risks. The view of the project manager relates to reaching agreements regarding cost and time limits, and also an acceptable quality level which is competitive with other user products. Developers, and in particular the project leader, have the completeness and manageability of the development process at the forefront of their quality considerations. Meeting the specified requirements, or the proving of such, is an important quality goal for this group.

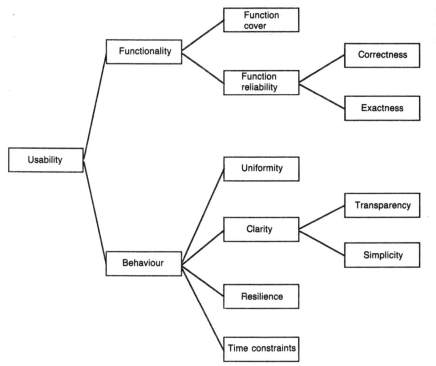

Figure 1.14(a) Relevant characteristics for users

Figure 1.14(b) Relevant characteristics for managers of software products

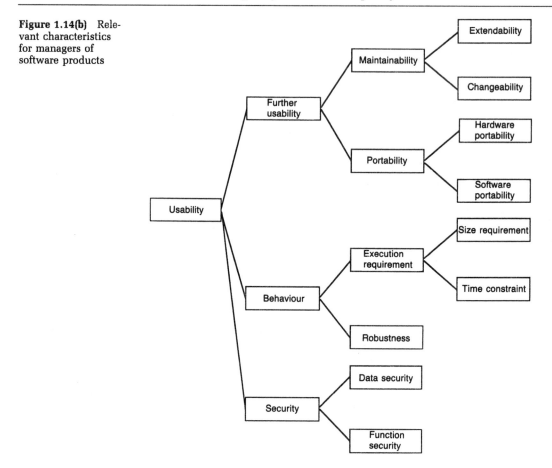

The limits of quality models today lie partly in the inability to describe software through quantifiable features, and partly in the poor structuring and formal description of development and maintenance processes. Many of the links between characteristics, features and metrics in quality models rest on values based on experience, most of them not systematically evaluated.

Summarising, we can say that, by taking into account the different views, applying a quality model becomes easier and simpler.

1.4.2 Pragmatic creation of a quality model

What possibilities are there when no mature quality model is available and serious quality planning and evaluation is to be carried out? I recommend a systematic handling process which takes into account the following rules:

- Identify the specifics of the application (classification of software products).
- Determine the important quality characteristics (maximum of 3).
- Define metrics for the individual features which can be easily found.

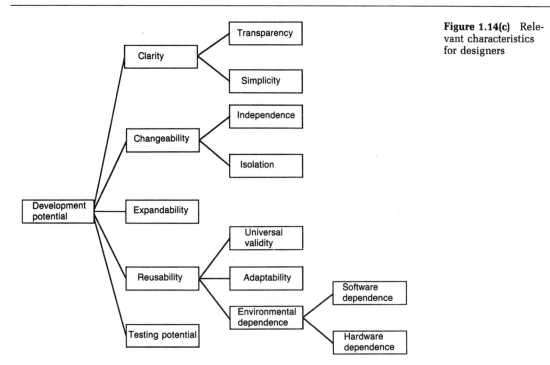

Figure 1.14(c) Relevant characteristics for designers

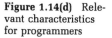

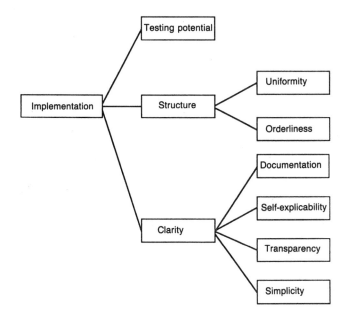

Figure 1.14(d) Relevant characteristics for programmers

- Organise the metrics into phases in which they can be measured and determined.
- Define measuring and evaluation methods and create checklists for the evaluation of unquantifiable features.
- Determine the point in time for measuring and evaluation.
- Select or develop simple tools which make measuring and evaluating easier.
- Try to prescribe limits and expected values for metrics. Discuss measures for reaching these limit and goal values.
- Find the values of metrics.
- Analyse the obtained values of metrics and compare them with the prescribed limits and expected values. The graphic representation of obtained values together with the limits and expected values promote the acceptance of quality planning.
- If there are deviations from the stipulated limits and expected values, initiate correction measures and check these.

The precondition for the creation and application of quality models is a stable development process with well-organised project management. The application of quality models leads to an increase in the error discovery rate during testing, to better productivity and to a reduction in maintenance cost [Azum87].

1.4.3 *Meaning of quality models in a quality assurance system*

Quality models are an actual research and development area of software engineering ([Azum85], [Asam86]). The better the development processes due to process models, the more possibilities there are for the application and use of quality models.

The central issues of quality assurance, such as quality planning, quality control and quality testing, can be solved only by metrics. Quality models offer a suitable foundation (characteristics, measurable and assessable features).

The three most important quality characteristics for a project must be chosen. Thereafter they are used for quantitative quality goals. This assumes that the respective features for these characteristics exist and that they are measurable. The relevant quality assurance measures can then be chosen in order to make sure that quality goals are reached. These measures comprise the application of methods, tools and aids, and quality control lies in their suitable practical application (see Figure 1.15).

At certain points in time which are defined in the quality assurance plan, intermediate evaluations are carried out in the form of quality tests on phase deliverables (Figure 1.16). They show us to what extent quality goals have been reached in each phase. At the same time, they cause the initiation of correction measures in order to reach the set quality goals. The principal concept here is to come to an acceptable quality level by using the systematic processes and practical aids of software engineering.

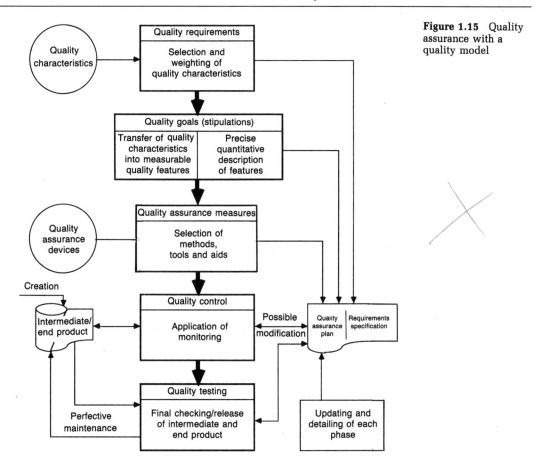

Figure 1.15 Quality
assurance with a
quality model

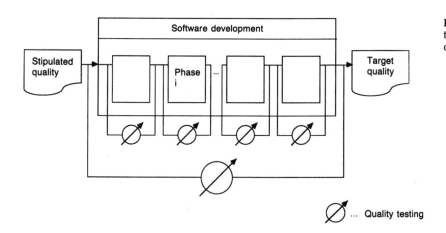

Figure 1.16 Quality
testing in the
development process

The following advantages [Azum85, Wall87a] can be achieved with the application of quality models:

- Quality goals can be specified by making available meaningful, quantifiable quality features for the product or the process.
- Quality can be evaluated objectively. In this way, the development factor quality can be planned and controlled.
- Management can see graphically to what extent quality goals have been reached [Azum85].
- The documentation of the product improves.
- Meeting user requirements becomes easier to check.
- Proof of the effect of quality assurance measures becomes transparent and therefore simpler.

Despite these advantages there are a number of problems which must be solved. Quality models have to be made to agree with the project infrastructure, the organisation structure of the developer, the management structure of the developer organisation, and social and psychological factors.

The selection of meaningful quantifiable features is different and diverse for different development processes, and validation of quality models is only in its beginnings. However, despite many unsolved problems, quality models are already a useful mechanism for improving the control of quality [Muri84].

2 Software quality and productivity

At present the demand for new applications surpasses the supply capacity of software development organisations in many companies and in the computing industry generally. This has been leading to an application backlog with many computer users for some time. At present software development processes are very labour intensive and demand well-trained and experienced developers, who will be in short supply in the not too distant future. This shows us that productivity is far too low in many computing organisations.

Attempts to increase productivity go in two directions:

- Application of methods, software tools and aids for the improvement of the conventional development process.
- Reduction of the labour-intensive process of programming by the application of fourth-generation languages (4GLs), generators and a development process which is not based on the classical life-cycle model (e.g. evolutionary prototyping). Here the end users are increasingly directly involved.

Both approaches can already look back on considerable practical results [Jone86]. In discussions about attempted solutions, the following questions occur again and again:

- What is productivity?
- What is the connection between productivity, its improvement and the quality of products?

So far, neither of the questions can be satisfactorily answered. An explanatory model for the development process is missing. In the following sections we can only give an overview of attempts to find solutions to these questions.

2.1 What is productivity?

The term 'productivity' has so far not been clearly defined. There are three aspects of productivity in connection with software development: time, return on investment and quality. If we want to increase productivity, we aim to:

- develop systems faster;
- develop systems which yield a better return on investment; and
- develop systems with better quality.

The first aspect points to a reduction in calendar time for the development of a software product. Many managers of computing organisations label this aspect 'efficiency increase'.

The second aspect can be formulated to say that a computing organisation simply wants to spend less money on the development and maintenance of software products with unchanged requirements.

The third aspect is concerned with quality assurance and is frequently mentioned in connection with the first aspect as one of the goals for a development organisation.

In order to reach these three goals, it is necessary to measure development productivity. For this we need productivity measures. Present acceptable productivity measurements are based on units delivered, lines of code per unit time or function points per unit time [Albr79]. Function points are only suitable for the evaluation of commercial information systems (low algorithmic complexity of solution). When calculating, then, the following application parameters are taken into account: number of user inputs, number of user outputs, number of user queries, number of files or databases, and number of interfaces to related applications or to other systems. Function points arrived at in this way are weighted by additional complexity parameters of the application and empirical constants of the development process.

The most frequently used productivity measures are as follows:

$$P_1 = \frac{CSI}{PY}$$

$$P_2 = \frac{Cost}{CSI}$$

$$P_3 = \frac{FP}{PM}$$

where *CSI* is the changed source instructions (new and modified lines of code), *PY* is person year, *PM* is person month and *FP* is function points.

The productivity measures based on lines of code (*LOC*) per unit time are unsatisfactory. The reasons for this are manifold:

- The actual creation process of code (programming) comprises only about 20 per cent of the entire development cost of an application [Case85]. Statements about the entire productivity of a development process must also take into account the activities of earlier phases.
- The problem of counting. How are comments, non-executable code and multi-used shared code to be counted? The counting of instructions is extremely problematic if one considers how, in modern languages such as Ada and Modula-2, instructions are delimited or grouped.
- It is not very sensible to motivate or evaluate staff on their *LOC* production. In most cases this leads to the production of useless code.

Productivity measures on the basis of function points have also come in for criticism:

- Estimation of the function points of an application which correlates with the number of produced instructions [Albr83] does not take into account the algorithmic complexity of the chosen solution.
- In the calculation of the function points, application parameters and weighting factors are used which are determined through subjective assessment and evaluation. (For example: are input, output, databases and queries complex?)

Each debate about productivity measures invariably leads also to the question of how the determined values are to be utilised. Should P_1 or P_3 values of a developer group be compared with those of another? Should management use these measurements also for the evaluation of individual developers or groups of developers? The answer to this question is a definite 'no'. The danger of comparing apples with pears is obvious and quickly leads to misinterpretations.

Boehm [Boeh87] defines productivity as follows:

$$P = \frac{\text{Produced results in the development process}}{\text{Cost}}$$

This points to the fact that we can improve the productivity of the development process if we either increase its results or lower its cost, or do both simultaneously. The cost of the development process comprises working and training cost, and the cost of computer resources and aids. Cost can be divided into the following cost classes:

- phases;
- activities;
- personnel;
- training; and
- aids.

Cost is best expressed in monetary units.

The critical discussion of Boehm's formula shows us the following difficulties and uncertainties:

- How are we to define the results, especially the phase-related results? What did earlier phases look like?
- How well are the results suited to evaluation and measuring? We have already discussed the advantages and disadvantages of the result *LOC*. However, there are also conceptional results such as a system concept or a requirement definition which cannot easily be evaluated quantitatively, and where a reduction in cost can lead to faults.
- The formula is not very well suited to the comparison of productivity values for different projects, since it does not take into account the different influences on productivity (see section 2.2).

We can therefore conclude that this attempt at defining productivity is also not devoid of difficulties. A closer examination of those factors which influence productivity appears necessary in order to be able to formulate an improved definition of productivity.

2.2 Productivity-influencing factors

A number of investigations have been made into the influence of different factors on productivity [Cont86]. We will now look at two of these in more detail, namely those of Packer [Lans86] and Remus [Remu82].

Packer of the MIT Laboratory for Manufacturing and Productivity has developed a qualitative method for examining productivity factors [Lans86]. This method was used for the first time within the area of productivity analysis by the Bank of America. For this Packer used a questionnaire approach with the four groups: programmers, analysts, managers and users. The questionnaires were used before and after certain technical and organisational changes in the system development process.

The questions centred on the organisational and company level and related to five groups of productivity factors which are used for interpreting the productivity of an organisation. They comprise the following:

1. Significance of work/job satisfaction/attitude to work.
2. Independence/adequate availability of resources/responsibility for the results.
3. Innovation/creativity/possibilities for organisational improvements.
4. Teamwork/management support.
5. Goals and feedback about the achieving of goals.

These five points were used for questioning the four groups involved. Through multiple-choice responses, all of which have a weighting, the average value of each group of factors (e.g. group 1) is determined and entered into a five-point scale on a productivity map. In the first step of the analysis, the ideal position from the viewpoint of management is shown (ideal organisational environment and working conditions), i.e. what does management need to meet its responsibilities? This initial evaluation graph (based on the weighted responses) can be used to analyse the differences between the ideal position of management and the strategic goals of the organisation.

For example, in Figure 2.1, group 3 has a considerably lower value than other groups in terms of the ideal management view. This points to an organisational weakness. If this is the case, the question of what can be done to promote innovation must be raised.

The second step shows the actual management view and compares this with the ideal. For example, there are significant differences in group 2. These were caused by a partial shifting of computer resources from development into production.

When all actual views of the four groups of people are available, the third step can begin with a comparison of these four views. The question is whether all

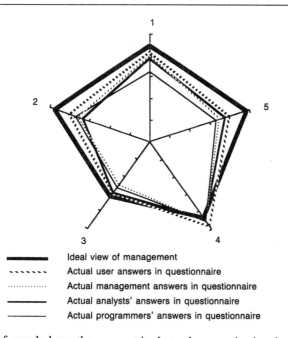

Figure 2.1 Packer's productivity chart for organisation

▬▬▬▬	Ideal view of management
＼＼＼＼＼	Actual user answers in questionnaire
·············	Actual management answers in questionnaire
────	Actual analysts' answers in questionnaire
────	Actual programmers' answers in questionnaire

four groups of people have the same attitude to the organisational environment and to the working conditions.

In Figure 2.1 the programmers give fewer points to cluster 1 than the other three groups. The cause for this might be that the relations between young programmers and senior programmers is bad or that no adequate incentive is offered to programmers.

In the fourth step, alterations over time in the organisation's productivity chart can be examined. For this it is necessary to ask the questions before and after an organisational alteration, to draw the charts and to compare them with one another.

In addition, specific productivity matters relating to areas of computing can be examined. The most important questions relate to the following six productivity factors:

1. Communication.
2. Strategic information systems planning (e.g. company-wide data organisation).
3. Project management.
4. Standards/quality assurance measures.
5. Staff leadership and promotion (e.g. specific further education courses in computing).
6. Technical development environment (e.g. personal development system).

When comparing the ideal with the actual viewpoints, Figure 2.2 shows the largest agreement on factor 6, while the greatest deviation lies at factor 2. The points 2, 3 and 4 carry relatively low values. This shows where improvements have to be made.

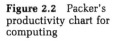

Figure 2.2 Packer's productivity chart for computing

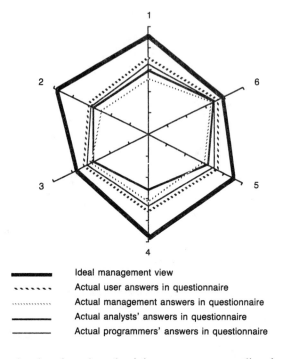

▬▬▬	Ideal management view
✕✕✕✕✕	Actual user answers in questionnaire
....	Actual management answers in questionnaire
▬▬▬	Actual analysts' answers in questionnaire
———	Actual programmers' answers in questionnaire

The predicted and evaluated productivity statements regarding the factors shown in the two diagrams are made before and after alterations on a productivity chart. They are then compared and their effects on the four groups discussed.

This is a useful approach which helps to evaluate technical as well as non-technical factors. It also becomes clear that high productivity can only be achieved by the four groups working together, and that it is influenced by the most varied factors. This systems engineering approach shows very clearly the complicated interaction of computing technology and organisation. However, it also puts quantitative individual terms such as *LOC*/unit time into perspective.

Remus, who carried out productivity analyses in the IBM Programming Laboratory in Santa Teresa, examined more closely the development and maintenance of system software. In doing so he differentiated between the types of influence on productivity which were due to the product itself, to the developer and to the management.

Product-dependent influence

- *Stability of requirements*. Vague and frequently changing requirements slow down the process.
- *Product size (LOC)*. When the amount of reusable code stays the same, or if there is no reusable code, productivity increases with product size. The explanation for this is that test overheads are larger for small products than for larger ones.

- *Type of code (new code/modified code).* The productivity is lower when modifying code than when writing new code.
- *Complexity/difficulty of setting tasks.* The complexity and difficulty of setting tasks influence the results of developers significantly. Experiments with different degrees of complexity have confirmed this.

Personnel-dependent influence

- *Ability and experience.* Checks have shown that the ability and experience of developers vary greatly. Controlled experiments by Chrysler [Chry78], Boehm [Boeh81] and Curtis [Curt81] confirm that experience has the greatest influence on productivity. These experiments showed that a programmer with several years' practical experience tends to be twenty times more productive than a programmer who has just finished his or her training.
- *Attitude and approach to work.* Apart from understanding the development process, the approach and attitude to work (in particular with respect to quality and productivity) are key elements in reaching better quality and higher productivity. Improvements can be made through assessment of working results and rewards to developers with a positive attitude.
- *Coding and design processes.* A significant difference can be noted when using different processes and tools. Suitable training and further training activities can lead to improvements.

Process-dependent influences

- *Process model.* An orderly process flow and knowledge of necessary process steps make a wide-ranging measuring and evaluation of the process possible.
- *Disruptions.* Disruptions and distractions to the workflow because of meetings, reviews, the training of new staff and unplanned events result in lower productivity (e.g. computer out of action, lack of support and agreements not kept which affect the developers).
- *Software technology solutions.* The choice of suitable software architecture is a decision for management. A bad decision leads to the revision of the phase deliverables and delays the development process. Prototyping and evolutionary development can help to avoid culs-de-sac during development.
- *Tools.* Tools which automate process steps (document and code generators, analysers, etc.) and support all phases (software engineering databases) can bring significant improvements. Management tools for monitoring product status are also a useful aid for the improvement of productivity. When applying tools the human factor is important. Tools must be user friendly: they should do what the user expects them to do.
- *Testing and measuring.* Regular measurements which are available to the developers for checking results lead to better quality and higher productivity. The development process becomes transparent through measuring and interpreting measured values, and involves all participants in the learning

process. The understanding of reasons for measuring/evaluating by staff and the avoidance of any kind of bureaucracy are important.

*   *Physical work environment and workplace equipment.* The effects of the following factors are recognised and must be taken into account for each development: equipment of the office workplace; availability of hardware; and easy access to computer terminals and work stations.

    The highest productivity acceleration is achieved (according to Remus) by the reuse of code and the application of tools.

Summary

On the basis of the above experiments, we see that the following factors influence productivity significantly:

*   Groups taking part in the development (management, developer, user).
*   Level of difficulty of task.
*   Development process model (processes, methods, tools).
*   Production requirements.
*   Development resources and especially their availability.

The achievement of better productivity is primarily a task for management and should consist of regular discussions with the developers (e.g. in the form of a working party).

2.3   Relation between quality and productivity

One might perhaps believe that measures for quality improvement cost more (e.g. the increased cost of constructive and analytical quality assurance measures), and that therefore better quality means lower productivity. These notions are purely speculative. They point to a missing explanation which might demonstrate in detail the link between quality, productivity and other development quantities.

The literature contains two simple explanatory models which show a connection between quality and productivity, one by A. Case [Case85] and the other by V. Basili [Basi84].

Case states that productivity is a function of efficiency and quality. By 'efficiency' he means the speed with which a resource solves a complete development task. The generation of 100 lines of specification, source code or documentation by means of, for example, a generator, is more efficient than the generation of 50 lines per unit time by using the same resource. This has no connection with productivity so far.

Assuming the same external and internal process conditions, faster execution of the development process increases the probability of defects in the product. These defects can be dealt with either in the development process or later in the maintenance phase. Both alternatives require additional cost. As mentioned before,

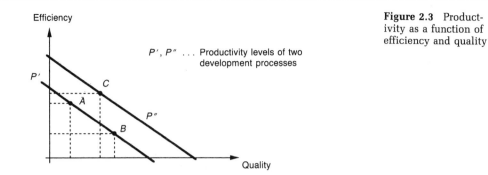

Figure 2.3 Product-
ivity as a function of
efficiency and quality

the more time that elapses between the cause of an error and its correction, the higher the cost. From this we conjecture that a delay in the identification and correction of an error decreases productivity. We can conclude that, when measuring productivity, efficiency as well as quality must be taken into account.

Productivity is represented as a linear function of efficiency and quality (see Figure 2.3). This reflects the fact that an improvement only in quality or only in efficiency will not improve productivity P'. This link is often overlooked in computing practice. The development manager often exerts pressure on the developers in order to get to the milestone results faster, and so causes poor quality results, which then have to be improved later with even greater effort. The overall productivity has not increased!

Another typical case is where one tries to improve quality with additional resources (i.e. more staff) (see also [Broo75]). The well-known effect of this process is extended development time. These efforts reduce efficiency. In Figure 2.3 this means that we move from point A to point B.

The development manager finds that he or she is in a 'goal conflict'. The actual improvement lies in the choice of a better productivity level (P'' instead of P'), i.e. efficiency and quality must improve simultaneously. Experience in different places [Arth85, Boeh87] also shows that quality and productivity improvements can take place at the same time. The productivity function is determined by the factors described in Figure 2.2.

The conclusions from this model for productivity improvements are as follows:

• Measurements of efficiency and quality are necessary. (How quickly does resource X execute task Z with technology Y? What error rates occur in which phase in a given project infrastructure?)
• An improvement only in quality or only in efficiency will not increase the productivity level. Implementing qualitatively bad systems hurriedly will not generate higher productivity.
• The area of productivity improvement must embrace all phases of development. If, for example, the programming activities take up only 20 per cent of project cost, an 80 per cent improvement of programming productivity brings only an improvement of 16 per cent of the entire productivity.

Basili's model (see Figure 2.4) is derived from the productivity formula

Figure 2.4 Basili's
productivity model

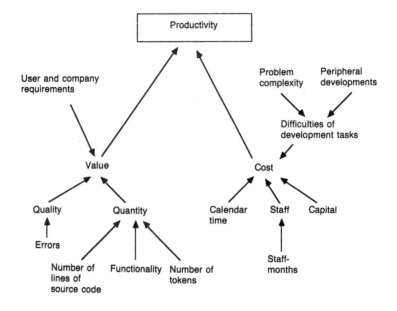

presented in section 2.1 (results produced/applied cost). The disadvantage of a
practical result in that section is cancelled out by the replacement of a number
of results by the product value. The productivity formula according to Basili is
as follows:

$$P = \frac{\text{Value of product}}{\text{Cost of production}}$$

Software production is looked upon as a process of value creation. The emerging
software product represents a value which, according to Basili, is determined
by user and company requirements, quality requirements, the reuse of components
and the amount of the product. The amount can be described according to the
size of the product, which is determined by the functional scope, the number of
source code instructions and the elementary source code items.

Nowadays, 'value' seems to be determined by the possible use (in terms of
satisfying requirements) of a software product to the user or to the company.

In Basili's model, value and cost are on a par. Basili sees staff (staff-months),
calendar time (time needed for any development), financial resources and the
degree of difficulty of the development task (complexity of the problem, external
interfaces in the development) as possible causes of cost.

On the basis of this model, some interesting points are made:

• Software development cost can be reduced at the cost of quality. However,
  this results in an increase in the life-cycle cost (40 per cent development cost:
  60 per cent maintenance cost) — for example, through error correction or
  lack of functionality. This was researched by Weinberg [Wein74]. Boehm also
  studied these empirical values [Boeh81] by analysing the COCOMO database

(63 development projects, 24 evolution/maintenance projects). This means in the model that, through lack of quality and reduced quantity, the value of the product is reduced in the long term.

- Through the application of constructive measures such as methods and tools in a project, software cost and software quality can be improved simultaneously [Boeh84, Vosb84, Mats87]. In this way, the product value increases and so does productivity.

If we summarise and evaluate these two described models, we find that Case's model can be easily applied as an aid for examining and testing product improvement with regard to efficiency and quality from the perspective of the computing practitioner. Basili's model provides an improvement on Boehm's productivity formula, but it also poses new questions which have not yet been answered. For example, what does a practical function for the creation of a value look like, and how is one to proceed in a project in order to estimate the value of a product at an early stage?

2.4   Possibilities for productivity increase

In the following, an overview will be given of existing possibilities to improve productivity. At the same time, many of the improvement measures affect the quality of the development process and the end product.

One measure for determining and improving productivity which appears to be promising for the management of a computing organisation is the regular use of questionnaires. Toshiba carry out two surveys per annum in their software organisation, Fuchu Software Factory, which in 1985 had about 2,300 staff. Each member of staff and each quality group comment in writing on how the demanded productivity target and quality target are reached.

The evaluation of this questionnaire for 1985 showed the results shown in Table 2.1 (see [Mats87]). This table shows very clearly where the largest productivity potential can be found, namely in the reuse of development elements. Despite this encouraging statement, a noticeable improvement in productivity through this approach seems to occur only during the introduction of object-orientated programming [Mart87].

Table 2.1   Results of the Fuchu Software Factory questionnaire 1985

% of interviewees	Factor
52.0	Use of reusable designs and reusable code
18.0	Improvement of steps in the work process, procedure and working environment
9.8	Use of software tools
7.2	Application of software engineering
6.7	Improvement of functional divisions of the systems
6.3	Use of very high-level languages (VHLL) (e.g. 4GLs)

Figure 2.5 Software
productivity
improvement tree

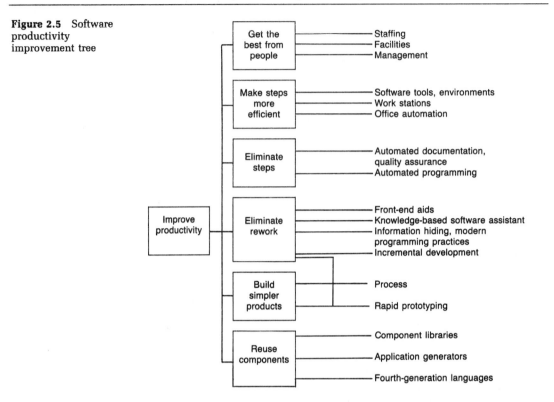

Boehm [Boeh87], who divides his improvement measures into six categories (see Figure 2.5), also looks at reusability.

'Get the best from people' can be interpreted as 'Support staff so that they may give of their best'. Qualified personnel play a key role and this means that an important policy is to employ the best people. Since development and maintenance are very work-intensive processes, capital investment to make work easier and to support the work process make it possible to improve the situation. An average capital investment of about $2,000 to $3,000 for an American software developer is only marginally different from that for an office worker. Large companies like IBM, TRW and Bell Laboratories invest between $10,000 and $30,000 per software developer in order to achieve their productivity improvements. Typical investments in this area are single offices and diverse office infrastructure improvements. Bad management can worsen productivity faster than other factors. Some examples of this are bad planning, narrow ability, inexperience in choosing staff and in supervising programmers, the lack of effort-orientated pay and the absence of career structures.

In the category 'Make steps more efficient', we are dealing with frequently repeated work-intensive process steps which are to be speeded up by the application of tools. The critical success factor here is the integration of these tools into an integrated project support environment (IPSE). Further improvements can be made by eliminating certain working steps. Examples in this area are test programmes for adherence to widely accepted standards and software designs, generator systems and 4GLs.

Eliminating reworking is very useful. According to some estimates, about 60 per cent of the entire cost in the life cycle of a product is spent on maintenance. Possible improvements are the use of methods and tools for the earlier phases, artificial intelligence (AI), information hiding, better process models and the construction of prototypes. Besides these technical aspects, the dialogue with the user should be made more efficient, perhaps through the creation of an organisation of user representatives or through regular meetings with users. The aim of all these improvements is to create good modules and consequently achieve better maintainability (see Chapter 5) during initial development.

One possibility already mentioned for the improvement of productivity and product quality is the reusing of software designs and of code. In this module, libraries, application generators and object-orientated languages play a key part. Endres [Endr88] shows four methods which lead to a planned reuse of software:

- program portability, e.g. the wide use of the UNIX operating system is to a large extent due to its portability;
- program adaptability, e.g. through use of macro preprocessors;
- polymorphisms (macros), e.g. in the form of generic abstract data types which are supported differently in Ada and Modula-2 (see [Pomb87a]), or through hierarchical data types (i.e. classes) in object-orientated languages like C++; and
- building block techniques, which are based on subroutines, macro and object libraries.

Many structural problems in reusability have not yet been satisfactorily solved [Wolf85]. Wolf and Schmid of IBM in Böblingen see the following pressing problem areas:

- reuse of software elements as one of the aims in development processes;
- application register of reusable contents and structures of software;
- categorising reusable elements;
- abstract steps of system description which are best suited for the reuse of components; and
- retrieval (in particular, finding) of suitable reusable software elements.

The solution to these problems can be found in technological advancement in programming languages, in the use of parameters and the standardisation of software systems, in program specification and the utilisation of knowledge bases.

The class of applications also plays a decisive part here. For a wide range of commercial applications, database systems with generators for data selection, graphics, control and report generation are generally adequate. Spreadsheet programs with pre-created solution models are, for some small commercial applications, the most suitable development tool for an increase in productivity.

Jones [Jone86] points to the size of a computing organisation in connection with productivity improvement. He notes that targeted improvement measures display a particular relationship with the factor 'number of developers'.

The basis for good productivity in small software organisations (up to 10 developers) is capital investment in the form of work stations and tools. In companies with 11 to 50 software developers, considerable improvements can be achieved by the use of work stations and tools. The application of standard packages, database generators and spreadsheet programs is also suitable. In companies of 51 to 200 staff, it may be worthwhile to employ specialists for testing, design and databases in addition to the measures suggested for smaller computing organisations. Application generators, reviews/audits and prototypes are particularly useful here for improving the performance of the developers. In even larger computing organisations, one can find the employment of specialist groups for quality assurance, testing, databases and software tools, in addition to the measures mentioned above. Regular attempts to measure quality and productivity are also helpful. The practice of reusing designs and code as well as the organisation of special processes for achieving this are important measures for the assurance of considerable long-term productivity gains in large computing organisations.

3 Constructive quality assurance measures

Constructive quality assurance means the application of technical, organisational or psychologically orientated measures and aids. The application of these measures and aids is aimed at the development and maintenance of a product which has a priori certain attributes and, during the development or maintenance of which, process shortcomings and errors are, as far as possible, avoided.

According to the German dictionary Duden, the word *konstruktiv* (constructive) has the following meanings:

- regarding construction;
- directed towards the maintaining, reinforcing and extending of that which already exists; and
- building, helping, making a useful contribution.

The first meaning of the word 'constructive' implies the possibility of designing and planning a software product, using engineering principles. Technically constructive quality assurance measures such as the application of methods and tools are particularly suited. In addition, measures by the project management must be mentioned which aim at the creation of and the adherence to plans (e.g. project plan, development plan).

The second meaning points to the quality-maintaining and protecting characteristics of these measures. For example, the application of aids for configuration management, be it only organisational instructions or a tool for code management, avoids inconsistent product configurations and makes possible the development of equally consistent versions of the product.

The third meaning of the word points to the building of software quality and its contribution to performance. For example, the application of modular programming languages (e.g. Ada, Modula-2) promotes the modularisation of large software products and facilitates their maintenance considerably. However, measures for training or for better communication between developers, contractors and users are also relevant.

From the above discussion, different types of constructive measure can be noted:

- Technical — for example, the application of principles, methods and tools of software engineering.
- Organisational — for example, the use of a process model or of a plan for configuration management.

- Human — for example, training and psychologically orientated measures which are essential as an aid to the developers in the execution or improvement of their work.

One of the most effective constructive measures of quality assurance is training, involving the continuing education and training of staff and management. Most of the technical quality assurance measures are ineffective without suitable training measures. Training and continuing education improve the qualifications of the staff. Boehm [Boeh81] has, in this context, also pointed to the effects of qualifications on productivity.

Examples of concrete constructive quality assurance measures are as follows:

- The application of processing models which include an explicit risk estimation for the development process in each phase.
- The application of an effort and cost estimation technique, such as COCOMO [Boeh81] or function point method [Albr79], with which the quality features of cost and time can be better planned and adhered to.
- The application of requirement definition methods, such as structured analysis (SA) [DeMa78], SADT [Ross77] or LITOS-A [Wall85, Färb87a], which help us to collate the requirements as a sequence of steps on several levels in a structured and clear way.
- A tool, such as LITOR-A [Wall85, Färb86], which guarantees that principles laid out in a method (LITOS-A) are adhered to. For example, LITOS-A promotes or forces the principle of abstraction, of specification of interfaces and of defined dummies.
- The application of a tool for determining cross references, which is applied to the analysis and evaluation of requirement definitions. In this way, quality features of a requirement definition such as completeness and absence of contradictions can be automatically checked in part.
- A document layout for a log book with a prescribed detailed scheme and instructions on how it is to be filled in, ensuring that all important points are dealt with and described.
- The use of a programming language which employs strong typing (e.g. Ada or Modula-2). This means that checks are carried out not only during translation, but also at run time
- The use of a tool for configuration management of source and object code.
- Adequate specialist further training and personal development for each participant on the project.

In section 3.1 we consider the constructive elements of software engineering more closely. In section 3.2 we consider the process model as a promoter of these constructive elements. Since a software product is useless without adequate documentation — bad user handbooks anger the user, and inadequate technical descriptions make maintenance activities difficult or impossible — the constructive contribution of documentation to quality assurance is demonstrated in section 3.3.

In sections 3.4 and 3.5 technically constructive measures (application of programming languages and software production environments) are considered. In section 3.6, organisational measures (configuration management) are described, and in section 3.7 constructive measures are explained which point to the influence of human behaviour on quality.

3.1   Constructive elements of software engineering for quality assurance

What lies behind software engineering? In this context we quote Pomberger [Pomb87a]: 'Software engineering is the practical application of scientific insights for the economical production and economical application of reliable and efficient software.'

Compared with classic production development areas — for example, industries which can look back on a long technological tradition of proven techniques and expert staff — software development and consequently software engineering are still in their infancy.

When we look at the state of technology in software engineering today, it can be said that, in the methodology of structured programming, the most important results so far are the restriction of program elements to clear and simple structures (in particular, eliminating go-to instructions) and the principle of information hiding in the modularisation of program systems.

In the area of programming languages, there are already examples such as Modula-2 and Ada which give appropriate support to the state of technology. Languages such as Lisp, Prolog, Smalltalk and others offer alternative possibilities for programming (functional, knowledge based and object orientated).

Constructive elements of software engineering for quality assurance include those of quality control (see section 1.2.4). These are:

- principles (concepts) on which we base our actions in software engineering;
- methods which support software engineering principles and lead the developers to predictable results;
- formalisms, especially languages, which are used at different levels of abstraction for describing results and which make possible the representation of intermediate and end results of methodical working;
- tools which support the application of principles, methods and formalisms and are useful to the software developer, to the project leader and to the software quality assurance engineers; and
- structuring of the development and maintenance process through standardised processes (processing models).

The connections between these elements can be expressed in the form of a triangle, as shown in Figure 3.1. The linking element is a standardised process which integrates all other elements via activities and result types. The description of the standardised process is called a process model. In section 3.2 we look more closely at the importance of process models for quality assurance.

Figure 3.1 Con-
structive elements of
software engineering
for quality control

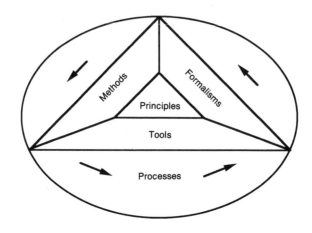

3.1.1 *Principles*

A principle is a basic tenet on which our activities are based. Principles comprise general rules of attitude, but they do not prescribe how a goal should be reached. For example, the principle 'Regular sport promotes good health' does not say anything about which kind of sport and how often or for how long it is to be done.

For the different tasks in the development and maintenance of software, some generally accepted principles can be offered. They came about on the basis of contemporarily available theoretical knowledge and practical experience obtained through logical analysis and generalised conclusions.

Balzert [Balz85] notes the following principles:

- constructive prediction;
- levels of abstraction with gradual refinement (making concrete) coarsening;
- structuring;
- modularising (building-block principle);
- locality;
- information hiding;
- integrated documentation (single-source principle);
- object-orientated design;
- well-defined interfaces;
- standardising (uniformity); and
- multiple use.

A notable success factor for practicable software engineering is the adequate support of these principles through methods and tools. The selection of formalisms, methods and tools should be guided by these principles.

From the perspective of constructive quality assurance, principles are a kind of 'catalyst' which supports or promotes the creation of quality. For example, a well-structured document (application of the principle of structuring) for a requirements definition (numbering of requirements, grouping of requirements by criteria) aids the analyst by the specification of clear, consistent and complete expressions. From the perspective of analytical quality assurance, these principles improve the testability of results.

3.1.2 Methods

Following Balzert [Balz82], methods can be defined as regularly applied processing instructions for specified goals (e.g. better quality and standardised results). Methods show the user how to reach a goal and how to avoid useless experimenting. The utilisation of methods leads to working systems which we can expect to comply with certain quality factors or standards.

A method can consist of several alternative processes or of a combination of processes. A process describes a concrete way to the solution of a problem or task. It often contains formal directives which support the creation of standards.

Methods usually rest on principles. For example, the method of structured analysis makes use of the principle of abstraction levels. In this process a rough data flow is divided into more refined data flows (hierarchy of data flow diagrams).

Examples of methods are the Jackson Structured Programming (JSP) and the Jackson System Development (JSD) methods [Jack83, Jack85].

The literature contains a number of characteristics which highlight methods [Ross75, Char86]. According to Charette [Char86] these are as follows:

- *Criteria*. Depending on method, set goals are reached under different criteria. Possible criteria are function orientated, data orientated, attitude orientated and object orientated.
- *Fields of application*. Many methods support only certain activities in the life cycle (e.g. specification or design). Also, these are frequently only applicable to specific problem classes.
- *Application*. The application of a method involves the use of principles which support the attaining of a goal.
- *Notation*. Methods of describing results use certain notations (e.g. natural, graphic or formal languages).
- *Manuals*. In order to be able to use a method, manuals are necessary (e.g. sequence of processing actions, decisions to be taken).

An objective of the application of methods from the viewpoint of quality assurance consists of the systematic and, therefore, testable generation of results, and the creation of documentation accompanying the project. In principle, we demand that the method makes uniform the documentation of the work and offers a systematic and goal-directed procedure which, if followed, leads to the set goal.

Several quantitative examinations of the effect of individual methods are in the meantime available, e.g. by Baker [Bake75], Fagan [Faga76], Walston and Felix [Wals77] and Black [Blac77]. They show an average productivity and quality gain of between 50 and 150 per cent depending on method: in other words, the effect is noteworthy.

3.1.3 Formalisms (languages)

Very often methods are directly or indirectly linked with formalisms or formal languages. By formalism we understand a specific textual or graphic notation. It is determined more or less formally by a system of rules which describe syntax and semantics. Examples of this are the different formalisms for structured analysis such as that of DeMarco [DeMa78], of Gane and Sarson [Gane82], and of Yourdon [Your78]. Further examples of languages which are not used for implementation are RSL (Requirements Statement Language) [Alfo85] and PSL (Problem Statement Language) [Teic77].

Programming languages such as Modula-2 and Ada [Pomb87b] offer language concepts for the design phase. This means that a language is used for both implementation and design. For example, designs for large systems are documented with the possibilities of module specification in Ada and Modula-2. Languages like C++ support the principle of object-orientated design.

The constructive quality assurance aspect of formalism and languages consists of the support of a formal description which provides methods. Formal descriptions are in turn prerequisites for automated testing (analytic quality assurance aspects).

3.1.4 Tools

For a long time editors, compilers and linkers were the only tools of the software engineer. With the development and spread of high-performance PCs and work stations, there was a sharp increase in the use of tools. The present problem is that there are many tools which are difficult to combine. In many instances the concept of a tool set is missing.

A classification of tools according to Denert [Dene86] differentiates tools for:

- text generators (e.g. editors, text formatting systems);
- analysis (e.g. specification analysers, static program analysers);
- translating (e.g. compilers, decision tables generators);
- testing (e.g. test systems); and
- administration (e.g. project library systems, data dictionary, configuration management systems)

from software and for the development of

- planning and controlling (e.g. PERT chart, spreadsheet systems).

Tools help to improve quality by preventing errors (constructive aspect) on the one hand, and to simplify and support the application of principles, methods and formalisms on the other. In particular, the use of tools in the early phases produces considerable quality improvements. Many tools have test functions which are suitable for the qualitative evaluation of results (analytic quality assurance aspects). Furthermore, tools give valuable support in the organisational and physical handling of large amounts of information, such as tend to occur in larger applications. Despite the many uses of tools, however, they cannot replace the thinking and creative work of the developers; they can only have a stimulating and supporting function. Charette [Char86] holds the view that, through the use of tools, the activities of the developer can become less administration orientated and more creative.

In section 3.5 we list a detailed tool classification and take a closer look at the software production environment.

3.1.5 Technique of prototyping

According to Balzert [Balz82] the term 'technique' may be used if individual constructive elements are combined and matched. One such technique is prototyping.

As already mentioned in section 1.1, problems in development occur in the classic life cycle. Since the early 1980s it has been attempted to solve these problems with the technique of prototyping [Seew82, Garm85, Budd86, Remm87, Färb87b]. Prototyping aids the discovery of missing and faulty requirements before design and implementation. For the developers and for management, the main purpose of prototyping is an early review to check whether the system development can be carried out in order to avoid the unnecessary use of resources and to make sure that the wrong product is not developed. Prototyping is therefore an effective technique of risk management in computing projects [Boeh79b].

The word 'prototype' stems from the Greek and means primeval type, idol or model. In industry, it means the first model (e.g. a vehicle or an aeroplane) which was created and tested before the production of a series.

In the literature, prototyping is separated into three types [Floy84, Budd86]:

- explorative prototyping;
- experimental prototyping; and
- evolutionary prototyping.

Explorative prototyping

The aim of explorative prototyping [Remm87] is to create, if possible, a complete system specification to enable the developers to gain insight into the application area, to clarify different approaches to solutions with the user, and to make sure that the planned system in a given organisational environment can be realised. With the use of the prototype, real examples of the application are run and the desired functionality is tried. In this context it is not the quality of the construction of the prototype which is important, but the functionality and ease of modification and development within a short time scale.

The prototype is created jointly by developers and users. It is made available in the life-cycle phases of requirement analysis and system specification (see Figure 3.2).

From the perspective of quality assurance, explorative prototyping has the following advantages:

Figure 3.2 Explorative prototyping

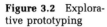

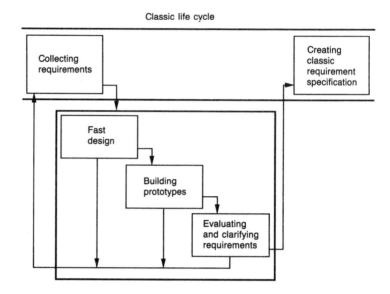

- Requirement and specification problems/errors are recognised and dealt with very early (and consequently at lower cost). The functionality is more widely specified and tried by the user.
- Besides the user interface of the system, the dynamics are also modelled and tested in the program execution.
- Language and communication problems between developer and user are minimised, and resulting potential error sources are eliminated.
- The user validates his or her wants and needs of the planned system by use of a working system model. This is a useful extension of static reviews of the written specifications of the requirements and systems.
- The developer can define sensible steps for the system together with the user, and can in this way avoid maintenance problems by use of a release step concept.

One disadvantage lies in the danger of generating permanent changes to the prototype and thus destabilising project planning. If insufficient explanation is given, the user could also assume that the prototype is the finished system.

For this kind of prototyping, the quality assurance contribution lies not only in early communication between user and developer and in the constructive area (avoidance of requirement errors, complete and consistent function specification), but also in the analytical area (validating the user's wants and goals in the form of a practical requirement and system specification).

Experimental prototyping

The aim in experimental prototyping is a practical design specification which forms the basis for implementation. This means checking technical goals for practicalities.

This is to prove the suitability and quality of the software architecture of the planned system, of inherent solution ideas and of the partitioning into system components (modules) as an experiment.

Pomberger suggests the following process [Pomb87a]. On the basis of the first ideas about partitioning of the system, a prototype is developed which allows the checking of the interaction between interfaces of the individual system components and of the flexibility of the system partitioning with regard to extensions in the experiment. Within the framework of the partial implementation of individual components, design and implementation requirements (e.g. performance, concurrency) can also be examined as well as their effects on system partitioning.

Building the prototype mainly involves the developers. Experimental prototyping supports the system and component design.

Advantages from the point of view of quality assurance are:

- early testing of the design and implementation requirements;
- improved maintainability through the verification of modules with regard to the characteristics of extendability and adaptability;
- consistent and complete interface specification of system components;
- extension to static design reviews.

A disadvantage is the additional effort and cost involved, which can delay the project. The use of suitable tools reduces this drawback.

Experimental prototyping offers the developer support in the constructive area of quality assurance (exploring function structure) as well as in the analytical area (reviewing of design decisions and verification of user requirements).

Evolutionary prototyping

Evolutionary prototyping differs from the two types of approach described above, in as much as we are dealing with an incremental system development, i.e. a gradual development strategy. The prototype is constantly modified to include new and discovered requirements. The development is not an isolated project, but runs parallel to the utilisation of the application. There is no partition between prototype and product. In this kind of prototyping the prototype is, as a rule, not discarded but enhanced [Pomb87a]. In contrast to throw-away and incomplete prototypes, we are dealing here with a complete prototype which contains all the salient functions of an evolutionary step.

The advantages from the perspective of quality assurance are as follows:

- The specification problem of the classic life cycle (always working with an incomplete specification) can be simplified in this way. The prototype is a manageable part of the system specification.
- Maintenance problems (difficulty in altering, and diverging and outdated documentation) are less severe because maintenance requirements are taken into account from the start.
- Quick validation of requirements by the user is immediately possible on a working system.

The disadvantages from the point of view of quality assurance are dangerous:

- The design structure can be inadequate (patchwork). The problem of system design is not solved by this approach.
- Developing becomes a permanent alteration process which is no longer target orientated and consequently is hard to control.
- Project management becomes much more costly.

Evolutionary prototyping is only suitable for those applications which are by nature subject to fast-changing requirements. Sommerville and others see the value of this kind of prototyping in the development of smaller systems where maintainability plays a secondary part [Somm85].

In conclusion, one method of constructive and analytical quality improvement from the viewpoint of quality assurance lies in experimental and explorative prototyping in the form of an extension to the classic life cycle. Prerequisites for this are tools which give sufficient support to both kinds of prototyping [Pomb88]. If parts of prototypes can be reused in later target systems, productivity will increase. The main value is in the inclusion of the user, improved communication with him or her, and an early introduction into the target system. In this way, the risk of developing a wrong or unwanted product can be considerably reduced.

Evolutionary prototyping must be viewed critically from the point of view of quality assurance, since it possesses the danger of chaotic and uncontrollable development.

3.2   Process models and their meaning for quality assurance

An important step in the transition from chaotic software writing to industrial software production is the introduction and utilisation of process models. Alongside a clear and systematic process, the time factor and the internal structure of the development process are important considerations. Through process models the software development process is divided into successive related phases, and for each phase activities and results are specified.

A process model describes the form of a model, i.e. it idealises and abstracts the software development and maintenance process. Examples of process models are 'software life cycles', 'phase models', 'project models' and 'process models'.

Process models are considered to be one of the most important constructive quality assurance elements after methods and tools.

3.2.1   Types of process model

According to Hausen [Haus84] and Boehm [Boeh79a, Boeh81, Boeh86] the following types of process model can be distinguished:

- sequential models;

- loop models (waterfall models);
- V-models (V stands for verification);
- viewpoint models; and
- spiral models.

Sequential models

In the case of sequential models, the phases are placed along a time axis. Within a phase, activities and intermediate and end phase results are specified. Phases are named according to the most important activity within the phase (e.g. analysis, specification, design, programming, testing). There is usually no rule which states who should carry out which activity, how the end results are connected and how multi-phase measures are to be carried out.

Waterfall models

The waterfall model [Boeh73] effects an improvement of the pure sequential model. Although the phases are defined as closed units, consisting of activities and results, it is nevertheless possible to improve the results of each earlier developed phase. This process is iterative in the sense that earlier phases can be carried out repeatedly.

One of the consequences is that certain activities for the planned milestones are never completely closed. Only when the last milestone is reached are the activities of all phases closed in the worst case.

The development and maintenance of documents ('document-orientated software development') is of great importance in processes which run according to a detailed waterfall model.

According to Boehm [Boeh89] waterfall models have much contributed to the fact that the process run has become disciplined, visual and controllable. Boehm sees a danger in that documentation might become more important than the actual system, that the risk factors of a project are not taken sufficiently into account and that reviews become too costly.

V-models

V-models have assumed a special meaning for quality assurance [Boeh79a]. Constructive activities (e.g. modularising the system design) are usually separated from test activities (e.g. testing the consistency of module interfaces). The test activities are verification and validation (see Chapter 4). Boehm was the first to suggest matching a phase of multi-constructive activities with a phase of the respective test activities (e.g. the phase component design of the phase integration). The phase allocation so developed can be represented in the form of a V, whereby the left axis contains constructive activities and the right axis the corresponding test activities.

Figure 3.3 shows an example of such a V-model. The symmetry of this model

Figure 3.3 V-model
based on Boehm

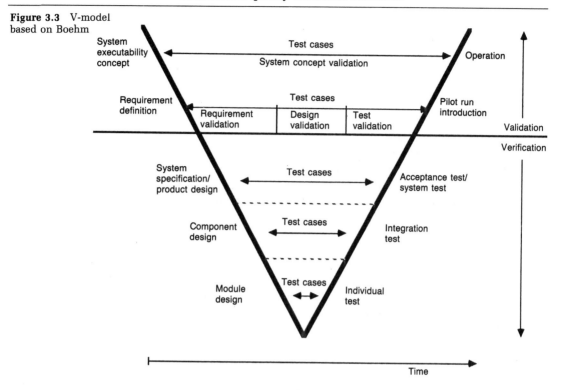

can be interpreted in the following way:

- The simplest way of finding errors is in the abstraction step where they were created. In a system development we proceed from the whole (task position) — this corresponds to the left axis in the V-model — towards detail (code), and then from detail (code) via integration (assembly) and test steps back to the whole (problem solving) — this corresponds to the right axis. It is therefore sensible to look in the phases on the right side of the V for those errors which were created on the left side in the symmetrical phase (same abstraction level). For example, in real terms this means that test cases are created in the module design phase and are executed in the individual test phase for error finding.
- The longer an error stays in the system, the more expensive its correction becomes. This time gap can be shortened through respective test measures at the end of each constructive phase.

The V-model shows how important a well-balanced process model is for the effectiveness of quality assurance measures.

Viewpoint models

Different groups of people take part in a development process (e.g. project leaders, users, analysts, programmers and quality assurance personnel). Each of these groups carries out activities from different viewpoints, and this is why they have

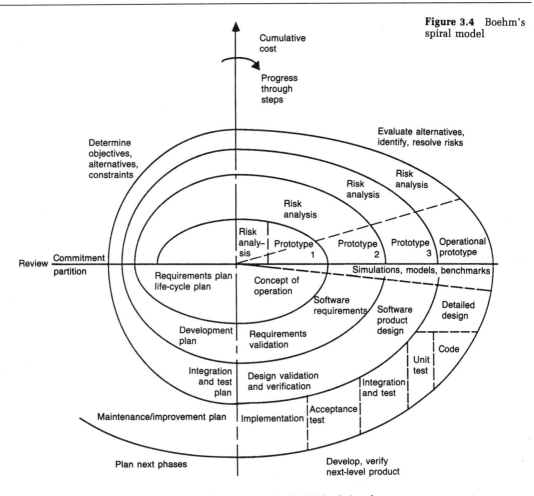

Figure 3.4 Boehm's spiral model

a different approach towards the system or towards the individual development results (user view, developer view, project leader view, etc.).

In a viewpoint model, we differentiate between activities, development results and views. This leads to a situation matrix which aids the decision of who is to carry out which activity. With the aid of the viewpoint model, a better selection of project staff for specific activities can be achieved. In this way, training and further training activities can be more suitably applied.

Spiral model

Boehm [Boeh76b] was one of the first to draw attention to the importance of being in command of risks in the development process. He considered this so important that he suggested a self-constructed process model [Boeh86], which takes risks into account. This is the spiral model (see Figure 3.4).

The radius of the curve represents accumulated cost up to a certain point in time. The angle indicates the progress of each phase.

A product develops in an evolutionary way in the form of product steps. Each cycle of the spiral begins with the identification of development goals for the product step which is being developed in this cycle. In addition, alternatives for the implementation of results of the product step are given, as well as restrictions which affect the alternatives (divided according to cost, time plan, interfaces, etc.).

In the next step, the alternatives relating to restrictions and goals are evaluated. In this way, insecurity and sources of project risks are determined, which are then examined more closely through risk analysis on the basis of a cost−use comparison. For this, techniques such as prototyping, simulation, user interviews and analytical models are used.

For further activities there are two possibilities:

- A plan can be made for the next prototype to be built, together with a rough specification for a product model. This prototype is then developed in order to eliminate the remaining risks.
- If all risks (bad performance, inadequate user interfaces, inflexible system interfaces, etc.) are removed, the development with the classical waterfall model can be continued.

Every cycle closes with a review in which organisations and the users concerned participate. The aim is for all parties involved to give their consent in order to be able to start the next cycle. Maintenance issues (i.e. production improvements) can be handled in the same way.

The spiral model, due to its risk orientation, is in many project situations superior to document-orientated or code-orientated process models [Boeh86, Boeh88]. It is particularly suited to the execution of very large complex development projects. The spiral model has been applied successfully by the company TRW for large projects for a number of years. However, Boehm envisages further improvements on the spiral model, e.g. with regard to the composition of contracts with suppliers, the setting of milestones, the supervision of project situations and the identification of risk areas.

Summarising we note that process models have been successful in practical computing situations, from the point of view of the project leaders as well as from that of the developer. Special advantages are:

- the standardising and uniformity of development process and results;
- staff independence;
- the existence of instructions and aids for solving complex development tasks; and
- a basis for efficient project planning and supervision.

These factors also affect productivity. Lai [Lai84] reports that, after successful introduction and consequent adherence to the process model, the productivity of developers rose by 25−30 per cent.

However, specific requirements which affect, for example, the size, complexity and constraints of software projects require adaptation and improvement of existing process models.

It has often been noted that the actual process in the project does not correspond with the process in the process model. This is dangerous for project planning and control (e.g. delays and postponement of milestones). Moreover, existing computer aids for the application of process models are inflexible and difficult to handle.

At the present time, the waterfall model is used more often than other models. Often waterfall models are complemented with prototyping-orientated processes. For very risk-orientated projects, the spiral model is suitable. It also provides a successful way of integrating techniques such as prototyping into the process run. Process models are nowadays accepted in computing practice and form the departure point for all types of improvement measure.

3.2.2 Requirements of process models from the perspective of quality assurance and improvement

A process model should be accompanied by a clear description of the 'what' (types of result) and the 'how' (types of activity) of the process. In particular, the process description should give detailed information about process direction (process control, project management), quality assurance and configuration management.

To each phase belong process-directing activities. They form a boundary around the production-orientated activities of the phase (Figure 3.5). Each phase is preceded by planning. The actual phase activities are accompanied by instruction, training and controlling activities. The phase is brought to a close by a formally stipulated termination process (release mechanism). This is the only way to ensure the orderly carrying out of a phase.

During phase supervision, the successive results (e.g. reviews) are checked. These checks are important prerequisites for the termination condition and the release of phase deliverables.

The activities of a phase are carried out with the aid of constructive quality assurance elements such as principles, methods, tools, examples and background information (see Figure 3.6). The execution of an activity demands specific information (e.g. results of other activities) and creates results.

The accompanying quality assurance activities, according to Radice [Radi85], must be linked by start and finish criteria to the actual development or maintenance

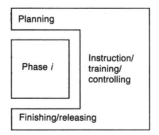

Figure 3.5 Process direction for a phase

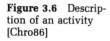

Figure 3.6 Descrip-
tion of an activity
[Chro86]

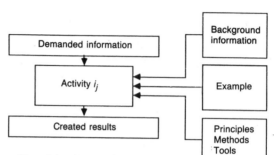

Figure 3.7 Schema
for description of
activities

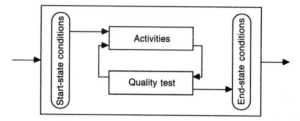

activities of a phase (see Figure 3.7). The following elements and their connection
form a schema:

- list of start-state conditions which must be complied with to make the work
  unit possible;
- description of an activity or a group of activities to be carried out;
- quality test or evaluation of executed activities; and
- list of end-state conditions which must be complied with to allow activities
  to be brought to a close.

The advantage of such a schema lies in better planning of parallel activities in
a phase, and this will result in increased productivity.

An important requirement of a process model is the support of process direction
through suitable types of activity for process leadership. These types of activity
are on the one hand inherent in the process model: for example, tests/evaluations
are prescribed for all important activity groups [Radi85]. On the other hand, the
process is controlled through collection, analysis and evaluation of statistical
product and process data (quality data) and can, if necessary, be improved if
anomalies occur.

Process models are described in manuals. The cumbersome handling of these
books (shelfware) soon demanded machine support. Examples of computer-
supported process models are ADPS [Chro89], Manager View [MSP88], GUIDE
[GMO87] and VIDOC [IBM85].

There is an attempt at present to provide computer support for the process models
in terms of methods and tool application [Chro86]. The integration of these models
into a software development environment (see section 3.5) has not yet been
satisfactorily achieved.

The following is a list of some quality features for the evaluation of actual process models [Dene80]:

* *Completeness*. The model spans all phases of development and extends also to maintenance and replacement of the product. All project leadership measures from project start-up to project finish are also supported.
* *Modularity*. The project is partitioned and clearly structured into well-defined instructions and results. Within these sections, working units (activity groups) can be easily handled, planned and controlled.
* *System*. All concepts conform with a uniform system. This makes them more comprehensible and facilitates easy construction. The concepts are appropriately chosen and clearly expressed, and complement each other. This promotes a good overview.
* *General validity*. Large as well as small projects, standard as well as special projects can be carried out. The application area of the product is not significant.
* *Adaptability*. The model is easily adaptable organisationally, is company and project specific, and can incorporate technical software innovations.
* *Machine support*. User-friendly, easily adaptable and easily extendable computer support for the process model is available. In particular, the incorporation of calls to tools is possible.

3.2.3 Demands on the definition and maintenance of process models

As computing practice shows, a balance between too little process support and too much regimentation must be found in the form of an acceptable compromise for each process model. This compromise is dependent on the situation and is influenced by the relevant process environment. Process models are the prerequisite for effective analytical and constructive quality assurance.

The following demands on requirements and definitions of process models arise:

* The process model must be conceptually consistent in its definitions and meet the quality features demanded (see section 3.2.2).
* The process model must take into account potentially usable constructive quality assurance measures, and regulate the conditions for their use.
* The process model must take into account potentially usable analytical quality assurance measures, and determine the conditions for their use.
* The process model incorporates measures for configuration management.
* The process model must make possible or regulate the availability which guarantees continuous process supervision. In this way, effects of process quality on product quality can be observed and evaluated. Analysis of these data suggests approaches for the improvement of the process [Radi85].

Demands on the maintenance of process models are as follows:

* The effectiveness of analytical and constructive quality assurance measures must be regularly checked by audits.

- Constructive measures inherent in the process model must be constantly adapted to the latest advances in technology. This is the only way in which it can be guaranteed that both quality and productivity are improved step by step.
- Descriptions of the result types (examples) must be regularly checked for their compliance with specifications and, if necessary, improved.

The fundamental significance of a process model must be maintained through training and further education measures. The first step in quality assurance training is to deal with comprehension of the entire development process and, in particular, of the process model. The next step is training in methods and tools.

3.2.4   *Introduction strategy for software engineering measures*

One of the most difficult tasks in computing practice is the introduction of software engineering measures. After purely technical problems there are a number of social and introductory problems to be solved. As a rule, considerable alterations in computing culture and in the working style of the staff are linked to the introduction of such measures.

Apart from proving the use of such measures — revealing the rational and quality assurance potential — the participation of all people concerned is an important prerequisite for the success of this process (co-operative introduction strategy). Further critical success factors for the introduction of software engineering measures are the observation of the maturity level of the development/maintenance process and the integration of software engineering measures into the process model. The introduction of a computer-supported process model is, for example, not to be recommended in the case of an existing *ad hoc* development strategy.

The frame of reference for all measures to be introduced is the process model. Experiments and the introduction of methods which are not co-ordinated with the process model are doomed or lead to the violation of established standards.

Chow [Chow85] gives a few rules for the introduction of software engineering measures:

- The simultaneous introduction of several different techniques should be avoided. An evolutionary process is preferable to a revolutionary process. A strategy of small steps which build on and extend positive experience is better than introducing too much too quickly. It is also important not to lose sight of long-term aims.
- The developers must be included in the selection and introduction process (co-operative introduction strategy). It is easier for them to come to a decision if they take part in the preparations for the decision process.
- Pilot projects with new technology should be carried out on small, risk-free applications. Enough time and adequate conditions must be provided for adaptation and introduction to the application environment.
- An initial cost, use and risk analysis is recommended before introducing new techniques. It is also important to examine how the new technique affects the computer performance (storage, response times, real-time behaviour).

- Before the introduction, training must also be planned.

The introduction of a new technique is, as a rule, not only a matter of specialist knowledge and familiarity with equipment on site, but is often more efficiently carried out by external advisers. They are usually better trained in method and psychological aspects than internal staff and can foresee problems and their solutions more quickly. (They do not have company blindness.) It is often more economical and a faster way of reaching the goal if tools or a training programme are created by external advisers rather than within the company. In addition, innovations suggested by external advisers are accepted faster than those developed by staff within the company (for reasons of personal prejudice and conflict of interests).

Siegmund [Sieg84] reports on experiences with introduction strategies for new methods and tools. He differentiates between the critical factors of process, management, sponsors, people concerned, training and support, pilot projects and tools.

Process

- Evaluate the use which is expected of the technology to be introduced. This use must be 'sold' to all participants in the respective form.
- Stake out realistic goals so that no false, excessively high expectations are raised with the developers and the management. This is often the cause of misunderstandings.
- Limit the scope of possibilities and the boundary of the technology clearly.
- Show the objective success actually achieved in the introduction. It has been known for individual members of staff or management to show subjective judgement of targets achieved.
- Recognise and analyse the actual problems and goals of all participants. Offer everybody a realistic approach to a solution.
- Analyse exactly the application environment of the new technology.
- The more intensively all participants are involved in the introduction process and identify with the set goals and the way to a solution, the greater is the chance of a successful introduction.

Management

- Management must create or arrange the financial, organisational, technical and idealistic preconditions for a successful introduction.
- Management has to ensure that the stipulated introduction strategy and the agreed measures are strictly adhered to. It is also important to provide a sufficient guarantee with the introduction, particularly if difficulties and problems occur in the beginning.
- Management should allow the necessary freedom for staff to accommodate added effort/cost when adapting to new technology.
- Management must see to it that the planned measures are carried out.

Sponsors

- A successful introduction is supported by active persuasion from its sponsors. These might be important representatives or managers in a company. This support is very important if success is not immediately obvious.
- The more difficult and complex a new technique, the more important it is to have influential sponsors at all company levels.
- Sponsors are useful not only in the introduction (pilot projects), but also later in the distribution of new technology to all projects, especially when the enthusiasm of the participants is waning.

People concerned

- Members of staff at the lowest levels often show great mistrust of the introduction of new techniques and new technology. This phenomenon occurs particularly among those who have developed their own working style over a long period of time.
- One cause of failure is the discrediting of the means by which former performance levels were reached. This causes the demotivation of participants, which at worst can lead to the sabotage of new technology.

Training and support

- Lack of training or insufficient training and support are often the cause of failure in the introduction of a new technique.
- Management is often of the opinion that training in the form of course attendance is sufficient. However, in many instances the application of knowledge in the actual project situation is enforced by time pressure and the changed task setting. Management should be aware of this problem, and the knowledge gained at courses should be reinforced by sample projects.
- The entire team must be trained step by step.
- Theoretical training knowledge should be put into practice straight away.
- The more complex a technology, the more support work must be done.
- Members of staff who are well conversant with methods and tools, and who can give practical support to their colleagues, are the surest way of securing successful introduction.
- Members with know-how are more useful than manuals.
- Complex help systems for tools are not yet a replacement for personal support by an expert.

Pilot projects

- Collected experiences — in particular, the advantages and disadvantages of the introduced technology — should be documented and consequently evaluated.

- Pilot projects also aid the decision of whether or not to introduce the technology on a broad basis. Equally, an idea can be gained of whether the introduction strategy should be improved, or whether the applied aids should be further developed.
- The limits and possibilities of the applied technology must be stated clearly.
- A successful pilot project tends to convince others more easily (snowball effect).
- The selection of members of staff and of the project determines the success or failure of the introduction in the long run.
- After completion of the pilot project, the participants must be allocated to other projects to spread the know-how. This reduces the learning effort considerably.

Tools

- Tools must be reliable. They help to achieve visible results.
- Data integrity and the consistency of results must be guaranteed by the tools used.
- Saving of working results must be simple.
- Response times must be satisfactory.
- User friendliness is important.
- Effort should be warranted by the set task.
- The tool should be adapted to the organisation running the development process, and should be supported by a methodical process.

Pressmann [Pres88] suggests the following steps for the introduction of software engineering measures:

- analysis and evaluation of the current state of software engineering;
- training;
- selection of software engineering measures;
- introduction and conversion; and
- evaluation of the measures introduced.

The first step involves an evaluation of the techniques practised so far, of methods and of tools used. The strengths and weaknesses of the development and maintenance processes are analysed and recorded. This evaluation step leads to recommendations which contribute to the achievement of certain goals, such as improved productivity, rapid response to developments, better product quality and better working morale among the developers. These goals are stipulated by management. The evaluations and recommendations are recorded in the first version of a plan of introduction.

The second step involves specific training in software engineering measures. Without a clear understanding of these measures, resistance to change would be very strong. Experience shows that good training conveys software engineering methods most effectively.

The third step involves the selection of specific methods and tools. First the

Figure 3.8 Introduction steps with feedback

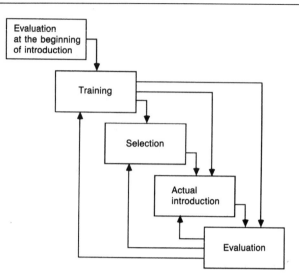

selection criteria are defined, then the possible candidates for methods and tools are determined, and finally the latter are evaluated with the help of the criteria. The selection should constitute a decision founded on rational thought and based on the consent of both management and developers.

In the actual introduction step, guidelines are created, the participants are trained in accordance with the specific selected software engineering measures, and measures are introduced with the aid of pilot projects.

By means of measuring and evaluating the product or process, as well as by consulting the participants, an evaluation of the introduction takes place.

Pressmann stresses that, with the exception of the evaluation at the beginning of the introduction, all steps can be repeated in any succession (see Figure 3.8).

Without doubt the introduction of a new technique or technology is a long process involving hard work. A strategy which treats the introduction of methods and tools as a project, and which looks upon the software developer as a human being, helps considerably in making good use of methods and tools and in minimising introduction risks.

3.3   The role of documentation in quality assurance

Present practice in the execution of software projects is marked by the fact that the larger part of the documentation (system, user documentation) is incomplete, often difficult to read and understand, and not up-to-date. Higher-level concepts and structure overviews which would make the initial stages easier for the reader are omitted and exist only in the heads of the developers: after a time they can therefore no longer be reconstructed. Together with high personnel turnover, these circumstances are to a high degree responsible for a general software crisis, and for the maintenance crisis in particular.

Software is a 'non-concrete', initially invisible product of the mind. If the material basis — that is, the documentation — is missing, then software remains merely notions in the heads of the developers or those responsible for the product.

Without adequate, good-quality documentation, a software product is without value and hence useless. All subsequent thought must lead to the maxim that each software development and maintenance process is simultaneously a documentation process. Documentation should not be seen as a separate phase in itself. As such it would not be quality promoting and is, therefore, not recommended. Many attempts at improving the documentation process have failed. This was, in many instances, caused by the use of unsuitable tools and by 'quality hostile' working conditions.

3.3.1 *Problems in the documentation process*

Many developers are of the opinion that sufficient documentation of results delays progress, since good developers are those who create as many lines of code per day as possible. From this point of view, the creation and maintenance of adequate and comprehensible documentation lowers productivity. Often it is the available tools which give insufficient support during the process of editing texts.

Cases are quoted again and again where, apart from code listings, no further documentation is available for large software systems. This points to the fact that documentation is at present a large and difficult problem in computing development.

Schweiggert [Schw85] mentions several reasons for a documentation crisis:

- It is the aim of management to achieve applications as quickly as possible. Strict adherence to timescales causes insufficient documentation.
- Software specialists believe that people who document their product sufficiently lay their work 'wide open'. They become replaceable.
- The actual writing of documentation is a monotonous process where nothing technical happens. The work satisfaction experienced in, for example, the first error-free run of a program can in no way be compared with the writing and releasing of a document.
- Software in the application process must be constantly adapted and altered. The maintenance programmer usually does not have the time for alterations to documentation. Often suitable tools are not available either. This causes the quality of documentation to suffer.
- Documentation is either not at all or only partly taught during training. Those who are preoccupied with such concepts are often watched by their colleagues with inane smiles. (This is an image problem.)

We have seen that the process of creating documentation and of maintenance causes considerable problems for the computing specialist. The solution of these problems is one of the main tasks of those involved in quality assurance.

3.3.2 Documentation requirements and creation from the perspective of quality assurance

In order to meet the tasks of quality assurance (quality planning, quality control and quality testing) at all, documentation and its creation and maintenance play a large part. Without sufficient documentation it is not possible to judge whether requirements are met.

During quality planning of a product, the relevant quality features with their limits and goals must be determined. This may take place, for example, in the requirements document. During the planning of process quality, it must be determined which features a document should contain and when it should be created and tested. This is noted down in the quality assurance plan. It must also be noted how the development document should be altered. In addition, measures (e.g. audits) must be specified which guarantee consistency between the working system and its documentation during maintenance activities. This can be done either via the quality assurance plan or in larger projects via the configuration management plan (see section 3.6).

Quality control determines the creation of the documentation. This is, in the main, a management task. For this control task, it is useful to differentiate between different working stages of documents (e.g. during definition, work, testing and releasing).

During quality testing, it is laid down to what extent the documentation meets quality requirements. This quality testing of the documentation usually takes the form of specific documentation audits. They are divided into test planning, test execution and test evaluation.

During the planning of the test, the timing and the cost of the test are determined. The test goals are defined as concrete requirements in the form of selected quality features. The result of planning is a test contract.

During the testing stage, the conception of the test process is important and should be included in the test plan. The availability of aids and tools must also be included. This is followed by the actual run of the test, with test results and documentation.

In the evaluation of the test, the test results are analysed, assessed and clearly documented. The test usually closes with a test report.

A good introduction to methods of documentation testing can be found in [Asam86]. The selection of requirements of good-quality documentation should be based on presently known quality features. In [DGQ86] the following quality features for documents are suggested, and their promotion through constructive measures is explained.

- *Modifiability* — suitability of documents for locating all of the document parts in order to perform alterations.
- *Integrity* — agreement between the description of the program in the documentation and the respective actual state in the program.
- *Clarity* — suitability of documents for the clear conveying of information to the reader.

- *Identifiability* — clear, unambiguous indexing of documents that give information on a specific topic which interests the reader.
- *Conformity to standards* — compliance with regulations and standards for the creation of documents.
- *Comprehensibility* — suitability of documents for the successful conveying of information to an experienced reader.
- *Completeness* — availability of sufficient information for the purpose of documentation.
- *Freedom from contradiction* — contradictory statements should be absent from the document.

Heidrich [Heid84] points to a close link between process and document quality. He uses the process features of completeness, relevance and consistency also as documentation features. He further differentiates between quality of content and, equally important for the reader, quality of structure.

For the evaluation of quality features, a scale with the following levels is suggested: without faults, slight faults, serious faults and unacceptable faults.

There are, at present, no theoretically based quality measures for these features of documentation. The existing approaches, such as measuring of test coverage [Smit70, Kinc81], have not yet been accepted in computing practice. To these belong methods which are based on readability formulae, reports on text form and reader−text interaction. These are the results of research work in the disciplines of psychology, education and linguistics.

It is advisable to count and classify the faults and errors which are observed in document testing. In this way, simple quality features such as error count per page of a document can be listed, and therefore simple quantitative stipulations for quality goals can be created.

3.3.3 *Document types and principles*

Documentation provides communication between all groups concerned with development on the one hand and the control of project progress on the other. General documentation also supports the evaluation of project and production costs as well as better planning of future projects.

Pomberger differentiates between three important reader groups to which specific forms of documentation must be addressed [Pomb87a].

Users

User documentation is important. It must offer sufficient information for those who want to inform themselves about the product. The system user should benefit from appropriate function-related instructions, and should be able to locate the necessary information quickly and thoroughly. User documentation is, as a rule, also a good indicator of the quality of interfaces, the thoroughness of the development process and the extent of quality assurance measures.

Developers/support staff

For those involved in development and maintenance, the system and maintenance documentation is important. The system documentation contains all the information necessary for knowing the structure and the actual state of the system. On the basis of this information, alterations and enhancements can be carried out. Documentation should give sufficient insight into the development process that has already been carried out, and consequently represents all important phase results in a brief and clear form. Maintenance documentation, if it is well organised, contains only those forms of information which describe the actual version of the system adequately.

Managers

Project documentation is important for managers because it contains information related to organisation, estimates and internal leadership. In the main it comprises project and organisation plans, such as reports, information about personnel and about the application of other resources, goals, target achievement and project progress. After completion of the project, the documentation serves for statistical evaluation and is meant to aid the planning and determination of the project environment for future projects.

It is important for such target group documentation to be directed towards the interests of the group concerned. For a qualitative evaluation of the documentation, see section 3.3.2.

The following documentation principles are recommended to Howar [Howa81].

Quality of contents

This means the width and depth of treatment of the respective text content. Both aspects must be geared to the target group concerned. Individual text sections should be given the same depth of detail. 'Width' refers to the degree of completeness of thematic content. One indicator for this is the extent to which exceptions and special cases are handled. The text should not contain anything superfluous, and consistency of the text content should be guaranteed.

Quality of organisation

The form and sequence in which the content is handled determine the quality of organisation. Readers should know at all times where they are in the document, from where they started and which reading goal they are able to achieve. Consistent numbering and clear headings help. The text must be divided into logical, self-contained sections. Good balance and structure avoid the readers being overwhelmed by a mass of detailed information. Introductions and summaries are useful aids, helping to feed information into the long-term memory of the reader.

Quality of format

The content of the document becomes more easily comprehensible through appropriate wording and illustrations. Simple vocabulary, or the explanation of specialist terms in a glossary, together with short and direct sentences in active form increase the comprehension of texts considerably. Illustrations or diagrams are a form of non-verbal comprehension, and are most effective if placed near the relevant text.

3.3.4 *Support measures for project-accompanying documentation*

In the introduction to section 3.3, the problems caused by inadequate software documentation were described. We now address the question of what can be done in order to fight this documentation crisis. In this context, Bartsch-Spörl states the following factors as keys to the elimination of the crisis [Bart84]:

- attitudes, goals and training;
- infrastructure of the workplace;
- documentation templates;
- tool support;
- quality assurance measures;
- management support; and
- acceptance strategies.

Attitudes, goals and training

Documentation is an activity which is fundamentally on a par with coding, analysis, design and testing. The time spent on the creation and revision of documentation must be planned and termed as productive in the same way as other activities. Pressure of time must not lead to neglect of the documentation process or hinder it. Software products are incomplete and not ready for release as long as their documentation is incomplete or does not comply with the requirements.

Documentation must also be taken into account in training and further education.

Infrastructure of the workplace

The workplace of the developer must have hardware and tools which support the creation of documentation. The hardware must be geared to the technical requirements of both programming and documentation.

Few developer systems are geared to the needs of the documentation process from the beginning. Correction and editing of documents is made easier if the workplace provides good facilities for text manipulation. Graphics must be supported by tools which are integrated into the environment of the programmer. Also a paper-free exchange of documents within and between groups of developers must be supported. If only PCs are used for documentation, for example, a network is recommended.

Document templates

A very helpful and quality-enhancing measure is the provision of document templates (see [Wall84]). These are tables of contents for all important phase documents together with explanatory texts about how the skeleton document is to be filled in. This 'package' can contain documentation guidelines which specify the numbering and order of headings. Document templates are suited for a life-cycle and document-orientated development method [Pomb89].

It is essential that documentation guidelines should not collect dust in filing cabinets, but should be made available as up-to-date and easily accessible data on the developer's work station. Text templates which might contain empty forms, title sheets, page headings, module headings and program templates increase the quality and productivity of the developer's work. They also contribute to a standard appearance of the document. One must examine them from time to time to see whether the templates are relevant to the actual situation or should be improved.

Phase documents continue to be necessary in a prototyping-orientated software development method (see section 3.1). Through prototyping, the contents of the phase document can be qualitatively improved: for example, by verifying the requirements definition on the basis of the prototype together with the contractor.

A prototyping-orientated software development without phase documents should be rejected because of the danger of constant alterations to the prototype ('trial and error' development). This danger exists with evolutionary prototyping. Without stipulated goals and requirements, the development method (prototype equals product) can become uncontrollable with regard to the cost of system development. Neither could certain quality characteristics (e.g. reliability, performance) be satisfactorily realised.

Tool support

Software tools can be used for the development and maintenance of project and product documentation. Adequate tool support brings a number of advantages. The documentation is:

- easier to create and modify;
- easier to format;
- easier to transfer without paper;
- easier to administer with configuration management tools; and
- there are retrieval functions which make the searching of documents considerably easier.

From the comments so far, it can be concluded that we need the following tools for the support of the documentation process:

- word-processing tools;
- editors that support the creation of hypertext and literate programming;
- information generators;
- graphics tools; and
- browsers.

Literate programming [Knut84, Lins89] and Hypertext [Bige88, Fris88] are among the methods and tools which could be contributing considerably to quality improvement in the future.

By literate programming we mean a design and documentation technique for programs. The aim of this technique is the development of well-structured programs which represent a high-quality document for the reader. By a well-structured program Lins [Lins89] means a program which consists of:

- small, easily understood parts; and
- a small number of easily understood (logical) relationships between these parts.

Knuth [Knut84] demonstrates his ideas on literate programming with the aid of the WEB system. This system uses a formatting language for documents (TEX) and a programming language (PASCAL). Further useful attributes of the WEB system are the utilisation of WEB Macros and the creation of keyword lists.

The user of the WEB system writes a PASCAL program while using the formatting language TEX at the same time. In one of the two steps, a document is created which describes the program and facilitates program maintenance. In the other step, an executable program is created. The program and its documentation are both created by the same source text. With this, consistency of programs and documentation is guaranteed.

Hypertext systems are systems for storing, linking and doing a selective search of graphical and textual information. The basic text is structured in the form of information nodes and dynamically activated links.

Hypertext systems are very suitable for the storing of development documents [Bige88]. Information nodes can be part of program documentation as well as part of the source code. The links between these are either 'lead-to' relations or dynamically activated links in the form of 'comment' or 'call-up' relations (see Figure 3.9).

In Figure 3.10 the link between the development documents stored in Hypertext is well illustrated. It is therefore possible at all times to jump from a particular

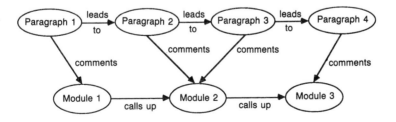

Figure 3.9 Comment source code with Hypertext representation

Figure 3.10 Connections between documents in Hypertext

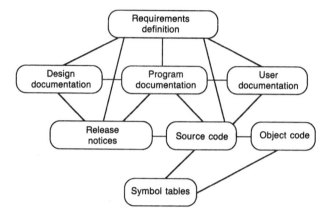

Figure 3.10 Connections between documents in Hypertext

place in the source code to the relevant place in the program or design documentation.

It is important that a simple and effective integration of these tools into the computer-supported working environment takes place. We shall consider tools in more detail in section 3.5.

Quality assurance measures

Each document must be subject to examination after creation in order to determine content and external formal quality, provided this is not at least partly done by the tool itself. Depending on the degree of importance of the document, graduated quality assurance measures can be selected.

Let us begin with a simple author—critic cycle. As soon as a created document is ready, the author hands it over to a colleague for critical inspection. He or she reads the document carefully, paying attention to detail. The critic should have expert qualifications for checking of content of the document. Criticism, faults and suggestions for improvement must be noted down in writing.

Reviews are more extensive checking measures, where several testers and a structured process are applied. In reviews, content as well as formal textual aspects are examined. The essential documents to be checked by reviews are requirements definition, design specifications, test plan, test cases, code and user manuals.

It is recommended to hand user manuals to a potential user, who does not yet know the system, for critical inspection.

Chapter 4 comments in more detail on different methods of checking documents.

Management support and acceptance strategies

None of the measures considered so far will be beneficial if they are not fully supported by management. If management sets priorities which neglect documentation, motivation and pursuasive powers can be destroyed.

Management must ensure that there is sufficient time for:

- the development and introduction of documentation processes;
- necessary planning and supply of infrastructure or tools; and
- necessary quality assurance measures.

Support by management is particularly important in the initial phase of new documentation processes.

The basis for an acceptance strategy consists of the availability of sufficient information and the inclusion of staff in the decision-making process. The benefits of new practices must be advertised with conviction. If necessary, adequate help from experts must also be provided.

Summarising, it is important to create a suitable climate for the introduction and execution of the selected measures. The transition process is long and difficult, but alternatives to these measures are not in sight.

3.4 Programming languages and their influence on quality

3.4.1 Significance of programming languages

The significance of programming languages chosen for a software project is nowadays rated lower than before. In a well organised software development process the cost of implementation only accounts for about twenty to thirty per cent of the project cost. Languages are now considered more important in the maintenance process. In this context the question arises as to which characteristic a language should have in order to keep maintenance costs as low as possible.

The application should, in any case, be written in a higher level programming language which offers the opportunity of creating a system of independent modules which communicate with one another via well defined interfaces. The language should, furthermore, have control and data structures which make well structured programs possible. Through a flexible data type concept the problem-related data is easier to read and more reliable.

3.4.2 Quality assurance concepts of programming languages

The following concepts and features of languages promote the creation of good quality software:

- a module concept with clear partitioning of module interfaces and module body;
- separate compilation which makes it possible to show possible interface errors at the time of compilation of interfaces;
- information hiding and abstract data types for clean separation of data

representation and data utilisation which promote object orientated development and increase re-use of code modules;

- structured control flow which leads to clear, easily readable and testable program structures and consequently improves the abstraction of the control flow;
- a data type concept and run-time checks which allow a problem related and clear representation of data and, therefore, promote problem abstraction;
- meaningful names for relevant labelling of program and data elements; and
- object orientated programming (information hiding, data abstraction, inheritance and dynamic binding), which makes altering, extending and re-use much easier.

Languages such as Ada [Barn82] and Modula-2 [Wirt80, Pomb87a] already offer good support regarding the above mentioned first six points. Object orientated languages like Smalltalk-80 [Gold83] or C++ [Stro86] promote in particular the application of reusable software components and hence increase considerably productivity and quality. For practical applications in computing we must check to what extent software systems written in these languages can be linked with conventionally created software and how easily they can be learned. This will determine the extent to which these quality promoting language concepts find their way into computing practice.

3.4.3 *Pragmatic criteria for selection of a language*

In many instances, the question of using of a new language does not arise, since the language is determined by already existing software.

According to Sommerville [Somm85] the most important criteria for selection of a programming language in practice are:

- customer requirements;
- availability of compilers and programming environment;
- portability of the language;
- training level of programmers;
- implementation language of earlier projects; and
- availability of development tools.

Application generators and their languages are frequently used in connection with databases instead of 'classical' higher programming languages. They are known as fourth-generation languages (4GLs). These languages have mostly emerged from database interrogation languages and make an impact through powerful commands for database access as well as for the construction and use of screens and interactive systems. They contribute considerably to increased productivity of the developer if databases and terminals play an important part in the application.

The important influence of these fourth-generation languages on quality assurance lies in their support of prototyping. Quick creation of prototypes makes possible the validation of user requirements early in the life cycle. The danger of applying 4GLs lies in the *ad hoc* development of applications which lack good modularisation. The consequences are often bad maintainability and a short life cycle of the product.

Summarising, we can say that the selection of the programming language is important for all development and maintenance aspects. None of the presently known languages are equally suitable for all applications. When selecting programming languages, attention must be paid to the specific application and to support from up-to-date quality-promoting principles of software engineering [Balz82].

3.5 Significance of software tools and the production environment for quality assurance

Tools have improved the quality and efficiency of processing considerably. If one imagines the excavation of a building site for a family house, a digger achieves the same as ten builders with shovels in a much shorter time.

Regarding software tools, the last twenty years have seen a development in the direction of increased user-friendliness and more extensive functionality. Let us look back at the past.

For a long time, editors, compilers, linkers and debuggers were the only tools available for supporting the development process. With the application and spread of software engineering principles and methods, the supply of support tools increased. Tools were introduced for guiding and supporting developers during the application of software engineering principles and methods. In addition, there are many methods which only became practically feasible through the use of tools (e.g. structured analysis).

The notable development of software tools can be demonstrated using the example of editors. At first, line editors were used. With these only one line at a time could be altered. In most instances this had to be addressed by means of a line number, whereby a number of errors could occur. If, for example, the line numbering was not correct, it could happen that lines were replaced incorrectly. A display of the control codes was absent and handling was cumbersome.

The introduction of the full screen editor brought an improvement. The area which could be altered was now a whole screenful. This made text input and alterations easier.

The next step was multi-document editors. With these several documents could be processed at the same time. Context-sensitive editors which allowed a specific input or alteration dependent on context (e.g. of module interfaces) brought a further qualitative improvement. This helps to avoid faulty input from the start.

Certain editors make it possible to store the actual state of working files (cursor position, writing and reading of files), so that work can be continued in the right place and the old state of working files need not be laboriously reworked (see the MAESTRO system [Soft84]).

Hypertext systems represent higher-level editors (see section 3.3.4). They allow a dynamic activated link to text sections in different documents, starting from a particular place in the text.

Experience with individual phase-related tools shows that they support only isolated parts of development work. They do not function at all if results have to be transmitted from one phase to the next, and the tools to be applied cannot continue to use the results without further manipulation. Here inconsistencies between results of different phases often occur. A further problem is the support of several developers if the requirement is consistency of working results. The inadequacy of individual tools affects the way in which they might be handled and how difficult it might be to come to terms with their use.

A big problem is the interface between the tools. Sometimes two tools cannot be combined because their interfaces are not compatible. Alternatively, difficulties are due to the fact that tools are based on different methods, the results of which are not compatible.

One solution to this problem consists in applying uniform software production environments into which the tools are integrated (see section 3.5.2).

According to the maxim 'The cobbler's children wear the worst shoes', many software developers still use inadequate tools for quality work. The situation encourages the development and application of further software tools and the use of a better software production environment.

3.5.1   CASE tool landscape

CASE (Computer Aided Software Engineering) is an attempt to improve the work of software developers and maintainers qualitatively and to increase productivity with the aid of complex hardware and software systems. CASE can be defined as: the creation and processing of software by means of tools (CASE tools) which are executed on computers. Through the use of CASE the development and maintenance process is automated as far as possible.

The market volume of CASE tools is constantly increasing. National and international support, research and development programs such as STARS [STAR86], ESPRIT and ALVEY take care of certain standardisation and divergence tendencies. Research analyses and market research [Rock89, McCl88] show the following CASE tool types today (see Figure 3.11).

Strategic information system planning tools

These serve company-wide planning and management of information systems. They are only used in this class of applications. A small group of specialists use them across a range of applications for business planning (including company goal planning), resource planning, technology planning and their supervision as well as computing architecture planning and administration.

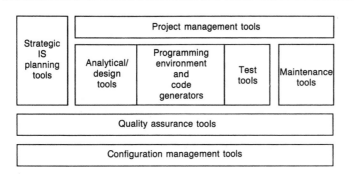

Figure 3.11 CASE tool classification based on market analyses

Analysis and design tools

Analysis and design tools, also called construction tools, are used for requirements collecting, analysis and definition as well as for the creation of technical design for specialist areas, for software and for company organisation. These tools comprise text and graphics editors for the creation and testing of specifications (specifications checker), prototyping tools and a repository. Prototyping tools help to determine and validate system requirements.

The 'test functions' of these tools are:

- checking the compliance of the syntax and semantics of a specification (e.g. of a diagram model);
- checking for consistency and completeness of a specification;
- checking model characteristics (e.g. functional decomposition on the basis of a tree structure representation of an application); and
- following requirements beyond different life-cycle documents.

A concrete example for a complex requirement system is Software Requirements Engineering Methodology (SREM), which was developed by TRW for the US Army (see [Alfo77]). SREM consists of a formal Requirement Specification Language (RSL) and a Requirements Engineering Validation System (REVS). This tool system was one of the first to have an integrated database which matched the tools. SREM is of restricted use in the phases of software requirements gathering, analysis and definition in data processing. Quality assurance is supported by aids for collecting and checking requirements, for prototyping and for reutilisation and debugging systems.

Programming environments and generators

The classes of programming environments and generators comprise prototyping tools, application generators, compilers for 3GLs and 4GLs, editors and debugging systems.

Many programming environments were created in connection with a programming language and are therefore labelled as language-dependent programming environments. Examples of such language-dependent programming environments are Interlisp for LISP, Integral-C for C, CDL2-Lab for CDL2, Macmeth for Modula-2, and Toolpack for FORTRAN [Müll89].

Generators are tools which create complete program systems or program parts [Kell89] from given specifications which can exist in textual form or as a formal language or in graphics. These either can generate executable code or have to be executed using an interpreter. In the first case, one speaks of program generators; in the second, of applications generators [Pres87].

A very widespread programming environment is the UNIX Programmer's Workbench (PWB, see [Ivie77]). This environment is available for different makes of computer. The programmer need not learn new details if the hardware is altered. UNIX/PWB is file orientated. Interfaces between tools are shared files or pipes, but there is no uniform database for the tools. In order to avoid this problem, solutions are sought at present which centre around a software engineering database system (see [Math87]).

Test tools

The category 'test tools' comprises the following types of tool:

- test data generators;
- test stubs and test driver generators;
- dynamic analysers; and
- result validators and file comparators.

Test data generators are used for the creation of synthetic test data. In the case of generators for test stubs and test drivers, the tester approaches the test system via the user interface. It is worth mentioning that the user interface of the test system in the tool environment of the developers can be complete and integrated. The user executes the tests by means of a start operation and the defined test cases are then run in sequence. The test object, which, for example, was monitored with relevance to C_1 measurements, is executed with the test cases. In this process the executed external calls are performed on the selected test cases. For the operation of the different functions and of the test object, dummy modules (stubs) may be necessary. These are 'inserted' into the test system. The test output routines which are used by the test system create the results. In addition, there is the possibility of comparing test results with the old or predicted test results (using a comparator).

Dynamic analysers deliver results which are obtained during the execution of a program. In general, they consist of the following parts: test generators, test monitors and report systems. [Snee83] gives a good overview of tools for dynamic analysis.

Large software systems requiring correspondingly high levels of quality assurance tend to use environment simulators. By this term we mean a program which simulates the environmental conditions of a test object (e.g. operating system, interrupts, DB/DC system). This tool is mostly used if it is too expensive or cumbersome to test in the real system environment itself. With these tools, users, hardware configurations and software interfaces are modelled. Environment simulators are used for:

- stress and volume tests, e.g. simulation of actions of 100 active terminals in a time-sharing system; and
- tests of software in space travel systems (e.g. space shuttle), radar systems or defence systems.

Maintenance tools

The category 'maintenance tools' (re-engineering tools) is gaining in importance [Hort88, Abi88]. The functions of these tools comprise program analysis, automatic documentation (analysis of source code and creation of documentation), restructuring and transporting of existing programs [McCl88]. The tools are complemented by test and debugging tools, code-tracing tools and file comparators.

Project management tools

These tools help the project leader to achieve better planning, costing, controlling and evaluating. The tools are therefore planning, costing and estimation packages, word processing, spreadsheets and tools for electronic communication. Planning and, in particular, estimation tools make the estimation of project cost possible. In addition, they allow 'what if' analysis for planning features such as project size or resource requirements. Examples of such planning tools are SLIM and ESTIMACS [Pres87].

Quality assurance tools

Quality assurance tools support quality assurance operations of a phase (e.g. testing of a software design) or across several phases. Special tools for software quality assurance are [DGQ86] tools for error prevention, error recognition, error evaluation and configuration management.

Tools for error prevention include:

- prototyping tools for determining functionality;
- documentation systems with document templates;
- syntax-driven editors;
- data dictionaries;
- database generators;
- assertion generators; and
- compilers for strongly typed languages.

Tools for error recognition and for error evaluation include:

- static analysers for complexity analysis (e.g. control flow analysers, data flow analysers, interface analysers);

- pretty printers;
- cross-references and listing generators;
- disassembler
- tools for checking standards;
- test coverage analysers;
- execution path listers;
- test data generators;
- test environment generators;
- test administration systems;
- test result comparators;
- assertion test programs;
- programs for symbolic module execution;
- debuggers;
- performance analysers; and
- software monitors.

Configuration management tools

These tools are described in section 3.6.3.

In conclusion, CASE tools offer automated support for the entire life cycle. Integration and uniformity of application are at present the biggest problems when working with these tools. But CASE is also a combination of tools with different methods of process support. The highest development level of CASE tools are software production environments.

3.5.2 Software production environments

The concept of Software Production Environment (SPE) has been known since the early 1980s. Synonyms for it are Software Engineering Environment (SEE), Software Development Environment, and Integrated Project Support Environment (IPSE). The concept [Char86, Öste88, Brer88] is also often mentioned in connection with CASE. A software production environment aims to meet the wish for life-cycle-embracing and integrated support for developer operations. For this purpose, an SPE contains a collection of integrated computer-supported tools which ideally support the operations in the life cycle completely.

CADES (Computer Aided Development and Evaluation System) of ICL [McGu79] was one of the first production environments which offered extensive support from the analysis and design phase up to maintenance. It was successfully implemented for the development of the operating system VME/B. CADES was one of the first operational usable software production environments which also took maintenance into account.

A mature software production environment has, according to Frühauf [Früh87b], a uniform user interface which makes available an information system for the project team, and which guarantees consistency of developed results by use of a software engineering database system. Generator and transformation functions support documentation and code creation, and help to transfer developer results from one development state (e.g.high-level design) into the next (e.g. detailed design) without the need for repeated handling of information.

Tool box type 1

The only tool available for requirements definition and design is a data dictionary. During the coding phase, a source code administration system is used. For verification and validation, a data comparator is used. This type of tool box is suitable for small to medium commercial projects (development time less than 2 years, with fewer than 7 project workers).

Tool box type 2

In addition to the tools of tool box type 1, a software engineering database system can be used. The data model of the software engineering database system is based on the entity−relationship−attribute approach. Entity types include a coded module, a test plan, a design document and other intermediate and final results. The database system of PSL/PSA [Teic77] is a forerunner of such a software engineering database system. In addition, there are evaluation tools which show the interdependence of stored elements. This type of tool box is suitable for medium-size projects (development time 2−3 years, with 7−14 project workers).

Tool box type 3

In addition to the tools in tool box type 2, further life-cycle tools are used which can be integrated in addition to the software engineering database system. These additional tools support verification and validation. If the tools cannot be integrated via the software engineering database system, they must have compatible interfaces. For example, a configuration management tool must be able to call up a compiler. This tool box is suitable for medium to large projects (development time 3−5 years, with 14−70 workers).

Tool box type 4

This tool box contains a software engineering database system which is also contained in type 3. In addition, tools for project planning and control are integrated. The software engineering database system also supports the configuration and version control.

For this type of tool box, the label 'software production environment' is justified. Large projects (development time more than 5 years, with more than 70 project workers) can be operated which comprise the project types 'commercial project' and 'embedded real-time system'.

Osterweil [Oste81], Habermann/Notkin [Habe86] and Balzert [Balz88b] have examined and defined typical features of software production environments. According to their studies, the following features for the planning and evaluation of an SPE can be noted:

- scope of application (different application types and project sizes);
- user-friendliness (uniform user interfaces, clear system messages, help system, recovery in case of software errors, at all times unambiguous identification of development status);
- automated configuration and version management;
- reuse of development elements;
- integration of tools;
- existence of a software engineering database system;
- support for project management activities;
- support for general office tasks (distributed word processing, diary, spreadsheets, report generators, electronic mail);
- extendability; and
- portability.

These features have shown themselves to be relevant during the development and application of software production environments such as Gandalf, R1000 and MAESTRO II.

Charette [Char86] characterises an SPE as follows: 'An SPE comprises the process, the method and the tools necessary to produce a software system.' He sees the purpose of the application of an SPE as being an ordered and controllable evolution of software systems.

According to Charette, an SPE can be represented by a three-layer architecture (see Figure 3.12). The bottom layer describes the development process. The layer above determines the methods to be applied. The top layer contains the necessary tools for the layers below.

Those software production environments presently in existence in computing practice can be differentiated with regard to the form of layers and their integration. A pyramid forms because the methods only partly cover the process. The methods themselves are only partially supported by tools.

This model is simple, but it allows discussion of all the important questions and problems of software production environments. For example, whereabouts in the process is method support lacking? How big is the gap between required methodology and the actual methodology which is supported by tools?

During the development of the programming language Ada [Barn82], an attempt

Figure 3.12 SPE model according to Charette

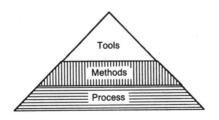

was made to develop a standardised layer model for a software production environment [Fish80]. Efforts in this direction culminated in the creation of a requirements document for the architecture of software production environments (STONEMAN) or of a standard proposal (Common APSE Interface Set (CAIS)) which defines the interface requirements [CAIS88]. The CAIS suggestion aims at portability of tools and transferability of the project databases. In 1987 the proposal was accepted as a valid standard, DOD-Std-1838 [DOD86].

An APSE (Ada Programming Support Environment) should be available on various computers, but will not necessarily be on the target machine. This requires cross-compilation. The application area for this is typical of the development of embedded real-time systems.

An APSE contains a predefined layered structure (see Figure 3.13). The innermost layer is called KAPSE (Kernel APSE) and forms the interface between Ada programs and software tools on the one hand, and the operating system on the other. A KAPSE serves to provide an environment independent of the host operating system (i.e. virtual machine). The kernel of APSE consists of an extended library system. An Ada compiler accesses the system in order to deposit separately compiled program units. The APSE library system manages source code as well as object code and documentation. Furthermore, a KAPSE contains the Ada run-time system and interfaces to peripherals such as screens and printers.

The next layer is MAPSE (Minimal APSE). It sits on top of the KAPSE and supports the Ada programmer with tools, such as Ada compiler, editor, linker, loader, static and dynamic program analysers, command interpreters and a configuration management system. All tools must be written in Ada. MAPSE can be described as a programming environment. The uppermost layer provides tools for all phases and creates, in our terminology, a development environment.

One advantage of this concept is that APSEs have been conceived as open layers for the acceptance of future tools. In the long term, Ada is interesting for the software industry because it is a portable language and its software production environment is also portable. In particular, any phase documents can be reused

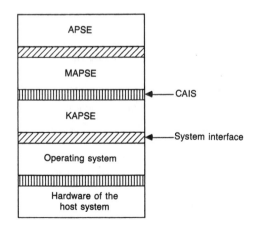

Figure 3.13 Layered model of the APSE concept with CAIS standard

or maintained if a hardware change occurs. Ada together with APSEs provides a powerful development and maintenance environment [Wehr88].

A further attempt at setting standards for tool interfaces is made by use of the ESPRIT Portable Common Tool Environment (PCTE) project. PCTE and CAIS are similar in their technical goals [Lyon87]. In both projects the object management system is based on an ERA model. PCTE differs from CAIS in that it is geared towards the operating system UNIX System V. The PCTE interface specifications lie in a C or Ada version. There are already some prototypes of software production environments, such as Emeraude, PACT, Entreprise and Eclipse, where the PCTE standard is implemented [Camp87, Boud88].

After looking more closely at various attempts to define and standardise the architecture of an SPE, as well as the tool interfaces the following task domains must be resolved:

- *User interface*. Uniformity, simple access to tools and an easily learnt structure are the key requirements of a user interface.
- *Tool integration*. Common calling of tools or of individual tool functions and arbitrary data exchange between the tools are important requirements to be implemented.
- *Data model for the underlying database*. Flexibility and extendability during object management and storage are relevant requirements of the database, which must be generated by means of a suitable data model and its efficient implementation.
- *Integrity of database*. The database must be consistent and always free of unnecessary storage of development elements.
- *Support system issues*. These include questions relating to networking capability, multi-host connections and the operating system.

It may here be critically noted that early and imperfect standardisation can hinder the development of an innovative and flexible solution. The absence of standardisation, on the other hand, leads to a wild explosion of possible solutions and to the wastage of research and development resources. A flexible strategy which distinguishes between standard proposal, prototype building and revision of standards may be the best way to a solution.

The integration of different types of tool is only possible via a software engineering database system. The terms 'repository' or 'object management system' (OMS) are also used. Examples of this are the OMS for the PCTE project and DAMOKLES for the production environment Unibase [Abra87]. The system architecture of an extensive production environment which is based on this concept is already recognisable today (see Figure 3.14).

The basis of this architecture is a repository which makes possible the efficient physical storing of development and maintenance elements. For this a very flexible data model (meta model) is used which determines which development elements are to be stored and what relationships exist between them.

The requirements of the repository are manifold:

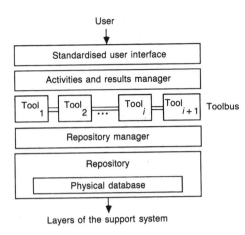

Figure 3.14 Architecture based on the repository of an SPE

- Complex elements must be managed. A complex element is formed hierarchically from simpler elements. Examples of such elements are modules which, apart from the source code, also include specifications, test drivers, etc.
- Elements and their attributes must be allowed to be of any length (e.g. file with source code or textual description of a function).
- Long transactions must be supported (e.g. a transaction in which a developer processes a module can take several hours or days).
- Different types of relationship between elements must be managed.
- Multi-user capability and the distribution of different access rights must be supported.
- Configuration and version management must be supported.

The layer above is known as the repository manager. This makes element management, supply and generation of new element definitions possible.

Above this management and control layer lies the layer of actual tools containing the required elements, which are passed via a standardised interface. Besides specified tools there is also the possibility of a number of generic basic tools (tool kit) for the development of any tool. The prerequisite for this is a standardised interface which controls access to the elements of the repositories [ESF89, Conn88].

A tool mechanism serves to activate the different functions of individual tools reciprocally, i.e. from one tool A it is possible to access the functions B1 and B2 of tool B.

For the user there is a standard, ergonomically tested user interface which supports high-resolution, bit-mapped graphics and contains a mouse, a pointer, a whole-page screen, multi-window technology, icons and pull-down as well as pop-up menus.

From the point of view of quality assurance, uniform element management and consistency and completion tests based on this are of great importance. Comparable to a fully automated high-bay storage system in a warehouse, continuous administration and clear access to all system development and maintenance elements is possible. The implementation of this architecture should give enormous support to those quality assurance measures which have so far been carried out manually, such as discovery of metrics and consistency tests. The implementation of software production environments is a field of current research and is therefore not yet closed.

3.5.3 Requirements of the software production environment from the perspective of quality assurance

The various definitions of an SPE show that the entire life cycle is supported by a software production environment. From this we derive the first requirement, namely that the SPE must support quality assurance tasks over the entire life cycle: for example, quality assurance tools must also be integrated into the maintenance of software products.

The aim of constructive quality assurance measures is the development of high-value quality product elements (products with as few faults as possible). In order to achieve this, the SPE must offer the following:

- computer-aided processing model with activity and result management (processing management);
- method-supported tools;
- templates of product components;
- aids for the retrieval of product components which are suited for reuse;
- aids for the assembly of reusable product elements; and
- sufficient help and learning support.

The aim of analytical quality assurance is qualitative and quantitative testing of developed units. An SPE must support these quality tests through automatic test functions. These test functions are integrated either into the tools or directly into the control layer (repository manager) (see Figure 3.15). A further aid of the SPE for test methods is evaluation. By this we mean the appearance of cross-

Figure 3.15 Quality assurance components of SPE

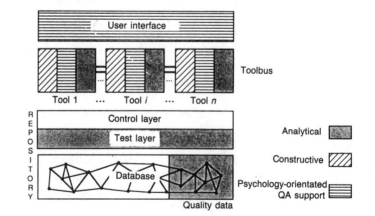

references between developed units and the researching and processing of quality data (values of process and product metrics, error data, etc.). The quality data must be stored in the database of the SPE and must be displayed using suitable aids (e.g. in the form of trend curves and statistics).

After automated test functions and evaluations, quality assurance is aided by the building of prototypes. This function is provided by prototyping tools. At present, tools for user interface prototyping dominate. Tools for architectural prototyping are only at the research and development stage [Pomb88].

In the area of psychology-orientated measures, support of an SPE is given by:

* uniform and simple-to-use user interfaces of the SPE;
* communication facilities in the form of electronic mail and help services for teamwork; and
* aids to developers and managers for better organisation of their own work.

The requirements of quality assurance with respect to the user interfaces of an SPE are high. In order to be able to check these requirements, it is advisable to differentiate between physical and logical user interfaces. Physical interfaces have been improved considerably in recent years. Pointers, a screen which shows a whole DIN A4 page, high-resolution graphic screens (Bit Map Display) and colour displays have proved to be extremely user friendly. The effects on quantitative and qualitative performance are considerable, as research has shown [Fole84, Niev81].

For logical user interfaces, the following requirements apply:

* *Uniformity*. The various tools have to be used via a uniform user interface.
* *Simplicity in use*. This must be implemented using icons, menus and window systems.
* *Comfort*. Graphical as well as textual representation of working items must be possible simultaneously.

The implementation of requirements to the logical and physical interface also facilitates an easy learning process.

The communication requirements of an SPE are concerned with the support of teamwork (work in groups on intermediate and final deliverables, transfer of results to colleagues, viewing of documents from others and electronic mail). In addition, a communication link to an international information service and network is desirable.

In the area of working aids and self-management of developers and managers, we are dealing with the organised planning, execution and control of the individual work results of SPE users. Further important requirements are a suitable report and document management system, a work planning tool, text and graphic tools.

Figure 3.15 gives an overview of the quality assurance components of an SPE.

The support of quality assurance through an SPE is an important factor in achieving effective quality assurance. If it were possible to implement this concept efficiently, the SPE would probably be accepted by developers as a working aid for the development and maintenance of high-quality software. The outcome would be a considerable increase in productivity.

3.6 Software configuration management

3.6.1 Why software configuration management?

Configuration management, especially administration of configuration, is a discipline which is applied traditionally to the development of hardware systems. It causes system development and related alterations to run in a smooth and structured way. Configuration management during the development of hardware systems consists of identifying individual hardware components, labelling them, administrating them and controlling alterations to them.

First of all, it is necessary to explain what is meant by configuration. The International Standards Organisation (ISO) defines the concept as follows: 'Configuration is the arrangement of a computer system or network as defined by the nature, number and chief characteristics of its functional units. More specifically, the term configuration may refer to hardware configuration or software configuration.'

The standard DOD-STD 480A gives the following definition: 'Configuration is the functional and/or physical characteristics of hardware/software as set forth in technical documentation and achieved in a product.'

The company Siemens defines the concept in the following way (see [End86]): 'Configuration is a designated and formally released number of developments which are brought into line with one another in their effects and their interfaces and which together fulfil a stipulated task.'

Summarising the above, software configuration is the entirety of software elements which are related in their actions and their interfaces at a particular time in a life cycle. A software item is either a software configuration or the smallest indivisible element of the product which is clearly identifiable within a configuration. For example, a software item can be a document, a module or a file, if this item is clearly identifiable as a whole and is subjected to a change process.

Configurations serve the following purposes:

- They regulate the collection of deliverables of part or whole systems.
- They bring order into the multiplicity of development deliverables.
- They form reference points for defined development steps, since they are tied in with the deliverables of previous development steps and hence represent a well-defined basis.
- They link intermediate results of a product for its entire life cycle and guarantee reusability and maintainability of the product in this way. In addition, a configuration forms a source of information for analysis of the development process and of the product. Configurations are, therefore, also suitable for computer-processed revision.

By software configuration management we mean the collection of methods, tools and aids which support the development and maintenance of a software product in a succession of controlled alterations (versions) and extensions (variants) of securely held process deliverables. In this way, the evolution of high-quality software is guaranteed.

Software is easily alterable. Deleting and modifying of program parts are no problem. Such alterations can have catastrophic consequences, however, if they are not systematically planned and tested.

The problem of alterations is particularly pertinent in maintenance (see also Chapter 5). In many instances, alterations are incomplete and insufficiently documented. The problem becomes worse if documentation is partly or completely missing, or if it is not up to date. The effects of this situation are not controllable and often lead to the necessity for the new development of systems sooner than need be.

The basic idea of software configuration management consists of keeping order systematically and with discipline. Four activities have to be carried out in order to achieve this.

The first activity of configuration management is to determine which items — for example, modules, files and databases — form a configuration. We are here dealing with the identification of all relevant elements of a software system at a certain moment in time.

In the second activity, change requests in the form of 'notices' are recorded. It must be possible to manage and reference these change requests. In a further step, requests for changes are converted into tasks for carrying out the changes. Prior to this a test must take place which examines the necessity of the change and rejects it if need be.

In the third activity, there are checks to determine if, when the changes are made, the consistency of software items and their relationships are retained. In principle, we are here concerned that originally specified requirements of the user or customer, and also the requirements which have emerged during system development relating to individual system components, are maintained after changes have taken place. It must also be guaranteed that all items affected by changes are processed in the required form and that, in principle, no unplanned changes are made.

The fourth activity is the recording of all changes. This activity makes possible the retrieval of information on alterations carried out so far on the system.

The following problems justify the application of software configuration management [Höft85]:

- *Problem of size*. Software systems, in the form of large-scale company information systems, consist of a large number of items (e.g. files, databases, modules, associated documents such as specifications, test cases, test plans, etc.). Among these there are a large number of relationships. These items must be managed consistently.
- *Problem of consistency*. Systems which consist of many items can be kept consistent only with difficulty. One and the same item appears in different places. For example, at first only a module specification of a building block exists, then a design for this building block is made and finally the code is

produced. In addition, there are test cases, test data and a test strategy which help to validate this building block. The consistency problem is aggravated by further development (revisions) of the system in accordance with the requirements, or because different versions of individual elements (variants) have to exist in parallel.

- *Problem of change*. Changes are unavoidable during the development and maintenance of software. Together with the above-mentioned problem of size, unplanned and uncontrollable changes are a potential source of faults and errors, often due to uncoordinated software elements.
- *Life-cycle problem*. During its life cycle a product may be used several times, or one might consider increasing the life cycle of the product. In consequence, as a rule, different workers or groups are responsible for maintenance and further development. Maintenance is only possible through adequate information about the system items and their interdependency.

Management responsible for the product must face these problems and make the necessary aids for their solution available. If this does not happen, quality will suffer considerably during maintenance and during the application of software products.

3.6.2   *Principles of software configuration management*

The effects of software configuration management on software quality and quality assurance are manifold. All-round development quality can be guaranteed early through organisational and technical aids and tools. This makes better control of the development process possible; project success can be more easily evaluated and it can be guaranteed that changes to the product are complete, achieved systematically and with the safeguarding of consistency in mind.

Concepts

The primary aim of software configuration management is the efficient management of software configuration in the life cycle of the product. A fundamental concept for this is the baseline.

Deutsch [Deut82] defines a baseline as follows: 'The data-processing resources produced by each phase of the software life cycle. These resources are controlled until superseded by a more current baseline. The data-processing resources of the baseline consist of both documentation and the software physical product.'

Bersoff, Henderson and Siegel [Bers80] see the baseline as a configuration (milestone) which is released at the end of each phase of the development process.

For baselines we apply the concept of reference configuration, by which we mean a configuration selected and released at a given point in time in the process. Tichy calls this 'baseline configuration' [Tich88]. Bersoff, Henderson and Siegel differentiate between requirement, concept, design, integration and product configuration (see Figure 3.16).

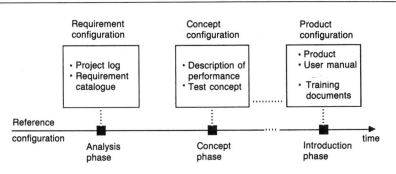

Figure 3.16 Reference configuration according to Bersoff, Henderson and Siegel

Important activities during the creation and maintenance of reference configurations are planning, execution and recording of all changes, with the aim that the actual configuration at all times reflects the changed state. This assumes that all reference configurations (of the software product) are defined and that the items in each reference configuration are identified and labelled.

The change process comprises registration, reporting of changes and verification with respect to one or several reference configurations (Figure 3.17). Verification is carried out through technical reviews or audits (see section 4.1.2). Deutsch calls these test measures 'functional and physical configuration audits' as well as formal qualification reviews [Deut82].

The development and maintenance of a product takes place through a series of planned and released reference configurations. They are frequently used as milestones by project management and by those responsible for maintenance. The product itself consists of a large number of software elements which form the configuration items of the individual reference configurations. Software configuration management helps to guarantee that products and their parts are visible, easily followed and controlled in a life cycle [Brya87].

According to Tichy [Tich88] a software item is an identifiable, machine-readable document which is created during the life cycle of a product. A software item

Determine the configuration structure of the system
(identifying and labelling all elements of the reference
configuration)

————————————————————— Reference configuration A

• Record changes in A
• Report on the status of the changes
• Verify the new reference configuration

————————————————————— Reference configuration B

• Record changes in B
• Report on the status of the changes
• Verify the new reference configuration

————————————————————— Reference configuration C

• Record changes in C
• Report on the status of the changes
• Verify the new reference configuration

————————————————————— Released product configuration

Figure 3.17 Changes system with reference configurations [IEEE88]

can be either a source item or a derived item. Source items, such as a design, are created by the developer through an editor. They can never be created completely automatically.

Derived items are created completely automatically by software from another software item. Examples of such software are compilers, linkers, formatters or generators for the creation of cross-references. Towards the end of this section we shall identify some typical examples of software items.

We shall now look at individual time-dependent software elements and introduce the concepts of version group, variants and revision.

As in technical drawings, it is useful to introduce a numbering scheme for software items. For example, this could consist of an unambiguous number, an unambiguous name and a revision number (Figure 3.18). The programming entity EM114-2-PR is the smallest identifiable software item subjected to a change mechanism.

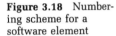 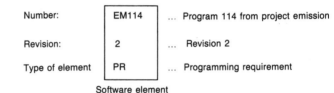

Figure 3.18 Numbering scheme for a software element

Useful for the introduction of the concepts of variants and revision are linked version groups of software items [Tich88]. A version group is a collection of software items which are linked by the relations 'is a variant of' and 'is a revision of'.

The relation '*y* is variant of *x*' is determined in the following way: *x* and *y* are existing software items which have an important characteristic in common. This might mean, for example, the same functional specification of a module. Implementations of this module are different. Variants are usually maintained in parallel, and the number of variants should be kept low for practical reasons.

The following example should clarify the concept of 'variant'. A software tool should be developed as variants on the computer types SUN and VAX for operating systems UNIX and VMS. The following tool variants are meaningful: V(VMS, VAX), V(UNIX, VAX), V(UNIX, SUN). Figure 3.19 shows a graphic representation of the possible variants.

Figure 3.19 Variants of a software tool

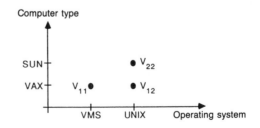

The relation 'y is a revision of x' is defined as follows: x and y are software items and y was created through changes to a copy of x. The reason behind this is the intention that y is an improvement on x and replaces x. For example, a module X was revised twice and hence a third revision is due ($X_{R0} \rightarrow X_{R1} \rightarrow X_{R2}$).

Activities of configuration management

So that the evolution of a software product stays visible, easy to follow and controllable, four tasks have to be carried out [Baze85, Bers80, Bers79]:

Configuration identification

- Identifying and defining items of a configuration.
- Determining individual configurations.
- Determining configuration structure (entirety of all configurations).

Configuration control

- Inputting change requests (messages) into the development process.
- Controlling the processing of changes through internally commissioned updates.
- Tracing all these updates (changes) up to their documented closure.

Configuration audit

- Guaranteeing the consistency and completeness of the reference configuration after input and execution of actual changes (configuration verification) and, if need be, recording deviations.
- Guaranteeing that after changes have been performed the results specified in the reference configurations meet the user requirements (configuration validation).
- Guaranteeing that product and documentation tally.

These activities can be carried out through organisational units such as quality assurance and system testing. With the help of reviews the reference configurations must be released after completed change control.

Configuration status accounting

- Recording and administrating all important information about all configuration items.
- Making information available about stored configuration items and their interrelationships.

The interplay of the above four activities is as follows. Determining the configuration is carried out within configuration planning. The results are defined configurations. During the development process there is a constant flow of reports about desired changes. Change control involves checks on these reports, initiation of their execution and monitoring of their completion. The change process is recorded by means of status accounting. Change control checks the altered configurations for consistency and releases them when the test is successful. In this way, change control can be seen as the central quality control. It is a formal process which follows all the internal development steps caused by change procedures up to the documented finish. The status accounting process is meant to record and collect all configuration items. Important here is the release date: only then can the change process be reviewed at all times.

Examples of configuration items

These include [Höft85]:

- released deliverables;
- reports;
- internal procedures; and
- plans.

The released deliverables and their interfaces are co-ordinated and solve a specified task together. All deliverables are looked upon as items which come about during software creation, such as requirements, design, and modules in source code and object code form.

The next important category of configuration items are reports. These are for dealing mainly with the administration of change and the implementation of planning and control of changes. The following categories of reports can be distinguished:

- problem reports;
- change requests; and
- error reports.

Commentary is added to reports in the course of processing; within this commentary, analysis goals, solution variants and implementation decisions are documented. Reports and commentary are processed by configuration management because they are responsible for the changes to configurations and their components.

Internal procedures are formal aids to configuration management in the control of the development and change process. They determine task setting, information on timescales and staff responsible for execution.

A further category of items which have to be administered by configuration management are plans. Two types of plan are known:

- plans which describe the activities and measures of configuration management; and
- plans which describe structures, i.e. which bring items into relation with one another.

The configuration management plan belongs to the first type; it describes the measures for effective execution of configuration management as part of the project plan. The item structure plan is of the second type; it breaks up a product into all the individual items which have to be created (individual development tasks), including items that are needed as aids and tools but which are not handed over to the customer.

Organisational requirements

In the following we are looking at configuration management in terms of the dynamics of the development process. From the organisational point of view, the following measures are useful:

- Introduce and establish organisation of the development process (process model).
- Determine processes for the determination of configurations.
- Establish directives.
- Determine internal task processes.
- Define change control.
- Introduce processes for software item management and information management.
- Determine the report structure.
- Introduce document management.
- Establish a project library.
- Execute configuration management planning.
- Determine conventions.

A configuration manager should ideally be responsible for task control in configuration management. Of vital importance for the selection of a suitable form of organisation is the volume of configuration items and the aids available for carrying out the configuration management tasks.

Present practice shows, however, that no manager is appointed specifically for the job. The project leader tends to carry the responsibility, and he or she delegates to an outside organisation or other staff for the execution of these activities; these consist mainly of status accounting (e.g. software librarian) and the distribution of software items.

Another form of organisation which is frequently found in practice is the change control board (CCB). This is a central decision committee for dealing with permission, postponement or rejection of requirements for new developments resulting from reports during the project process. The CCB decides on the basis of considered decisions:

- which requirements and requests for change are inserted into the current or into the future development process;
- which error reports need no longer be taken into account in the current development process; and
- which configurations are released for integration and after a successful system test will be released to users.

The CCB initiates the necessary activities through the distribution of internal tasks to the respective project teams. The project leader should either be in charge of the CCB or assume a leading role in the CCB.

A frequent fault of current development processes is the absence of adequate system planning, in particular with regard to the planning of configurations, which is a necessary condition for the successful execution of configuration management. Elimination of this fault can be effected either through project leadership or through the use of tools and aids of configuration management.

3.6.3   Aids and tools of configuration management

Suitable aids and tools are an important prerequisite for the execution of configuration management. Without these configuration management would be difficult to execute. Not only programs, but also specifications and design documents as well as test data and test procedures are handled with these aids and tools. In addition, error reports and change requests must be registered and administered. The following aids and tools are at present known:

- configuration management plan;
- project documentation system;
- project library;
- tools for new configurations of software systems; and
- tools for version control and administration.

Too little evidence about the application of these aids is so far available. Most experience comes from version and configuration administration of object and source code. With the increasing spread and maturity of software production environments, the application of aids for configuration management will also increase.

Configuration management plan (CMP)

The CMP regulates the working areas of configuration management, project organisation with reference to configuration management, the selection of suitable processes and tools, conventions for the support of configuration management and the kind of co-operation involved with suppliers. The introduction of configuration management in a software project is suitably regulated by a configuration management plan.

There is an internationally recognised standard for a software configuration management plan, drawn up by the IEEE (IEEE Std 828-1984). If the configuration management plan is to be used for the introduction of configuration management, it should also contain a suitable introduction strategy. The IEEE standard contains the following points:

Introduction

- Purpose
- Scope
- Definitions and acronyms
- References

Management

- Organisation
- SCM responsibilities
- Interface control
- SCMP implementation
- Applicable policies, directives and procedures

SCM activities

- Configuration identification
- Configuration control
- Configuration status accounting
- Audits and reviews

Tools, techniques and methodologies
Supplier control
Records collection and retention

In IEEE Std 828 there is an introduction which contains statements about how the standard is to be interpreted for a specific project. At the beginning of this introduction, four examples of software configuration plans are given: software for integrated systems, software for commercial systems, software maintenance projects and CAM software.

Project documentation system and project library

The project documentation system plays an important part in software configuration management. In each project a large number of documents come into being. The system deals not only with development results, but also reports, contracts and plans. Whether the project goals are reached depends to a considerable extent on the orderly creation and quality of these documents. In connection with the project documentation system, there must be directives for document management and for document administration. Here it must be noted how the documents are to be classified, how they are identified and what the guidelines are for the external appearance of the overall structure, the structure of contents, distribution, storage and the ongoing status of the documents (e.g. in planning, in review, on release). At the centre of configuration management is the project database, which we also call the project library. It also contains data which does not come into configuration management (e.g. private work versions produced by developers), and all elements which are identified within the realms of document administration and document management. The project library goes far beyond the activities of configuration management. It is a general instrument for storage and administration of elements for all project participants from project leader to developer.

The separation of items from information administration is considered to be an important characteristic of the project library, since the administration of items and the evaluation of information require very different functions from the project library. Item management means that items are put into the library in an orderly fashion, that they are stored or can be made available. In contrast to item management, where the set items can only be retrieved, information administration must allow free evaluation of stored information in the sense of logical interlocking.

Tools for new configurations of software systems

These tools help with generating a new configuration of a software system where there have been changes. Only those parts of the system which have changed or are derived from changed parts (e.g. compiled and linked) are newly configured. In order to determine the identity of configuration items before and after the new configuration, time-stamps are used. The relationship between software items and the necessary or desired processing is described by a specified syntax. Examples of these tools are MAKE on UNIX and MMC on VMS.

In the last fifteen years a number of tools have been developed which support the different tasks of configuration management. One of the first tools was the Source Code Control System (SCCS) [Roch75], which was available under UNIX as well as under OS/370. A functionally improved system for SCCS was the Revision Control System (RCS) [Tich82], which was developed by Purdue University and AT&T. One of the most powerful tools of configuration management currently available is the Domain Software Engineering Environment (DSEE) of APOLLO [Lebl84]. It is known for its good integration into the distributed development environments of APOLLO computers. It is language independent and can be combined with every word processor.

Tools for version control and administration

Tools for the economic storage of several revisions and versions of software items are not yet widespread. In one scheme which puts items under the complete control of tools, only the differences between versions are stored. In essence there are two strategies for the storage of files: either the first or the last version is stored completely. Examples of such tools are SCCS, running under the UNIX operating system, and SMS, running under the VMS operating system.

3.7   Quality influences of human behaviour

In this section we look in more detail at aspects of work psychology and human relationships in quality assurance. At the centre of our observations is the developer as a human being; he or she is not viewed as a means of production, but as a person with specific interests, aims and needs. A psychologically unpleasant working environment and discord among members of staff have negative effects on the quality of work performance and the productivity of the developer. The following three areas are sources of disturbance which can have a negative effect on quality and productivity (see Figure 3.20):

- company culture;
- human communication; and
- workplace environment.

Computer experts are inclined to neglect problems in these areas due to their technology-orientated priorities. We shall now examine these three areas.

3.7.1   *Company culture*

At the centre of each computing organisation are people who take part in the development and maintenance processes. In spite of the CASE view of a future

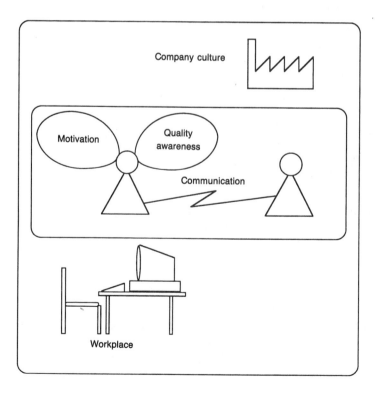

Figure 3.20 Sources of disturbance which influence human behaviour

software industry, it is my conviction that automation trends in the development process will always be limited to parts of the development area, and that the creative, 'thinking' members of staff will hold the key position in the development and maintenance of high quality products. The most valuable assets of every computing organisation — despite increasing software technology — are the devotion and qualifications of members of staff.

A team works under certain specific conditions which are specified by standards and values. The values may vary slightly in different units of an organisation (e.g. department, section or group), but the principal values, such as attitude to quality, to the customer, to profit and to colleagues, are similar. This means that the basic attitude of members of staff is to some extent determined by the company culture, and this, in turn, is affected by the example set by company leadership.

By company culture we mean the entirety of thinking [Stad88] (ideas, standards, views and opinions), of feeling (attitudes to values, ethics), and of acting (attitudes, transfer of knowledge strategy, working practices) which are inherently created and initiated by the company. These influence activities and most of the relationships between staff.

What is the connection between company working climate and quality? The hypothesis offered here, which refers to [Stad88], is based on the idea that the mental and actual attitudes of the developers have a direct effect on the quality of their performance and hence also on the quality of the product.

Company culture, according to Stadler [Stad88], affects the following areas:

- communication (senior with more junior colleagues, members of staff with each other);
- ways of proceeding when carrying out tasks (participating, directed by the superior);
- working mentality (complacency, identification);
- textual quality of documents (superficial, thorough);
- order (restricting, rigid, functional);
- architecture and layout of buildings and work rooms (functionality, cleanliness, security); and
- degree and quality of training opportunities.

Inadequacies in these areas invariably lead to lower quality. In particular, the area of document generation is often an indicator of the attitude towards quality and of existing quality awareness within a company culture. The quality of manuals is marked by the influence of company culture and especially by the attitude of management to quality assurance. It is, therefore, not surprising that individual actions to improve document quality are often unsuccessful in the medium and long term, if changes in the company culture do not occur in parallel. In section 3.7.2 we shall give detailed attention to the area of communication.

The question arises of who is responsible for company culture. It is primarily determined by the company owner and top management. However, a secondary influence can be seen in the prevailing political and economic situation. In addition, the staff themselves and the medium and lower management also set values in the workplace.

Figure 3.21 Staff factors for quality work

In Figure 3.21 conditions for staff are listed which would promote good-quality work [Stad88]. If these conditions are met, according to Stadler, good-quality work and working results will ensue.

We have already seen that the relationship between senior and more junior staff is an important ingredient of company culture. This relationship is influenced by leadership style. A run-down of leadership styles and leadership attitudes is unnecessary here; we shall limit our deliberations to the influence of leadership style on quality.

Leadership, according to Grunwald and Lilge [Grun80], is the goal-orientated influencing of human behaviour with the aim of reaching company goals as well as the personal goals of the staff.

The attitude of staff can be influenced on the one hand through the stimulation of interests and the availability of identification potential, and on the other through the creation of fear. Both possibilities are used as elements of leadership style. By manipulation, the member of staff is compelled to act in a particular way in order to reach the stipulated goals. Through motivation, the member of staff shows a willingness to behave in a particular way and to work towards stipulated or agreed goals.

Division of labour in product development, where the worker solves ever smaller tasks, stands as an obstacle to reaching the goals of quality assurance through increased motivation. Simply being part of a whole can lead to loss of work satisfaction and cause the interest in quality work to decrease. A key task in quality assurance, therefore, lies in examining the needs of workers for initiative, recognition of good-quality work and self-initiated responsibility, and in promoting oportunities for these.

3.7.2 Communication between members of staff

Communication is one of the major activities of the members of staff when work is shared in software development and maintenance. According to a study by Jones [Jone86], discussions and agreements on work results account for more than 35 per cent of the activities of software developers. The following aspects of communication must be differentiated:

- communication with users;
- communication among/between project teams; and

Figure 3.22 Basic model of simple communication

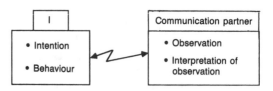

- communication with representatives at different levels of the company hierarchy.

Communication also plays an important part in quality assurance measures such as reviews, inspections and quality circles.

First of all, we will take a closer look at shortcomings in communication. For this we need a communication model [Birk82] (see Figure 3.22).

During the transfer of messages from sender to receiver, misunderstandings can be created on both sides. Here the maxim applies, 'Truth is not what I say — truth is what the other hears or understands.' In order to avoid misunderstandings, it is necessary to send a message that is receiver orientated and to receive a message that is sender orientated. This means, in actual terms, that I have to bear in mind the receiver when I send a message, and that the receiver must always interpret the message relative to my intention.

Each conversation takes place on two levels which are characterised by the terms 'climate' (level of relation) and 'subject matter' (material level). Expert discussions can be useless if problems and difficulties exist on the climate level. A positive attitude to the communication partner helps to create a good starting point on the climate level as well as on the material level. During communication (e.g. discussions, negotiations) it is necessary consciously to take into account both the social climate and the material level. A successful conversation where messages are sent and received in the desired way demands a balance between the two levels. An elementary prerequisite for successful activity in the subject matter is an acceptable conversation climate.

Everyone has a sense of self-esteem which is linked to the desire to be accepted and recognised by others. The self-esteem of the communication partner will be increased if we make him or her feel that their contribution is important. If we threaten his or her sense of self-esteem, then we worsen the climate of the conversation.

Examples of threats to the sense of self-esteem are: talking down, imposing one's opinion, repeated interruptions, lecturing, direct opposition, laying open weaknesses, cynicism, personal injury, preoccupying oneself with something different, favouring a third person, showing off, high-handedness and ignoring.

Examples of increasing the sense of self-esteem are: listening actively, taking the conversation partner seriously, showing understanding, having time, taking up the partner's thoughts, apologising, recognition, praise, admiration, putting the partner into the centre, asking for advice, addressing with name and title, friendliness and politeness.

By avoiding threats to the sense of self-esteem and by deliberately increasing it, the communication process can be considerably improved, and errors which appear in the form of misinterpreted or unnoticed information can be reduced.

The effects of inadequate communication on quality are underestimated in software projects. A computing organisation is, therefore, well advised to send management and developers on training and practical courses where weaknesses in communication and possibilities of positive communication are pointed out.

3.7.3 Influence of the physical working environment

There are a number of psychological studies [Paul80, Wald81, Oldh83] which show that the physical working environment has a bearing on the actions and attitudes of members of staff.

The following factors in particular tend to influence staff behaviour:

- how closely people are sitting together;
- the arrangement of the workplace, such as lighting conditions and how the workplace is enclosed; and
- personal space.

How closely members of staff are sitting together in a working area is significant. Paulus and Sundstrom [Sund78] proved that the individual reacts more negatively the closer he or she is located to colleagues (not being able to concentrate, not being interested in the work of the colleague). Furthermore, they established a link between working in close vicinity and the rate of turnover of workers.

The lighting conditions and the colour of the walls in the office also affect the behaviour of the workers. Darker rooms and dark office walls are looked upon as disturbance factors by members of staff (little work satisfaction and low performance rate [Oldh83]). However, attitude to colour and light/artificial light differ from individual to individual. Problems in this area can only be solved by the participation of all colleagues in the creation of the physical working environment.

Enclosure of the workplace is defined by psychologists as the number of walls and partitions which separate the workplace of the worker from his or her environment. Studies show a positive correlation between enclosure and individual job satisfaction, happiness with the working environment and degree of intimacy. In addition, it was noticed that more work interruptions (e.g. coffee breaks) occur if the enclosure of the workplace is insufficient (open-plan offices without partitioning).

By personal space we mean the physical distance in the workplace between one worker and the next. Research work has shown that workers can feel cramped, claustrophobic and distracted if there is little personal distance between them [Paul80, Sund80].

The results must be taken into account in any analysis of the qualitative and quantitative performance of software developers. Frequent inadequacies in the working environment of computing specialists are:

- machine noise (printer, ventilation of computers) in the immediate workplace environment;
- insufficient storage area for documents next to the computer terminal; and
- no facilities for displaying graphic material and pictures in the immediate field of vision of the worker.

This list is only an example. In this connection, the experiences of software ergonomy [Schö87, Balz83] are also of interest, and are not taken into account often enough at present.

When arranging workplaces for computing specialists, these observations should be taken into account in the form of checklists. The worker should have a say in the arrangement of his or her workplace.

In this section, we have tried to show a picture of the human aspects of the development process. Many of the disturbance factors listed here have been researched. Further interdisciplinary research is necessary in order to broaden our understanding. It is important for those involved in quality assurance management to take these factors into consideration.

4 Analytical quality assurance measures

The quality of software can be examined and evaluated using analytical quality assurance measures. These measures can lead to the improvement of a product. There are a number of reasons for such investigations:

- The buyer or contractor wants to know whether a software product meets his or her requirements.
- The project leader is interested in the quality of intermediate and end deliverables of a phase.
- The developer wants to know whether his or her work has reached a high level of quality.

An important prerequisite for analytical quality assurance measures is a practical quality plan. This determines which requirements the product has to meet. From this the test objectives can be derived.

It is not sufficient to observe after the development of a software system whether it possesses the required features and meets the specified requirements (validation aspects). Testing of the quality of software involves not only the testing of intermediate and end products (e.g. through reviews), but also an evaluation of the development process (e.g. through a process audit). The different forms of the software must be tested from the requirements definition to the working system. However, the correspondence of these forms must also be tested (verification aspects), such as the requirements definition with the design specification.

Software testing plays an important part in verification, validation (V & V) and certification. These three concepts can be defined as follows:

- *Validation*. By validation we mean testing and evaluation of a software product at the end of the development process in order to prove whether product requirements match with the product as implemented.
- *Verification*. By verification we mean the testing and evaluation of an entity against the previous intermediate and end results of a phase in the life cycle (e.g. specifications).
- *Certification*. By certification we mean the testing and evaluation of a software product or quality assurance system to confirm previously stipulated requirements (e.g. conformance with standards). When the stipulated requirements have been met, an independent testing agency will issue a certificate.

For example, the German Society for Certification of Quality Assurance Systems (Deutsche Gesellschaft zur Zertifizierung von Qualitätssicherungssystemen, DQS) and the Swiss Association for Quality Assurance Certification (Schweizerische Vereinigung für Qualitätssicherungszertifikate, SQS) issue quality certificates to the standards ISO 9001−9003. For application software products which meet the quality criteria in standard DIN V66285, a certificate can be issued [Schm84] (see Appendix A7) via authorised test institutes from the Software Quality Association.

In historical context verification and validation were first used for evaluating the functionality and performance of a product. Questions which arose in connection with verification and validation in the past were as follows:

- Do the product design and the product itself contain all the specified functions, and have these functions been correctly implemented?
- Does the chosen design or product guarantee the specified results with specified precision and under the specified time restrictions?
- Does the product work satisfactorily with the available resources?

Because of the growing and complex requirements of software products, the central importance of verification and validation has been recognised, and the field of activity has been modified and extended considerably. At present, attempts are being made to answer the following questions through verification and validation:

- Does the product meet the specification?
- Can the product be produced within the specified time at the stipulated cost?
- Can the installed product be easily modified and adapted to meet changing user needs?
- Can the product operate efficiently in the user environment?

The central position and increasing significance of verification and validation can also be recognised by the fact that an international standard Software Verification and Validation Plan (SVVP) already exists (IEEE Std 1012-1986 [IEEE86]).

By means of verification and validation activities, which are recorded in a software verification and validation plan, we attempt to:

- discover and remove errors as early as possible in the life cycle;
- reduce project risks and cost;
- improve product quality;
- improve the transparency of the development process for management; and
- achieve a swift estimate of proposed alterations and their effects on product quality, cost and timescales.

The content of the verification and validation plan to IEEE Standard 1012 is structured as follows:

Purpose
Referenced documents
Definitions

Verification and validation overview

- Organisation
- Master schedule
- Resources summary
- Responsibilities
- Tools, techniques and methodologies

Life-cycle verification and validation
Software verification and validation reporting
Verification and validation administrative procedures

The standard lays down the necessary preconditions, minimum tasks and results of each phase, in order to achieve the goals of verification and validation. As an example, this is represented for the design phase in Figure 4.1.

Each test has a certain goal which is determined by the software requirements. The goals are many layered. For example, a design evaluation includes checking adherence to standards and directives, or features such as correctness, consistency, completeness, precision and testability.

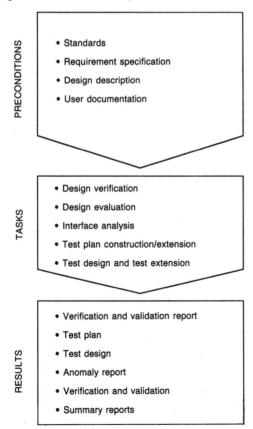

Figure 4.1 Preconditions, tasks and results of verification and validation for the design phase [IEEE86]

The available test methods can be divided into two categories: static and dynamic tests. The important difference between the two is that the test object in the dynamic test is executed, and this is not the case in static tests.

4.1 Static tests

Static tests include audits, reviews (inspections, walkthroughs), static analysis with software tools, proofs of correctness (mathematical program verification) and symbolic program execution.

4.1.1 Audits

With reference to ANSI Standard N45.2.10.1973 an audit can be defined as: an activity to determine through investigation the adequacy of, and adherence to, established procedures, instructions, specifications, codes, and standards or other applicable contractural and licensing requirements and the effectiveness of implementation.

In connection with quality and quality assurance we differentiate between the following kinds of audit:

- *Audit of product quality*. In this kind of audit, a quantitative evaluation of conformity of the product with the requested product features is carried out. Examples of product features are physical and functional completeness.
- *Audit of process quality*. In this type of audit, the elements of a process and tests for completeness, effectiveness and necessary improvement are suggested. By process we mean the management and development process.
- *Audit of quality assurance system*. In this kind of audit, we examine whether the existing elements of a quality assurance system are complete, effective and documented in compliance with the specifications. If necessary, improvement measures are suggested.

Audits of product quality are often used in the software industry. Audits of process quality and quality assurance systems are rare and vary in their execution. Typical examples of audits from computing practice [Craw85] are development process audits (frequently called project audits), which test the productivity and performance of a project team and the effectiveness of the applied methods and tools, and project management audits, which test management practices and performances (of the management process) and project organisation.

Important features of audits are [Evan87]:

- product, process or system evaluation;
- evaluation from a neutral, uniform point of view;
- suggestions for improvement measures; and
- application of checklists.

What are the important results of audits? Audits should identify concrete problem situations (deviations of the actual state from the target state) and induce target-orientated suggestions for solutions and improvements.

The audit procedure consists of the following steps:

- Define aims.
- Define the scope and field of application.
- Put into practice.
- Review and collect data.
- Analyse collected data.
- Work out suggestions for solutions and improvements.
- Create and present a results report.

In the first step, which is the definition of aims, the specific aims are identified. These aims depend on the nature of the project, the experience of the project personnel and the purpose of the audit. In principle, the definition of an audit should answer the following questions:

- What is the area, or which results should the audit supply?
- Why is the audit to be carried out?
- Is this a routine audit, or is this audit to identify and solve specific project problems?
- Who is responsible for carrying out the audit?
- What are the particular expectations of the receiver of the audit results?
- Is an open evaluation of the project status welcome? (This is not supposed to influence the set goals of the audit, but it does influence its execution.)
- How and for what purpose is the audit result used?
- Will there be subsequent audits for further project evaluations?

After the aims of the audit have been clearly set out, the extent and application area of the audit is defined. In order to get more practical statements concerning the time and cost for planning, it is useful to characterise the product with regard to the product type (e.g. business information system, technical process control), the size (e.g. number of staff, number of person-years), the complexity (e.g. commercial application with many interfaces) and the planned development phase (see section 3.2.1), so that on this basis an audit plan can be mapped out. This plan should be kept brief and should describe the aims of the audit, the way the audit is to be executed, the required project staff, the field which is to be evaluated and the expected results. Furthermore, it should be specified what data is to be collected and how data collection is to be executed.

During the setting up of the audit, the relationship between the audit team and project personnel should be established. Preconditions for successful execution are a clear representation of the aims of the audit and avoidance of the impression that the project personnel are being cross-examined. The setting up of the audit usually takes place in the form of an opening conference ('kick-off meeting').

During the assessment phase, raw data is collected which might come from reviews, for example. The project history is analysed and project development is examined. For this, interviews with project personnel are necessary. One of the main problems is that the audit team is confronted with a large amount of data, from which it is difficult to select relevant data.

The analysis of collected data must be directed by one person, and analysis results must be compressed. ABC analysis and multi-moment procedures have proved useful as practicable methods for compressing analysis data [Deym84]. The compressed analysis results must be evaluated in parallel by different audit workers. The individual results must then be compared and for larger deviations the cause must be found.

On the basis of analysis results, suggestions for improvement are worked out which determine the ensuing procedure for the auditing of elements.

The creation of the report is the last step. The results or the situation identifiable from the audit must be clearly presented. Presentation of this report terminates the audit itself.

4.1.2   Reviews

Referring to IEEE Standard 729-1983 [IEEE83] a review can be defined as: a formal meeting and structured analysis where project results are presented to the user, customer or other interested parties for comment and approval.

The particular merit of this examination procedure lies in the fact that software development and maintenance consist, to a large extent, of the creation of documentation and the maintenance process. Each document should be checked in some form or other. At present, informal documents are in the majority in the development process, while semi-formal and formal documents are rare. Reviews are particularly useful for informal documentation, and offer the best opportunity of determining faults and deviations from quality specifications. Reviews are today the only effective check which can be usefully applied during the earlier phases.

In 1981 Diesteldorf, Bons and van Megen [Dies81] launched a survey of companies which used reviews. The project contained, among other things, an exact analysis of the aims of reviews. The main reasons for the use of reviews were:

- immediate quality improvement of the test object;
- indirect improvement of process quality; and
- better control of the project factors of cost and time.

With regard to the immediate quality improvement of the object under review, the following sub-aims were determined in descending order of importance:

- early error recognition;
- securing the required quality characteristics;
- testing with regard to adherence to development standards and directives; and
- testing of interfaces and system building blocks.

With regard to the second aim, indirect improvement of process quality, it was discovered that, through the use of reviews, communication within the project team improved considerably and communication with specialist departments could be more easily arranged.

Regarding the factors of project cost and time, it was discovered that reviews facilitated exact and reliable project control and that program testing required considerably less cost and time.

Review process

The individual review steps are represented in Figure 4.2.

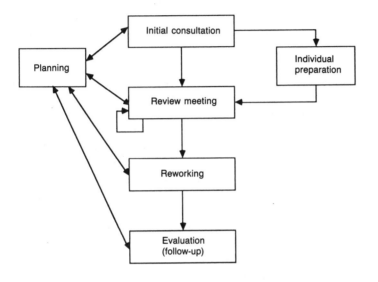

Figure 4.2 Review structure

Planning. First of all, the test aims and the release criteria for the review are determined. The latter determine under which conditions the review object can be considered ready for examination. Planning is mostly carried out by an independent moderator. The review should be carried out without interruptions or encumberance with regard to time and place. It must also be guaranteed that the participants are available for the review meeting.

How much time should be planned and used for the review process is an important issue. Empirical research data are available for code inspection. Buck states the following productivity values for code inspection [Buck81]:

- for the consultation meeting, about 500 instructions per hour;
- for preparation, about 125 instructions per hour; and
- for inspection, about 90 instructions per hour.

The maximum inspection rate is about 125 instructions per hour. It was discovered that if this rate is exceeded, the error discovery rate is considerably reduced. In most cases this leads to re-inspection (i.e. repeat of inspection).

Initial consultation. For complex or new test objects, it is sensible to have a consultation meeting before the review. This gives the review participants an overview of the test object.

Individual preparation. The consultation meeting is followed by individual preparation for the review. Sufficient time must be made available for this. The complete documents for a review must be dispatched in good time before the review meeting with a note that they should be perused before the meeting. The review participants should give the review document close attention, taking into account test aims and a checklist which is attached to the documents. It must be pointed out that additional suggestions can be added to the checklist. Questions, faults and errors of a formal nature (e.g. typing errors) should be recorded in writing.

Review meeting. At the beginning of the review meeting, records of so-called formal errors are collected by the moderator because of time constraints. Then the author gives an overview of the review object. During inspection the participants read the document under the guidance of the author. During walkthroughs the functionality of the test object is played through with the aid of test cases and examples. Faults found are recorded in an action list for further attention. For highlighting discovered faults (in the action list) overhead transparencies or a flip-chart are suitable.

The length of the review meeting should be limited to two hours. During the meeting, faults should be identified but not corrected. The participants should be advised to give constructive and factual criticism only. One of the important tasks of the moderator is the careful control of these last two points.

At the end of the review meeting, the participants assess the results of the review. There are various possibilities:

- The review is closed. No serious faults have been discovered.
- The review is closed after obvious faults have been eliminated in a follow-up phase.
- The review is not closed because of serious faults, and must be repeated. It must be ascertained whether the review object presented is in a state ready to be tested.

Follow-up work. In the follow-up phase (rework) the author must deal with the correction of faults in the review object. A fault report summary should be written and a list of performed corrections presented.

Evaluation. As the last step, an evaluation takes place. The aim of this evaluation is to determine whether all corrections have been carried out and whether any new problems were caused in the process. This evaluation is carried out by the moderator. When the review is closed, management receives a report.

Selection of participants

The first step during selection is the search for a moderator. Taking into account the decisions a moderator has to make, Schnurer [Schn88] states the following criteria for finding a suitable moderator:

- expertise, so that errors can be recognised and evaluated;
- conviction and persuasiveness, so that decisions sound credible; and
- neutrality, so that no person or method is preferred.

Experience has shown that staff from an independent quality assurance institution make good moderators. Because of their organisational independence from the developers and because of their expertise, they are better suited for the task than members of the development team.

Having been selected, the moderator and the author of the test object select other participants. The selection of participants should be carried out with great care and with special regard to their abilities. According to Parnas [Parn85] who stated exact rules for this selection process, the following people should take part in a review:

- specialists, i.e. people with specialist knowledge and long standing experience in the area of databases, aeronautics, etc.;
- possible users of the system; and
- all those who have the ability and enjoy discovering logical contradictions in a systematic way.

Parnas also emphasises the necessity of making the selection of participants dependent on the aims of a review.

Reviews with a large number of participants (more than eight) are difficult to moderate. Regarding the number of participants at inspections, Schnurer [Schn88] recommends:

- 5−8 for inspections of the specification;
- 6 for inspection of the high-level design;
- 5 for inspection of the detailed design; and
- 4 for code inspection.

The higher the degree of work components in a project, the greater the number of participants required at the review meeting.

Role of management

The software project manager who has the responsibility for a software project is also interested in the evaluation of its quality. There are two different models for the role of management in a review.

In the first case, the management review, the manager is responsible for planning the review, putting the review team together and making sure that the participants are available. He or she decides, further, whether the review object can be passed or should be reworked. The manager is present at the actual review meeting.

In the second case, the author of a document sets up a review and invites the review team and also the moderator. The review team itself decides about the acceptance or reworking of the review object. In a report, the moderator informs the management about the results of the review.

A review is not meant to evaluate the performance of team members. However, there are sufficient indicators that management tries to use reviews to this end.

The danger of staff evaluation is greater in the first case, since the manager is present at the review meeting. Weinberg and Freedman [Wein84] suggest in this connection that those who have the task of evaluating the developers of a product do not attend reviews where technical expertise predominates. This is because a considerable part of the review would be spent on the self-representation of the developers, which would mean a loss of valuable time.

Without sufficient management support, the introduction of reviews is endangered. It is therefore advisable to offer special training for management, including:

- foundations and principles of reviews;
- utilisation for management;
- importance of management to successful review procedure; and
- motivation to make adequate resources available and to secure the attendance of participants.

Aids for reviews

Reviews can be more efficiently planned and executed with the assistance of tools. These are mainly static analysers and various forms (see Appendix A3).

Static analysers help to filter out those parts of a document or of a software product that exceed a certain degree of complexity, or which contain anomalies (e.g. dead code). These sections are particularly suitable candidates for reviews.

The following forms can be used:

- review profile;
- review preparation;
- review fault list;
- fault report summary; and
- management report.

The review profile serves as the plan for reviews. The review preparation form is filled in by each review participant during the personal preparation phase. It contains faults, problems and items lacking clarity which the review participant noticed.

The review fault list is completed during the review meeting by the moderator or a secretary named by the moderator. Here faults are listed which were discovered during the meeting. The faults are listed by giving their position in the document, a verbal description, class and type.

The fault report summary is filled in by the moderator. This contains an exact classification of the discovered faults and is forwarded to the quality assurance organisation.

The management report form, which is also filled in by the moderator, contains a summary of review activities and results, and is forwarded to management. It constitutes formal evidence about the actual review itself and also contains the signature of the moderator responsible.

The fault report summary and management report forms have to be filled in up to the time of the follow-up. When the follow-up is concluded, all corrections should have been dealt with. The creation and distribution of both forms constitutes the final action in the review process.

Walkthroughs and inspections

In this section we concentrate on different review processes. We differentiate in principle between walkthroughs and inspections. The significant difference between the two lies in the fact that inspections are more formally planned and processed than walkthroughs. In a walkthrough, the functionality of the test object is worked through with the aid of examples and test cases. In inspections, on the other hand, the documentation of the tested object is read line by line. Walkthroughs are used, among other things, for the training of staff and the promotion of team communication. They can stimulate discussion and lead to increased interaction between the presenter and participants.

During the planning of an inspection, it is important to ensure that inspection aims are specified and are dealt with in a limited number of questions. A further feature of inspections is that each participant is assigned a specific predefined role. Involved in the inspection are the moderator, who plans and leads the inspection, the author whose document is inspected, and the inspectors.

In the following, we shall consider inspections in detail. A code inspection will serve as an example.

Start-up. So that an inspection can be started, the object to be inspected must meet a number of conditions or additional information must be available.

In order to set up a code inspection, the following four conditions must be met:

- The source code must be free of errors, i.e. the program listing should not contain any syntax errors.
- All design alterations must be documented in the code. The source code is accompanied by all design documents and a list of alterations.
- The documentation in the module heading must be completed and up to date. It contains, among other things, details of the author of the module, pre- and post-conditions, the history of alterations and technical detail.
- The code must be commented clearly enough for an independent reader to understand when using the program documentation.

Completion criteria. In order to finish an inspection, completion conditions must exist. Examples of such completion conditions are 'All code faults have been corrected' and 'All faults not corrected are to be found in the problem record system of the project'.

Strategies for fault discovery. On the basis of earlier experiences, it makes sense to develop a strategy for fault discovery as early as the preparation of an inspection. Such a strategy can be supported through checklists and directives. For example, in a code inspection the causes of the most frequent programming and coding errors must be pointed out in the form of a checklist.

Fault evaluation and classification. For later analysis of the development process, it is important to divide faults and errors into classes and types. A sensible classification, for example, is into missing statements, incorrect statements and others. Faults and errors can be divided into those related to data, functionality, interfaces, etc. Further criteria for the division of faults and errors can be the degree of difficulty (form, content, 'open questions') and the error source (which activity in the process has caused the error?).

During classification, attention must be paid to consistency and uniformity. This provides the only way of comparing inspection results. It is, therefore, advisable to work out classification directives and to train moderators and project leaders regularly.

Reviews in the development process

Large manufacturers such as IBM have long recognised the importance of reviews and apply these very successfully in the development process [Faga86].

Depending on the object being reviewed, reviews can be divided into technologically-orientated reviews and management-orientated reviews (so-called project reviews). In technologically orientated reviews, a software product is tested and evaluated according to form and content. In management-orientated reviews, adherence to cost and time plans in particular, and to project progress in general, is examined and evaluated.

We will now consider project reviews, technologically orientated reviews and their application in more detail. The important test objects of technologically orientated reviews are requirement specification, design, code, test plans, test cases, test results and the user manual.

Project reviews

Project reviews are reviews which evaluate projects at particular points in the development process from the point of view of the management. They are frequently called project progress meetings. Since these are often used in practice, we need to look at them in some detail.

The aims of these reviews, which are determined by management, are as follows.

Control of the project. Typical questions regarding this aim are:

- Has the project team understood the project task in hand?
- Must the project task be modified?
- Is there determinable or measurable project progress?
- Is the work done so far complete and correct, and does it form a reliable basis for further work?
- Have the prescribed standards and directives been adhered to?
- Can the time and cost plans be adhered to?

Project control. The project staff discuss specific approaches to solving existing problems with the management. The project manager presents the solution strategy in conjunction with the project leader.

The planning and execution are not nearly as strict and formal as they are for example, in an inspection. The participants are:

- the project manager, who is, for example, responsible for the direct organisation of the project (e.g. head of section, head of department);
- the project leader;
- the project members; and
- external specialists who are involved in the project.

It is significant that in a review meeting the project manager leads the review, the project leader presents it, and this is followed by a discussion.

Success criteria for the project review are as follows:

- The project results are 'reviewable' (readable and comprehensible).
- Project planning and execution occur in small and clear working units which can be easily reviewed.
- A well-structured development plan with milestones exists, which serves to evaluate project progress (it contains no '90 per cent ready' entries).
- There are well-documented project results which have already been evaluated by technical reviews.

The last point in particular often presents a weak point in project reviews. Lack of time and the reluctance of management to delegate cause a situation where technical reviews do not take place. This makes it necessary to examine the product's technological evaluation in more detail and more thoroughly in a project review. Time does not usually allow for this. Consequently, important technical problems and weaknesses in the development process are overlooked, and the project manager makes subsequent decisions on the basis of a very unsafe technical evaluation.

The ideal situation in the interrelationship of technical reviews and project

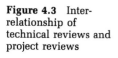

Figure 4.3 Inter-relationship of technical reviews and project reviews

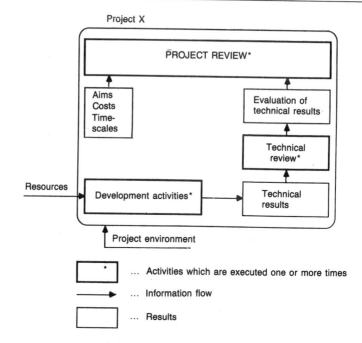

reviews is represented in Figure 4.3. The aim is to transfer technical evaluations as far as possible into technical reviews, and to guarantee that the results of technical reviews are adequately discussed with the project team in project reviews.

The results of project reviews for the management can be summarised as follows:

- project progress control;
- developed risk evaluation related to cost, timescales, resources used and product quality; and
- general product evaluation.

Well balanced planning takes into account both project reviews and technical reviews.

Review of requirement specification

Inadequate requirements have delayed many computing projects considerably and have caused the termination of projects. The following types of requirement error can often be found:

- unclear, contradictory requirements;
- missing and incomplete requirements;
- erroneous, untestable requirements;
- requirements which lie outside the task; and
- requirement errors due to typing mistakes.

Some of these errors can be removed by using structured methods involving a precise requirements definition language and the application of software tools for requirements searching and testing. Boehm found [Boeh84] that the elimination of a requirement error can be up to one hundred times more costly when the software is already in use than if the error was discovered in the requirements specification and dealt with then. Reviews of the requirements specification are a very useful aid for the discovery of errors in earlier phases.

An important aim during a review of the requirements specification is the testing of whether certain quality features are met. The following quality features of a requirements specification must be tested:

- *Freedom from internal and external contradictions*. Absence of internal contradictions is tested with regard to conflict between the elements of the specification. Absence of external contradictions is tested with regard to contradiction between the elements in the specification and external specifications or entities.
- *Completeness*. The requirements should contain no gaps; there should be no references to non-existing functions, inputs or outputs; no elements of the documents, no functions and no part-products should be missing.
- *Implementable/processable aspects*. The requirements should be processable with respect to ergonomics (human engineering), technical and economic resources, and risks.
- *Testable/precise aspects*. The requirements should not be formulated in a vague form. All requirements should be clearly identifiable and able to be referenced.
- *Comprehensibility*. The requirements should, by the use of graphics and/or semi-formal specifications, be formulated in such a way that they are comprehensible to the customer/user as well as to the software engineer.

As mentioned earlier, checklists are a useful aid to the carrying out of reviews. A checklist for reviews of requirement specifications should take into account the structure of the examined document and the categories of typical requirement errors. Such a checklist in the area of data processing could contain the following questions:

- Are the requirements complete and specified without contradictions?
- Are all necessary hardware resources specified?
- Are the specified response times realistic?
- Are all hardware and external software interfaces covered?
- Are all interface items specified with respect to their inputs and outputs, and to their formats, value ranges and declarations?
- Have external interface programs been specified?
- Have input rates been specified in terms of volume/unit of time or, if necessary, in the form of a statistical distribution?
- Have all the functions that the user needs been identified and specified?
- Have all the algorithms stipulated as functional requirements been specified?
- Have requirements regarding time constraints in the processing of each function been specified?

- Do acceptance criteria exist for each specified function?
- Has the acceptable level of accuracy been specified for results?
- Has the initial state of the system been defined?
- Are all necessary set-up operations specifiable?
- Are there requirements for validating input data?
- Are the requirements comprehensible for those who have to design the project?
- Are the requirements overspecified?
- Were requirements for later extensions specified, and are these requirements specially marked?
- Have the necessary experience and training needs of development personnel been specified?

Many tools for the creation and maintenance of a requirements definition have test functions which can support the testing of the above questions.

Design reviews

Depending on the type of design, there is a distinction between high-level design reviews (preliminary design reviews) and detailed design reviews (critical design reviews). Design reviews have the following aims:

- determination and evaluation of the respective state of a design (completeness of feature); and
- discovery of errors and contradictions (e.g. contradictions between specification and design, or between module interfaces).

The following is a checklist for high-level design reviews.

Performance

- Are there any hints of non-fulfilment of performance requirements?

User interfaces

- Are the layouts of the user interfaces uniform?
- Are the screen layouts not overloaded with information?
- Are the screen outputs clear?
- Are the user guidelines adequate?
- Has user input been kept to a minimum?

Data

- Has the data model been tested?
- Are there missing or unused variables in an input, output or update module?
- Are there erroneous or missing data types in an input, output or update module?

Interfaces (in older, third-generation languages)

- Is there one parameter too many or too few in a procedure call? (In modern languages such as Modula-2 or Ada, the compiler and the run-time system offer sufficient interface checking in order to localise or prevent these types of error.)

Functionality

- Is an element non-existent, superfluous or faulty in a processing module?
- Are logical conditions non-existent, superfluous or faulty in a processing module?

Documentation

- Is the design description incomplete?
- Is the design description ambiguous?
- Are the algorithms in a module clearly specified?

Standards

- Has a relevant development standard in the project manual not been adhered to?

Syntax of design description

- Has the syntax of the design notation been applied incorrectly?
- Does the design description contain spelling errors?

Miscellaneous items

- Are there other errors which do not belong to the above-mentioned types? Similar checklists exist for detailed design reviews.

Code inspections

IBM introduced code inspections as far back as 1972 [Faga76]. The intention was to improve software quality on the one hand, and to increase the productivity of the programmers on the other. A further goal of code inspections is to test whether the code matches the detailed design. The same type of review is used for examining adherence to program construction and coding standards.

Possible examination areas in a code inspection are:

- interfaces of the examined object;
- structure of the program;
- use of variables or their names;
- calculation formulae;

- input/output;
- comments; and
- adherence to coding standards.

An important prerequisite in code inspections is the ability to read code correctly. In this context, we can list a few interesting facts:

- Programmers often have problems with the appreciation of their own work. The reason for this is that nobody else reads the source code. The correct execution of the program is often sufficient reason for programmers not to be motivated to improve their work. Code inspection solves this.
- The reading of code should be taught before the writing of code. This leads to a more readable code.

Good readability of the code can be achieved through simple, clear and logical structure. Programs full of 'tricks' are difficult to read.

When reading a program, the following rules must be observed:

- Attention should be paid to program structure.
- The recognition of one error is no indication that other errors do not exist.
- Comments can also contain errors.
- Code which is difficult to read requires an examination of the causes.
- All details in code are important.
- Nothing in code should be taken as true if it has not been tested.

Studies [Faga86] show that 67 per cent of programming errors can be found before the module test, and that programs which have been subjected to a code inspection contain 38 per cent fewer errors. This result was obtained on the basis of seven months' operation after product release.

Test reviews

We can differentiate between two types of review for testing, namely test design reviews and test inspections.

The aim of test design reviews is to check the adherence of the test design to the test goals. Each test case should be subjected to a completion test. In this context, the following questions arise:

- Which characteristics of the test object should be tested?
- Have all test goals of the test plan been taken into account during creation of the test cases for the project?
- Were the test cases chosen in such a way that economic aspects were also taken into account when fulfilling test goals?
- Which environment is necessary for test case execution?
- How are input values made available to the test object?
- What output values are expected?

The aims of test inspections are:

- appraisal and correction of test cases;
- checking for correct execution of the test, conforming to test procedure and test protocol;
- discovery of faults in interface specifications of individual modules; and
- discussion of the success of the individual tests.

Test inspections are mainly designed to examine the success of test activities. Test inspection takes place after test execution.

Larsen [Lars75] has published the results of his experiences with reviews for different test functions. For a product of about 20,000 lines of code, the following results were achieved through inspection:

- reduction of functional test groups in about 30 per cent of test cases;
- discovery of 176 serious faults in test plans and test cases; and
- saving of testing time through the discovery of these faults in inspections rather than in functional tests.

These results show vividly that the productivity of the project team as well as the quality of software can be increased through reviews.

Summarising evaluation

Experience in recent decades has shown that reviews provide a very effective error discovery method. The effectiveness of reviews is due to the following facts:

- Four eyes see more than two.
- In explaining his or her work, the developer often notices irregularities.
- Testers not taking part in the development often raise questions which are alien to the developer, since the latter's view has in the meantime narrowed to focus on the test object.

Error discovery rates lie at between 60 and 90 per cent before release of the software [Faga86]. Reviews give programmers very useful hints for the improvement of their future work.

The cost of design and code inspections together is estimated at 15 per cent of the project cost.

The following advantages can be noted when reviews are used:

- Reviews make possible the utilisation of human ability to think about and analyse (cognitive abilities) the evaluation and testing of complex situations.
- Reviews are suited to formal documents (e.g. program listings) as well as informal documents (e.g. verbal design descriptions).
- Reviews are checking procedures with a high success rate.

There are the following disadvantages when using reviews:

- The success of a review is very dependent on the people taking part. The role of the moderator is of decisive importance.

- The communication climate is important for activating the human ability to think and analyse.
- Preoccupation with solutions to problems can lead to the passing of valuable review time, so that no further faults may be discovered.
- There is a danger of judging staff. This can cause the reduced credibility of this very useful checking procedure.

The importance of reviews in the development process is often underestimated. Important effects in the development process are:

- early and comprehensive fault discovery;
- cost-saving fault prevention;
- effective control and directing of the development process;
- increased productivity through a reduction in testing costs; and
- compulsory tidy documentation.

Static analysers can increase the efficiency of reviews still further. Error rates of less than one error per 10,000 LOC can be realised.

4.1.3   Static analysis with software tools

The use of software tools increases the possibility of computer-based static analysis of phase deliverables such as requirements, design documents and the source code. With this analysis technology, all process documents that are built in a specified formal manner can be analysed.

In the following, static analysis with software tools is seen as involving the testing and evaluation with computer supported tools of quality features of a product: in particular, its form, structure, content or documentation.

Through static analysis, statements can be made about characteristics such as the 'syntactic correctness' and the 'semantic correctness' of an analysed object. Semantic correctness can be analysed only if the semantics are formally described (using denotational semantics).

It is an advantage of this test that complex documents can be analysed and that the analysis process is faster than it would be if carried out manually. Information which is created through static program analysis, for example, can be classified as follows:

- Syntactic information (complexity measures, dependency graphs such as procedure calls, data import graphs and structure trees, evaluations of the source program format, etc.).
- Semantic information (control flow and data flow anomalies, declared but not used variables, uninitialised variables, etc.).
- Lexical information (length of procedure, frequency and length of program elements such as instructions, comments, nested data blocks, etc.).

The significance of these tools within quality assurance lies in the discovery of faults which are likely to be overlooked in large volumes of code if tested manually.

Typical faults which are recognised with such tools are:

- wrong use of local or global variables;
- non-matching parameter lists;
- illegal nesting of loops and branches;
- wrong sequence of processing steps;
- undefined variables;
- infinite loops;
- calls of non-existent procedures;
- missing code or missing labels;
- unused variables;
- unreachable code (dead code);
- unreferenced labels;
- complex calculations; and
- violation of coding standards.

Many of these faults can be avoided through the use of modern languages like Ada or Modula-2.

Static program analysis is also increasingly used for maintenance of old software. Static program analysers are an essential tool for each maintenance organisation. However, it is also evident that each language requires its own specific analysers, which are adapted to the syntax of the language. This fact limits the application of modern analysers considerably.

Examples of static program analysers are ASCOT [IBM87b], RXVP80 [Deut82] and INSTRU [Huan81].

Examples of tools for static analysis of requirement documents are SREM [Alfo85], TAGS [Siev85], LITOR-A [Färb86, Wall85, Wall87b] and PSA [Deut82]. In addition there are a number of CASE tools such as IEW,[1] Excelerator,[2] Software Through Pictures[3] and Teamwork[4] which have integrated analysis functions for requirements as well as for designs.

Summarising, it can be said that static analysis with tools has already passed the stage of experimentation. Within the area of systematic fault discovery, it represents an extension of analytical quality assurance measures.

4.1.4 *Proof of correctness (mathematical program verification)*

With this test method, the consistency of a program with its specification is proved by using mathematical proofs. The class of documents where this can be applied is limited to those which can be specified using purely formal descriptions.

---

1 Product of the company KnowledgeWare, Inc.
2 Product of the company Index-Technology, Inc.
3 Product of the company Interactive Development Environments, Inc.
4 Product of the company Cadre Technologies, Inc.

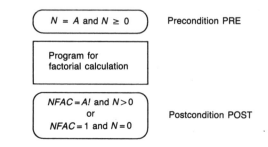

The principle of correctness proofs lies in the step-by-step observation that the description of the postconditions of an action has been derived from the described precondition. Program proving also means that the program must terminate if the precondition holds. The pre- and postconditions are also referred to as assertions. This can be demonstrated on a program for factorial calculation (Figure 4.4).

All possible input values are named A. Within the program, further assertions are given at different points to show that the postcondition *POST* results from the precondition *PRE*.

$$PRE = \{Z_1\} \ a_1 \ \{Z_2\} \ \ldots \ \{Z_i\} \ a_i \ \{Z_{i+1}\} \ a_{i+1} \ \{Z_{i+2}\} \ \ldots \ a_n \ \{Z_{n+1}\} = POST$$

Z_i is in this context the condition which results from Z_{i-1} if one takes into account that operation a_{i-1} has been executed.

Examples of methods of program verification are the inductive assertions of Floyd [Floy67] and Hoare [Hoar69] and approaches which are based on abstract data types [Zill74, Gutt77, Beie88].

The disadvantages of proof methods are as follows:

- A purely manual proof is liable to contain errors. The application of computer-supported tools for the proof (e.g. generator of verification conditions, theorem prover) reduces the probability of errors.
- Even if the proof is found and the proof is formally in order, no statement gives any indication of whether the specification is right and whether the program has solved the original task.
- It is often difficult to find assertions from which verification conditions can be created.
- Even if verifiability or partial correctness can be theoretically proved, it is not certain whether a proof can be found within an acceptable time.

Summarising, it can be said that correctness proofs can be recommended only for specific tasks of real-time data processing, such as for control systems in aircraft. In commercial application development, they should be used only for extremely critical program parts, which should be subject to a formal specification. The reason for this is the high cost of the time-consuming verification activities.

4.1.5 Symbolic program execution

This method is included in the class of static tests because of the close link between program verification and the use of symbols.

Symbolic program execution can be defined as: a method of execution of program paths in which a number of symbolic expressions are verified in accordance with a quantity of predefined conditions and assertions.

Symbolic program execution, also called symbolic evaluation or symbolic testing, is a program analysis method which uses symbolic expressions (consisting of names of variables) instead of actual data values for the execution of program paths. This means that all manipulations of variables and decisions in the program are carried out symbolically. An example will clarify this [Fair85].

This Ada program calculates the sum of N elements of an integer array A. The values of field A are represented by the symbolic values $a_1, a_2 \ldots a_n$. The symbolic execution of this code can be explained using a tree representation (see Figure 4.5).

The symbolic execution can be represented by the symbolic formula

$$S = \sum_{j=1}^{I-1} a_j$$

At the loop exit, I has the value of $N + 1$. In replacing I by $N + 1$ we get

Function SUM(A: INTARRAY; N: NATURAL) return INTEGER is
   S: INTEGER :=0;
   I: NATURAL :=1;
Begin
   while $I< =N$ loop
      $S := S + A(I)$;
      $I := I + 1$;
   end loop;
   return (S);
End SUM;

Figure 4.5 Representation of a symbolic program execution

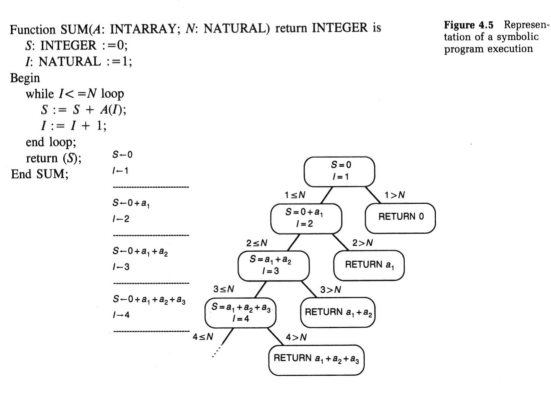

$$S = \sum_{j=1}^{(N+1)-1} a_j = \sum_{j=1}^{N} a_j$$

which corresponds to the desired result.

The result of a symbolic execution is usually a long, complex expression. This can be divided and interpreted as a tree structure in which each leaf of the structure represents a path through the program. Each node in the structure represents a point of decision in the program. The tree structure can then be used for the creation of test data for dynamic tests, so that each path in the program is executed. For reasons of simplicity, we will only look at programs without loops. The predicates for each node in the tree structure are combined for each path in the form of a common path expression. Data which affects the execution of a specific path is found by determining this data which sets the path expression during evaluation to the value 'true'.

The results of the path evaluation can be compared with the external specifications of the program. Provided that the external specifications are strictly formally described, it can be shown whether the symbolic path expressions are congruent with these external specifications, or whether there are any differences which point to possible errors.

Examples of tools which support symbolic program execution are DISSECT [Howd77] and ATTEST [Clar81]. Symbolic manipulation is carried out automatically. Only at decision points (i.e. nodes) must the user intercept and input a value for the continuation of the program run.

There are two main problems when applying this test method. First, the number of paths in larger programs leads to a considerable calculation effort. Second, there is a problem in determining whether there are values which deliver the value 'true' for the combined path expression.

The method of symbolic program execution is used as a basis for research work in the selection of test paths and test data [Clar84]. It is also used for mathematical program verification: in particular, for the creation of verification conditions [Hant76].

4.2   Dynamic tests

During these tests, the test object is executed. A program is tested with a selection of input values. This serves to test whether the program behaves in accordance with the specification. Testing is a most important verification process.

For the sake of completeness, all those methods must be mentioned where the test object or a model of it (e.g. implemented as a prototype, or a design in the form of a Petri-net) is executed, interpreted or simulated. For example, a comprehensive prototype approach makes possible a hybrid execution of a test object [Bisc89]. In this way, designed but not yet implemented modules are simulated, partly coded modules are interpreted, and modules which are coded and tested are executed directly. The possibilities and limits of prototyping were discussed in section 3.1.5.

Simulation models for software systems are, among other things, used for the evaluation of designs [Zinc84] and performance requirements, or take the form of environment simulators. The latter serve to test the behaviour of the test object in relation to its environment. More details about simulation as an aid to the dynamic testing of software can be found in [Deut82] and [Dunn84]. Testing will now be described in detail.

At the present time, there is no accepted theory or method for testing. But there are a number of methodological approaches for organising testing and for making it more efficient.

Before going into detail, we need to define two concepts with regard to methodological approaches. Testing can be destined as: a process where a program is executed for the purpose of finding errors [Myer79]. Debugging is: a process where the cause of an error is found, correction is determined, the effect of correction is checked and the correction is carried out.

After the debugging of an error, the test is generally repeated in order to test whether the error has actually been corrected and no new errors introduced. This is the process of retesting.

We can differentiate between the cost of finding an error and the cost of correction. The finding of an error is on average considerably more costly then its correction (the 80:20 rule).

The following opinions about testing can frequently be heard in expert discussions:

- Testing is an experimental process which tries to prove empirically with a limited number of inputs that the deviation of a program from its specification lies below a certain tolerance level. The tolerance depends on the quality requirements (H. Balzert).
- Testing is the process of exercising or evaluating a system or system component by manual or automated means to verify that it satisfies specified requirements, or to identify differences between expected and actual results [IEEE83].

Testing requires, as a rule, a considerable amount of effort. In a larger project this can occupy 50 to 60 per cent of the entire effort put into a project. From this we may conclude that testing can be very costly, and that therefore only those tests which reveal errors are worthwhile.

The English language distinguishes between error, defect, fault and failure. In this context, the definitions in ANSI/IEEE Std 729−1983 [IEEE83] and Birolini [Biro85] are useful.

According to the IEEE, an *error* is a discrepancy between a computed, observed or measured value or condition and the true, specified or theoretically correct value or condition. An example of an error might be when a program produces an output value of 30 when the actual value is 20.

A *defect* is a deviation from the expected value or characteristic of a feature. Defects can (but must not) influence the functionality of the item under consideration (e.g. a program). For example, there can be good functionality in spite of bad maintainability in a program. Defects can occur in connection with all features used for the specification of product quality.

A *failure* is the termination of the ability of a functional unit to perform its required function. The failure of a unit can either affect the operation of higher-level units or have catastrophic consequences. Failures affect reliability.

A *fault* is an accidental condition that causes a functional unit to fail to perform its required function. A fault can be caused by a failure, a defect or an error. For example, the failure of a database system can cause a fault in a program which performs monthly accounts. A fault in this program can also be caused by a software error in an accounts program which delivers data for the monthly accounts. Faults affect the availability of a facility.

Testing is in itself a destructive process. In other words testing is not, as many developers believe, designed to show that the software is free of errors; testing is a process to be carried out with the intention of finding errors. This basic principle does not, of course, conform to the conceptions of the software producer, who naturally has the intention of solving a task with as few errors as possible. This conflict between the destructive testing and the constructive production of software often leads to unsystematic or careless testing, and is often further exacerbated by the obligation to meet deadlines.

Experience suggests the following principles for software testing:

- Each test must have sensible and quantifiable aims. Testing without set goals is a waste of time and money.
- Test goals are acceptable only if they are obtainable and measurable. In order to meet these requirements, the test goals must be prescribed in quantifiable form: for example, 95 per cent C_0-test coverage (i.e. 95 per cent of all instructions are executed during the test run) or 100 per cent functional coverage of a program (i.e. all specified functions of the program are carried out at least once in the test cases).
- For each test a termination criterion must be given. At present there is the problem that no theoretically determined criteria exist. Nevertheless, there are already heuristic approaches for finding criteria for test termination (see section 4.2.2).
- Because of the impossibility of testing a test object for all possible inputs, we must test 'economically', i.e. just as much as is necessary. Testing economically is an optimising task and is made possible through systematic and controlled test case selection.
- It is important to test against something, i.e. we have to specify the expected test results a priori for each test case.
- The results of each test must be carefully checked.
- The developer should be responsible for the tests of the individual modules (unit test, module test). When the modules of the program system are integrated, an independent test group should take over (familiar names for these tests are integration tests, system tests, etc.). In practice, the developer and the independent test group work closely together, so that the tests are carried out as smoothly as possible and the discovered errors can be corrected immediately.

In an experiment, Basili [Basi87] showed the advantages of preparing personnel and organisations for development without program execution and testing. In doing so, he used the 'cleanroom' development approach of Mills [Mill87]. This approach includes incremental development, the application of formal methods for the specification and design, development without program execution (testing completely independent of the development) and the use of statistical processes during testing.

- Test cases must not only cover the area of expected and valid input data; they must also take into account unexpected invalid input data (see section 4.2.1).
- Test cases and their results must be collected in an archive. They are a valuable investment which will come in useful later in the maintenance phase for the retesting of programs or program parts that have to be altered or extended during maintenance.
- A test case can be considered successful if a new error is discovered. For this it is necessary to keep an exact error log for each program.
- 'Throwaway test cases' must be avoided at all cost, unless 'throwaway software' is written. In this case, testing is in itself less meaningful.
- When setting up the test plan, one should always assume that difficulties will arise. During test planning for a project, sufficient time as well as financial and staff resources must be made available for the test process.
- It must be possible to reproduce a test. This is particularly important not only when changes are made, but also in the maintenance phase of software. In principle, each change in the program is a reason for repeated execution of the test cases.
- The number of hitherto undiscovered errors in a module is proportional to the number of errors already found. This means that special care must be taken when testing modules where frequent errors have already been noted. For example, 47 per cent of all errors in the IBM OS/370 operating system were found in only 4 per cent of the modules [Myer87].

In conclusion, we can say that testing is a creative and intellectually demanding task. Practical experience of testing also shows that, in order to be able to test a system, we must understand it thoroughly. Present-day applications are neither simple in themselves nor simple to understand. Testing is, therefore, costly and difficult. It requires not only a large measure of insight and knowledge, but also experience. It is often the case that the best testers are those with good expertise in the business area of the application.

4.2.1 Testing methodology

Before we look more closely at different test methods, we have to ask ourselves which tests have to be set up within which parts of a life cycle. These test tasks — in their entirety referred to as the test plan — depend, of course, on what has to be tested. With reference to IEEE Standard 1012−1986 [IEEE86] we arrive at minimum tests on the basis of the following (see Figure 4.6):

Figure 4.6 Test method with test tasks and results

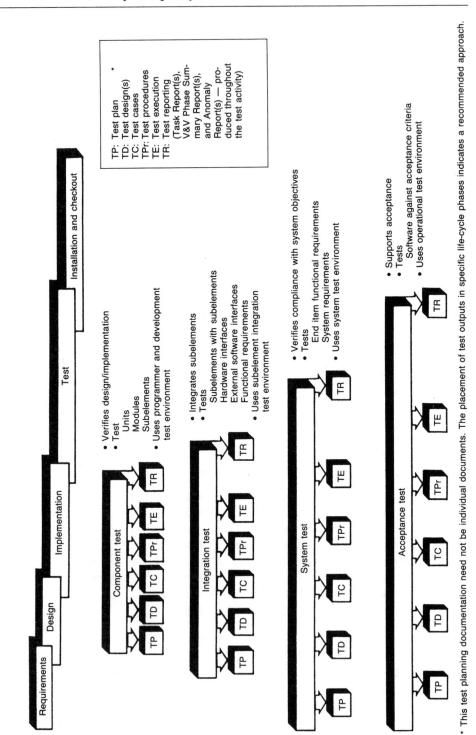

TP: Test plan   *
TD: Test design(s)
TC: Test cases
TPr: Test procedures
TE: Test execution
TR: Test reporting
    (Task Report(s),
    V&V Phase Sum-
    mary Report(s),
    and Anomaly
    Report(s) — pro-
    duced throughout
    the test activity)

Requirements | Design | Implementation | Test | Installation and checkout

Component test

TP TD TC TPr TE TR

• Verifies design/implementation
• Test
    Units
    Modules
    Subelements
• Uses programmer and development test environment

Integration test

TP TD TC TPr TE TR

• Integrates subelements
• Tests
    Subelements with subelements
    Hardware interfaces
    External software interfaces
    Functional requirements
• Uses subelement integration test environment

System test

TP TD TC TPr TE TR

• Verifies compliance with system objectives
• Tests
    End item functional requirements
    System requirements
• Uses system test environment

Acceptance test

TP TD TC TPr TE TR

• Supports acceptance
• Tests
    Software against acceptance criteria
• Uses operational test environment

* This test planning documentation need not be individual documents. The placement of test outputs in specific life-cycle phases indicates a recommended approach.

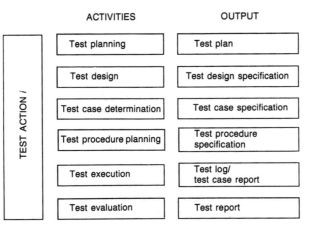

ACTIVITIES   OUTPUT

Figure 4.7 Standard-
ised activities and
results of test actions

$i \in$ {module testing, integration testing, system testing, release testing}

- module testing (component test);
- integration testing;
- system testing; and
- acceptance testing.

An exact explanation of these test tasks and hence the structuring of the test plan will be detailed in section 4.2.2.

In these test tasks, standardised activities are suggested for carrying out testing, together with their results (see Figure 4.7). These are as follows:

- *Test planning/the test plan (TP)*. With this activity a document (test plan) is created which records the goals, the size, the method, the resources, the schedule and the responsibilities for the intended tests. Since test planning is of particular importance for systematic testing, we shall comment in detail on planning and organisational aspects, and on the test plan itself, in section 4.2.2.
- *Test designing/the test design (TD)*. In the test design, detailed instructions related to test methods are given. It must be stated clearly how the goals contained in the test plan are to be reached, i.e. which methods are to be employed and in which way. It is also to be stipulated which test objects in which tests and on the basis of which criteria are to be used, in order to come to a decision on whether the test object does or does not pass the test.
- *Test case determination/the test case specification (TC)*. Test cases are specified based on the test design. It is stated in detail which test object in the execution of each test case is to be fed with what input, and what output should be generated. In parallel with this, particular requirements are specified for the test environment (hardware, system software, etc.).
- *Test procedure planning/the test procedure specification (TPr)*. With this activity the steps for the actual execution of the test are fixed. The requirements

for the execution of the test runs, the sequence of the test runs, and records
and termination tasks for each test run are specified in detail.

- *Test execution/the test case report (TE)*. The planned test runs are executed
  and their associated test log is established. All incidents and problems which
  require an examination are recorded in the test case report.
- *Test report (TR), test analysis and evaluation*. The test results are analysed
  and collated. The aim is an evaluation of the executed test and a decision on
  whether the test goal has been reached or whether the test has to be repeated.

Through these standardised activities and their results, exact time and cost planning
is possible. The risk of an uncontrollable test process is reduced in this way.

The standardised activities and their results also create the conceptual
prerequisites for the test method. Goals are established by means of test planning,
and attempts are then made to reach them through the selection of suitable test
cases. Determining test cases makes test methods necessary.

In the following we shall concentrate on the methodological basis of testing.
The central question which comes up in connection with methods of test case
design is: how many of all conceptual test cases offer the greatest probability
for maximum error discovery?

At present, there are two groups of methods for test case investigation: black-
box methods and white box methods. In black box testing, the test object is seen
as a black box (see Figure 4.8). This means that the tester does not draw upon
any information about the structure of the test object during application of the
method. Only the performance description of the test object (functional description)
forms the basis for the derivation of test cases. A complete test comprises each
combination of input values (valid and invalid), and this is therefore practically
impossible because of combinatory explosion.

Important prerequisites for the application of black box test methods is an exact
specification (functional description) of the test object. This is often referred to
in this context as functional or design-orientated testing.

White-box testing assumes that the structure of the test object is known. White-
box test methods are also referred to as structural test methods (see Figure 4.8).
A user of the white-box testing method uses the information about the structure

Figure 4.8 Black-box
and white-box testing

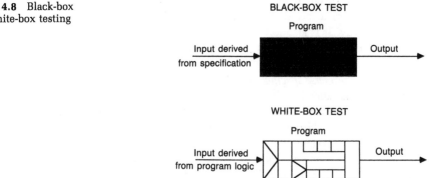

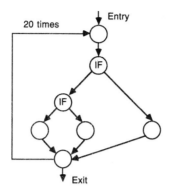

Figure 4.9 Program graph with 3^{20} paths

of the test object (e.g. detailed design, source code) for the derivation of the test cases. A test can be said to be complete when each path from each entry point to each exit of the module has been traversed. The small segment in Figure 4.9 contains a loop which is run through twenty times. This loop contains two 'if instructions'. From this process structure, 3^{20} paths result. We can therefore conclude that it is impossible to cover all paths.

Even if each path of the program were tested, the program could still contain errors. The possible reasons for this are:

- the program does not correspond to the specification;
- paths are missing; and
- during path testing no data-sensitive errors are discovered.

For example, the comparison of two real variables for equality (if $a = b$ then ..., a, b are of the type 'real') can be wrong due to the machine representation of a and b. Instead the statement: if $ABS(a-b) < eps$ then ... (*eps* is a very small positive real constant) is more reliable.

A complete test based on black-box test methods is superior to path tests (White Box Methods). Neither of the two maximum requirements is practicable, however. The usual way to proceed is therefore to start by designing test cases with black-box methods and to complement these as much as is necessary with white-box methods.

In order to execute software tests in accordance with these methods, all necessary documents must be available. For black-box tests these are:

- product description;
- user documentation (user guide); and
- installation instructions.

For white-box tests the following must also be available:

- design documents; and
- program documentation (including program listings).

These documents should contain precise information about the structure and internal construction of the test object as well as its technical particulars.

Black-box methods

The most important black-box test methods are:

- function coverage;
- the equivalence class method;
- boundary value analysis; and
- the cause/effect graphing method.

Function coverage. This is also referred to as specification-orientated testing. Based on the actual application itself, the functions of the test object are identified. For this purpose an input/output specification is created for each function. Tests are executed by employing test cases which are based on these specifications, in order to show that the functions exist and can be executed. The test cases are chosen with reference to the normal behaviour of the test object (no exceptions or boundary values).

A very sensible and useful aid for collating test cases when applying functions is to use a test case matrix (see Figure 4.10). With the aid of a test case matrix, test cases can be deleted when function coverage is duplicated. For example, in the test case matrix of Figure 4.10, the test cases 4, 5 and 6 can be deleted. This helps to minimise the number of test cases and therefore to improve the effectiveness of the test process.

Equivalence class methods. An ideal test case uncovers a class of errors during a test (e.g. wrong processing of the input values of a string of characters). This helps to reduce the number of test cases.

An equivalence class is a set of values in a given range. For all values of an equivalence class, it is assumed that testing with one value of this class would lead to the same effect as testing with another value of this class. The program

Figure 4.10 Functional test case matrix

Test object: Module 'Regular Customer Administration'

Function	Test cases					
	1	2	3	4	5	6
Initialising regular customers	x					
Updating regular customers		x	x		x	
Selective output of regular customers			x	x	x	x
Cancelling regular customers		x		x		

Input/output ranges	Equivalence classes			
	Valid		Invalid	
Date	≥ 1	≤ 31	< 1	> 31
	TC1	TC2	TC3	TC4

Figure 4.11 Help schema for the equivalence class method

Actual test cases: TC1: 25
                   TC3: 0
                   TC4: 40

would execute (i.e. follow the same execution paths) irrespective of which value in the equivalent class was used.

If the values of the equivalent class lie in a specific input or output range of values, we speak of a valid equivalence class; if they lie outside, we call them invalid.

The following are necessary for the design of test cases:

- The ranges of input and output values must be divided into equivalence classes (thereby determining equivalence classes).
- A value must be chosen from each equivalence class (determining a test case).
- The partitioning of equivalence classes must be tested for completeness and its effectiveness in uncovering errors with the chosen values must be evaluated.

When splitting into equivalence classes, for every valid one an invalid one must be chosen.

When the valid and invalid equivalence classes have been determined, the test cases are defined with a help schema (see Figure 4.11). This help system contains three columns, one for input/output ranges, one for the valid and the third for the invalid equivalence classes.

Because of the heuristics involved in forming equivalence classes, no guarantee can be given that the classes do not overlap. The concept of equivalence cannot therefore be understood in the strictly mathematical sense.

Boundary value analysis. We know from experience that the handling of boundary values frequently produces errors. Boundary value analysis provides test cases which cover the boundaries of value areas of inputs/outputs, variables or their environment (see Figure 4.12). The method of boundary value analysis builds

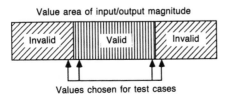

Value area of input/output magnitude

Values chosen for test cases

Figure 4.12 Boundary value analysis

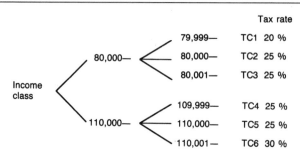

Figure 4.13 Example of boundary value analysis

on the equivalence class method. It differs from the equivalence class method in the fact that no single element of the equivalence class is selected as representative but several elements are selected to the effect that each 'boundary' of the equivalence class is tested.

This can be demonstrated using the tax calculation on income. For the income categories DM80,000 to 110,000, the tax rate may be 25 per cent. Any income below this will be taxed at 20 per cent; any income above at 30 per cent. In Figure 4.13 test cases are shown which evolved through boundary value analysis.

The method of boundary value analysis can also be used for white box testing (minimum and maximum number of value inputs in a data structure, minimum and maximum number of iterations of a loop, etc.).

Cause/effect graphing method. The cause/effect graphing method is a method which is not limited to input and output values. The specification of a program is changed into a graphic formalism when this method is applied. The notation of this formalism is based on Boolean algebra (see Figure 4.14). The nodes of the graph are cause and effect, whereby a cause which has a certain effect is linked to it by an edge or path. Causes may be input conditions or equivalence classes for input conditions. Effects can be output conditions, equivalence classes for output conditions, transfer points in databases or events.

Figure 4.14 Symbols of Boolean algebra

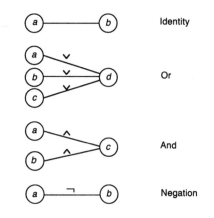

First of all, the specification is expressed as a graph. The graph is then converted into a decision table whereby the causes are the conditions, and the effects are the actions. Each column of the decision table represents a test case.

This can be demonstrated with an example. The input vector for this transaction has two input values. If the input character in column 1 is an A or B and the character in column 2 is a digit, a data update is carried out. If the first character is not valid, the message E12 is output; if the second character is not a digit, the message E13 is output (Figures 4.15 and 4.16).

One advantage of this method can be seen by virtue of the fact that a combination of input values and their common semantics is observed. A useful effect is an early validating of the specification. The disadvantage of the method lies in the fact that it is difficult to create a graph for a complex specification and that errors may occur.

Intuitive test case search. Intuitive test case search (error guessing) is based on human intuition or on heuristic processes. Some people are capable of finding errors intuitively. But there are error categories which occur frequently in almost all applications (e.g. a loop is executed once too often or not often enough, a system interruption occurs after a dialogue input). This approach is suited to the qualitative improvement of systematically created test cases and is also suitable for black-box and white-box tests.

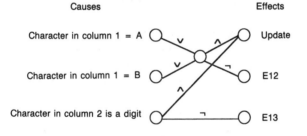

Figure 4.15 A specification represented as a graph

	R1	R2	R3	R4	R5	R6	R7*	R8*
Character in column 1 = A	1	0	1	0	0	0	1	1
Character in column 1 = B	0	1	0	1	0	0	1	1
Character in column 2 is a digit	1	1	0	0	1	0	-	-
Update	x	x	-	-	-	-	-	-
E12	-	-	-	-	x	x	-	-
E13	-	-	x	x	-	?	-	-

Figure 4.16 A specification represented as a decision table

? Hitherto undefined side effect
* Rules which are impossible because of syntactic or semantic facts
— Irrelevant (either 1 or 0)

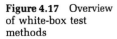

Figure 4.17 Overview of white-box test methods

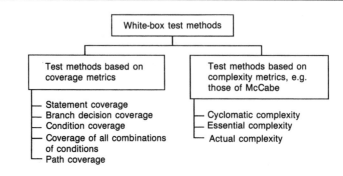

White-box methods

These methods involve using information about the internal structure of the test object (detailed design, control and data flow graph) in order to test whether a specification has been met.

The white-box test methods are based on known values which provide test coverage on the one hand and structure complexity of the test object on the other (see Figure 4.17).

In test methods which are based on coverage metrics, the processing of the test object (program/module) is represented as a graph. The nodes represent the statements or collections of sequentially executed statements. The control flow is represented by arcs which link the nodes.

In a complete white-box test, all paths of the program graph must be executed. Because this is costly in practice, the achievement of targets for the various coverage metrics is considered sufficient. Depending on the achieved degree of test coverage, further test cases are selected from the control and data flow, the tests are executed with these test cases and consequently test coverage is increased.

The following test coverage metrics are common:

- *Statement coverage* (C_0). This constitutes the number of statements dealt with relative to the complete collection of statements of a test object.
- *Decision coverage* (C_1). This constitutes the proportion of branches dealt with relative to all possible branches of the test object.
- *Condition coverage* (C_2). Test coverage of 100 per cent C_2 means that in each conditional expression used in a conditional or looping statement, each term must be evaluated at least once.
- *Decision condition coverage* (C_3). In order to obtain test coverages of 100 per cent all possible combinations of elementary conditions within a complex condition or loop condition must be run through at least once.
- *Path coverage* (C_4). All possible paths of a module must be run through at least once.

These test coverage metrics are used as test goals for module tests. Specifications of test goals are given in the form '$n\%$ test coverage factors C_x' ($0 < n \leq 100$,

$x = 0,1,2,3,4$). The probability of discovering errors increases if we increase the value of test coverage metrics or use combinations of test coverage metrics. Practical testing shows that the measuring of test coverage without tool support is not practicable. For the determination of C_0 there are, for example, for conventional programming languages such as PL/1 or Cobol, special compiler options which help to monitor the execution of statements.

It must be agreed with the contractor which values of test coverage factors are to be attained for the contractor's product. Typical examples from practical experience are the statement coverage (C_0) of 95 per cent and branch coverage (C_1) of 85 per cent.

Test coverage of 100 per cent is no guarantee that the test object is free of errors. In particular not only missing paths, but also errors in the specification cannot be uncovered by means of this type of testing.

A further means of test case generation is based on complexity metrics, such as those of McCabe. The underlying idea states that the more test paths there are, the more difficult it is to test a test object. From a graph theory perspective, McCabe derives the cyclomatic number $V(g)$ which constitutes the smallest number of independent paths[5] whose combination produces all test paths (section 1.3.6). For a test object with only one entry point and one exit the cyclomatic number is 1 + the number of binary branches in the test object.

In order to obtain test cases in this way, the following procedure is recommended:

- The program graph of the test object is created. Then the factors $V(g)$ of the test object are computed. This number is called c.
- c independent paths in the process graph of the test object are sought.
- The test cases (test data) are selected so that c independent paths can be executed.
- For each of the c test cases, the expected results are determined.
- The test cases are executed.
- The actual results are compared with the expected results.

McCabe suggests limiting the complexity of the structure of a module (e.g. to a $V(g)$ of 10). This is a dangerous suggestion, especially when a module contains sizeable case statements. This action could lead to an artificial fragmentating of the program structure which might reduce clarity.

McCabe uses basic and actual complexity metrics for determining test cases alongside his well-known cyclomatic complexity metrics. In basic complexity metrics which are an indicator for the lack of structure in a module, all those partial graphs in a program graph which contain a single input and a single output node are determined, i.e. those which can be reduced to a single node (see Figure 4.18).

---

5   The test object is represented as a graph which deals with execution flows only. Independent paths are considered as non-overlapping edge sequences in this graph.

Figure 4.18 Example
of the reduction of a
graph for determining
basic complexity

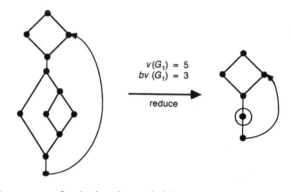

$$v(G_1) = 5$$
$$bv(G_1) = 3$$

reduce

$v(G) = e - n + 2p$ (cyclomatic complexity)
$bv(G) = v(G) - m$ (basic complexity)

m number of partial graphs in G which can be reduced
e number of edges
n number of nodes
p number of connected components

It transpires that, for a structured program, $bv(G) = 1$. The basic complexity factor $bv(G)$ is used by McCabe to estimate the effects of modifications. He suggests that a modification should not be made if $bv(G)$ increases as a consequence.

Actual complexity $av(G)$ of a program means, according to McCabe, the number of independent paths which are executed during the test runs.

If, after a series of executed test cases, the actual complexity is smaller than the cyclomatic complexity, either more paths have to be tested or the complexity $v(G)$ can be reduced by eliminating $v(G) - av(G)$ decision nodes.

The following procedure is recommended for module testing:

1. Checking the specifications using the cause/effect graph method.
2. Equivalence class method.
3. Boundary value analysis.
4. Improving the quality of the test cases by intuitive test case creation.
5. Completion of test cases through use of white-box test methods.

Combinations of both black-box and white-box methods are called grey-box testing.

Taking into account the different possibilities of the methods mentioned so far, it is necessary to examine the question of effectiveness. In order to assess effectiveness, two methods that spring to mind are error seeding and mutation analysis.

In error seeding, a specific number of errors are planted into the test object prior to the test procedure [Mill72]. We can then examine how many of these errors are uncovered.

Assuming that:

• the statistical characteristics of the planted errors and other errors are the same; and

- the testing and error inputs are independent of each other we can estimate the number of errors in the test object by the formula:

$$E_s = \frac{I \cdot S}{K}$$

where

E_s is the estimated number of errors in the test object,
I is the number of errors not planted which are uncovered,
S is the number of planted errors, and
K is the number of uncovered planted errors.

A justification for the above formula is given in [Toms 77].

During mutation analysis, minor changes which cause errors are carried out on the test object. With the existing test cases we then check whether the errors planted in this way are uncovered. The number of test cases is increased by the number of uncovered mutation errors.

The possibilities and limits of these test methods are clearly characterised by a quotation from Dijkstra [Dijk75]: 'Program testing can be used to show the presence of bugs but never to show their absence!' The abovementioned test methods do not enable us to show that a program is free of errors.

4.2.2 *Organisation and management of test processes*

We can assume that the test process is integrated into the process model as part of the validation and verification process. In spite of this conceptual foundation, organisation and management concepts are necessary to make the test process efficient, plannable and controllable. The test group should be independent of both the developers and the organisational measures at the time of test planning and test control.

Seen historically, job descriptions in computing show up extreme specialisation in the area of testing. In large development processes, test specialists with extensive know-how and long experience in testing are needed. In larger computing organisations the maxim holds that, in projects which will take longer than six calendar months to complete, at least one independent test specialist should be involved.

The responsibility of these test specialists lies mainly in the execution of the following tasks:

- creating, maintaining and assessing test plans;
- organising test activities;
- developing test specifications and test procedures;
- creating and maintaining collections of test cases;
- creating and maintaining test documents;
- ensuring the availability of test tools and aids;

- executing test reviews;
- testing post-release changes; and
- continued development of and training in company-specific test know-how.

Because of the need to deal with the integration and networking of applications nowadays, the success of many projects in reaching the project goals depends to a large extent on test specialists.

Especially in the area of testing, the tasks of computer managers are of great importance. Present management experience shows that there are some critical success factors in the three areas of leadership, support and control which are important for an efficient test process (see Figure 4.19). It should be emphasised here that testing is not only a technical task, but also a leadership task. A balanced package of measures must exist in all three areas in order to make the test process more efficient.

Leadership is responsible for motivating staff to reach the set goals and to meet expectations and plans. In the area of control, it must be ensured that the computing organisation keeps to its goals and that the set milestones are reached qualitatively and quantitatively. This requires permanent process and result control, mutual evaluation of results and well-organised reporting, and may also involve a change of direction. In the area of support, staff performance must be guaranteed and improved through training and the availability of aids, methods and tools.

Test planning

When testing large systems, numerous problems occur. For example, a large system consists of hundreds or thousands of modules, thousands or tens of

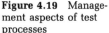

Figure 4.19 Management aspects of test processes

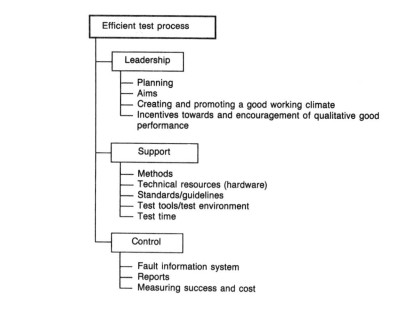

thousands of test cases, and hundreds of errors which have to be pinpointed and corrected. Several dozen people may work for a year or more on such a system. The main danger in the planning of testing lies in the fact that those responsible assume that resource planning, time and milestone planning, procedure planning and tool planning are not accompanied by shortcomings or negligence. Experience with large projects shows that the resource requirements are often wrongly estimated and the risks inadequately estimated.

Since resources are limited in every computing organisation, and because the project team has to meet the most varied requirements, detailed and extensive test planning is essential.

The most important products of test planning (documents) are:

- main test plan (test concept, master test plan);
- test plan;
- test design specification;
- test case specification; and
- test procedure specification for each test task.

The test process also has to be tested and evaluated from the viewpoint of quality assurance. Therefore suitable features for quality testing (testing of the test process) must be determined. The three most important features for the quality of testing are as follows.

Specification. Specifications which evolved in the development process serve as a basis for determining test goals and test plans. For example, for a module test, module specification and module implementation are relevant. These are used for determining test goals and test cases.

Ability to reproduce results

- Each test case must be repeatable.
- For each test case there should be exact instructions for execution and evaluation.
- For each test case there should be an expected test result.

Comprehensibility for people outside the project development

- Clear test documentation for external groups.
- Self-explanatory test cases.
- Complete and valid description of the test run.

It is not sufficient to carry out *ad hoc* test runs with specially selected input data. Good test planning leads to tests which result in trust in the test object and which justify the cost incurred. They result in a test process with a high probability of problem and error discovery. Good test planning means that the time spent on it can be justified, and it also means that it helps less experienced staff to improve their performance.

It is important to consider when test planning should begin. This can happen as early as the requirements analysis phase. Important configuration items are the release conditions which are to be worked out between the customer and contractor. These conditions must be recorded in a document, such as the requirements definition or a log book. The aim of this procedure is to guarantee product release on the basis of an agreement between contractor and development team.

The planning of system testing can take place immediately after the release of the systems specification. Since extensive organisational and technical preparations are necessary for system testing (special test kit, creation of test environment, availability of independent test teams, etc.), it should be planned as early as possible. The test case design for system testing should be made by an independent test group which is not involved in implementation.

The planning of integration testing can begin at the design stage. Analogous to step-by-step partitioning in the structured design, the system can be put together and tested step by step during the integration process. The basis for integration testing is formed, on the one hand, by the integration plan (when are which modules put together?) and, on the other, by the respective module specifications. For those modules which are not part of the integration process, test harnesses and dummy modules must be planned.

Module testing in the detailed design phase (module design) can only be function orientated (black-box methods). The test case design for white-box tests (structure tests) can only be carried out during the implementation of a module. As one of the test goals during the planning of module testing, the extent of test coverage must be determined.

Figure 4.20 gives an overview of test methods which may be suitable for test case creation. This shows that white-box test methods can only be used for module testing and integration testing (module dependence). For all other tests, black-box test methods are applied. The left-hand side of the diagram shows constructive activities which deliver development results (e.g. system design). These results contain errors. Corresponding test activities (e.g. integration testing) can make error discovery possible.

Figure 4.20 Application of black/white-box tests

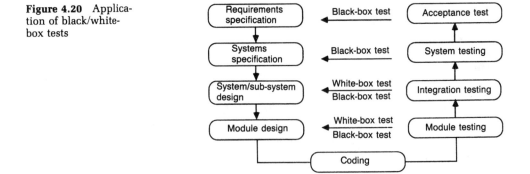

The risk of serious consequences at product release time and during product operation must be taken into account during test planning. It makes sense to allow all programs or modules of an application, or the application as a whole, to undergo risk analysis. One of the goals is to find a list of all test objects which represent a high risk factor at release time and in operation. For example, in commercial applications, erronous programs which access databases used by other applications often represent a risk factor.

For the selection of test goals and test methods, it is also important to know to which risk class a specific test object belongs. The Rheinisch-Westfälische TÜV [Pabs85] has created a useful division of risk classes (Figure 4.21) for this purpose. These can, if necessary, be adapted to the specific application environment. There are five classes (A–E), ranging from program classes without application risk (for example, a program for the creation of acetates) to program classes where, as a consequence of malfunctioning, people can come to harm (control programs for flight safety).

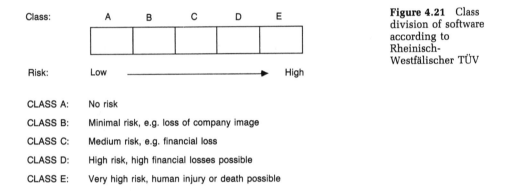

Figure 4.21 Class division of software according to Rheinisch-Westfälischer TÜV

CLASS A: No risk

CLASS B: Minimal risk, e.g. loss of company image

CLASS C: Medium risk, e.g. financial loss

CLASS D: High risk, high financial losses possible

CLASS E: Very high risk, human injury or death possible

Such risk analysis offers a well-founded base for the selection of suitable test methods or combinations of these, and for the sensible allocation of limited test resources.

Figure 4.22 shows possible combinations of test methods for the respective risk classes.

CLASS A: None

CLASS B: Black-box tests

CLASS C: Black-box and operations tests, static program analysis

CLASS D: Black-box and operations tests, static and dynamic program analysis

CLASS E: Black-box and handling tests, static and dynamic program analysis, additional risk observations of the entire system (environmental influence, organisation procedures, etc.)

Figure 4.22 Application of test methods showing relationship to risk classes

Test goals

By a test goal we mean a desired value of an objective, a measurable metric which is used for assessing the scope and the results of a test. Using test goals enables us to achieve an objective test procedure and to facilitate management of the tests.

With reference to Schmitz [Schm82], the following two test metrics can be defined. A test coverage metric (TCM) is an activity-orientated test metric which results from observation of test items as well as from their inclusion in the test. A test result metric (TRM) is a result-orientated test metric which results from the outcome of test activities.

Examples of test results metrics are the mean time between errors found, the necessary calculation time for a test, the necessary calculation time for a test/number of found errors, and the cost of a test or the cost of a test/number of found errors.

Examples of test coverage metrics for the specification of test goals are:

$$TCM_1 = \frac{\text{Number of executed branches}}{\text{Number of existing branches}}$$

The actual test goal for a module test might be: 90 per cent TCM_1.

$$TCM_2 = \frac{\text{Number of executed modules}}{\text{Number of existing modules}}$$

The actual test goal for a program test might be: 100 per cent TCM_2.

The application of these metrics depends on the respective test (in particular, on the applied test method) and on the availability of tools for determining these factors. The application of white-box test methods promotes the use of test coverage metrics.

Criteria for the selection of test metrics are the test requirements, the degree to which it can be executed and cost.

Test termination criteria

An important issue in test planning is the question of when testing should stop. Completion and termination criteria must be established for the test process. Bad criteria are, for example, 'the planned test time has run out' or 'the test cases are not successful, i.e. no errors were discovered'.

What possibilities are there for determining the completeness or the end of a test process in the individual phases? In principle, we can assume that a combination of different test methods leads to succcessful test cases. There are two ways of terminating the test process:

- through a given number of errors which had to be found; and
- through observation of the error rate in the course of the testing phase.

In the first method, the entire number of errors is estimated (remaining error estimation). Large computing organisations have historical values: for example, systems with more than 10,000 statements contain five errors per 100 statements according to the code review. Next, the effectiveness of testing of test tasks is estimated. Let us assume that we find:

- in module testing, 65 per cent of coding errors and no design errors;
- in function testing, 30 per cent of coding errors and 60 per cent of design errors; and
- at system testing, 3 per cent of coding errors and 35 per cent of design errors.

This means that altogether about 98 per cent of coding errors and 95 per cent of design errors are found. In a system with 10,000 statements, the remaining errors can be estimated at 500. In module testing about 130 errors have to be found, in function testing about 240 errors, and in system testing 111 errors, so together 481 errors have to be found.

The second way of ending a test process is by use of an error/time statistic. The number of errors found per unit of time (e.g. week) is entered into a diagram (Figure 4.23). On the basis of this diagram it can be determined when the efficiency rate of testing is passed: that is, when the limiting value has been reached.

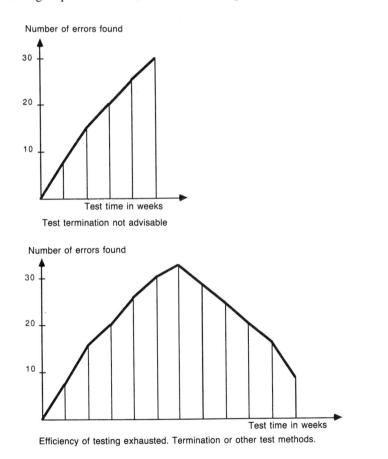

Figure 4.23 Error rate as test termination criterion

A prerequisite for these procedures is an error collection system (see pp. 182–4) and a test case design which takes into consideration a combination of different test methods.

Structuring of the test process

The procedure of a test process is determined by the establishing of test features (name, activity, results) and their schedule. All large test processes can be distinguished by categories of test tasks.

It makes sense to speak of small-scale and large-scale testing. During small-scale testing, elementary objects are defined and tested. The relevant test task is then labelled as module testing (e.g. procedure and program testing).

By large-scale testing we mean the combining of elementary test objects into larger units and the testing of these linked test objects (i.e. subsystems and systems). The first of these test tasks we call integration testing. If we look at the system as a whole and concentrate on system performance and capabilities, we refer to the test task as system testing. During acceptance testing we look at the whole system as a test object together with its application environment (e.g. user organisation), and concentrate on the aspects of system requirements and applicability. Figure 4.24 gives an overview of different categories of test tasks.

Module testing. Module testing is the test of the smallest program units, the modules. This takes place before the integration of the modules into larger units.

Figure 4.24 Categories of test tasks with features

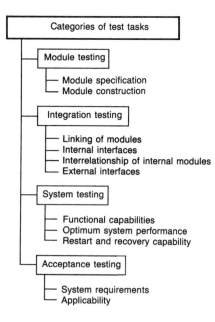

Module testing is usually carried out by the module developers. The test design would be made on the assumption that the implemented module does not correspond to the module design. Typical test aspects which are relevant for the setting up of test cases comprise:

- module functions;
- module structure;
- exception conditions, special cases, etc.; and
- performance.

Typical error classes which are recorded during module testing are:

- missing paths;
- computation errors; and
- domain errors.

Domain errors are errors which come about when executing the wrong paths. This is caused by a set of wrongly formulated conditions.

The prerequisites for module testing are as follows:

- A module specification ('what' description) exists and corresponds to the actual version of the module.
- The detailed design and program listing ('how' description) exist and correspond the the actual version of the module.

It is advisable to carry out a static module test before the actual module testing. This can be done in the form of an inspection of the module or by using a source code analyser for the discovery of code and design faults.

Integration testing. A synonym for integration testing is subsystem testing. After the first modules have been released, the planned integration of the modules into larger units or subsystems can begin. In integration testing, we assume that the individual modules have been well tested individually, and that we can concentrate primarily on testing module interfaces and the interrelationships of modules (module communication). If the subsystems have been adequately specified or documented during the design process, on different abstraction levels, then it is relatively simple to find suitable test goals and test cases for integration testing.

Closely linked with the problem of integration testing is the question of the order in which the different modules should be integrated. This is referred to as the integration strategy, which also influences the test strategy. In this process, we need to take into account organisational as well as technical criteria. Organisational criteria include development strategies, deadlines for module testing, availability of personnel to carry out the tests, and the selection of personnel. Technical criteria are the type and use of applied tools, the verification of test results, the cost/time/effort of making test data available, the time spent on integration testing and the machine time necessary for the test process.

Integration strategies known today are as follows:

Processing-orientated strategies

- *top-down*. Modules on the highest design level are handled first and the other modules are inserted into the hierarchy of module calls.
- *Hardest first*. We start by integrating the system-critical modules and then deal with the rest of the system.
- *Bottom-up*. We start with the modules on the lowest design level and then build larger elements from the modules.

Strategies with goal-orientated criteria

- *Function orientated*. All modules necessary for a selected system function are integrated and tested.
- *Availability*. Modules where module tests have been completed are integrated.
- *Big-bang*. A larger number of modules are integrated.
- *Transaction orientated*. All modules of a transaction are integrated and tested.

With the exception of big-bang testing and transaction-orientated testing, all other test strategies in the process are similar and are referred to as incremental testing. It is significant here that only one module is added per test. The two last test strategies are referred to as non-incremental testing. The procedure is that each module is initially tested independent of the others and that all modules are subsequently integrated and tested.

The advantages of incremental testing are:

- low cost (not as many drivers and stubs necessary);
- early recognition of interface errors; and
- single debugging of interface errors.

Advantages of non-incremental testing are:

- less machine time is necessary than in incremental testing; and
- parallel testing of modules is possible.

There are no generally valid answers to the question of which module should be assembled and tested at what time. This account has pointed to different criteria which may apply to integration according to the project situation involved.

System testing. In system testing, the entire system is tested with regard to its functional performance on the one hand and the limits of its capabilities on the other. Aspects such as loading of the available application hardware environment, integration into the user organisation and maintenance of the software system are observed.

The following test goals must be observed for system testing:

- *Completeness*. It must be examined whether the system meets all functional and non-functional requirements in accordance with the performance specification (e.g. log book).

- *Volume*. The system must be tested with extensive quantities of data (bulk test). One potential weakness is the size of files or databases.
- *Load*. The system must be tested over a longer period of time under maximum load. For example, an on-line customer information system should be tested over several days, during which transactions should be carried out from all terminals simultaneously over several hours.
- *Handling/user-friendliness*. Error messages, help techniques, acknowledging of input, displaying of system conditions and arrangement of layout must be checked with regard to user-friendliness.
- *Security*. It must be tested how far data protection mechanisms and data security tests are provided through the software system or through the surrounding software.
- *Efficiency*. It must be tested whether the response times and the throughput meet the specific requirements under a severe system load.
- *Configuration*. If the software is to be suitable for different hardware configurations, it must be tested to see whether it can also be configured correspondingly.
- *Compatibility/data conversion*. Many systems are these days integrated into older systems of long standing. It must be tested to what extent the interfaces are compatible, or whether conversion procedures exist for the transfer of data into other systems.
- *Documentation*. Accuracy and quality of user and maintenance documentation must be tested.
- *Maintainability*. All requirements must be tested with regard to maintainability.

In highly integrated applications (as, for example, in bank applications) the aspect of compatibility/data conversion is often observed through a special test task which is inserted before the system testing, and which is referred to as application integration testing. In this instance, comprehensive tests of interfaces to related applications are planned and carried out.

In order to test the limits of a system, huge quantities of test data are needed. These are suitably created with simulators or test data generators.

The extensive test data quantity in system testing is eminently well suited to regression tests in maintenance. Good test documentation, which also contains the test results, facilitates considerably the testing of changes in the maintenance phase.

As experience in system testing shows, the cost in resources can be very high.

System testing ends when those responsible have measured the system performances, have solved recurring problems and have sufficient trust in the product to carry out acceptance testing.

Acceptance testing. Acceptance testing is the third level of large-scale testing.

The aim of acceptance testing is to demonstrate that the trust put into the product by the customer or contractor is justified. In order to prove this, the following conditions must be met:

- concentration on user requirements;
- user participation or participation of user representatives; and
- testing of the system under normal operational conditions (hardware/system software).

Acceptance testing is usually carried out by the user organisation. Based on the contract with the customer, test cases are created which attempt to show that the contract is not fulfilled. If the test cases are not successful then the system is accepted and released. Acceptance criteria must be stipulated in the original requirements specification or in the contract with the customer.

Test cases for acceptance testing are characterised by:

- release criteria from the requirements specification;
- some test cases from system tests;
- test cases for the processing of business data over a typical time period (e.g. day, month, year) or an accounting period; and
- test cases for permanent tests with the aim of testing a permanent operation over a longer period of time.

Errors and faults which can arise during release testing are:

- non-observance of specified goals of acceptance testing (testing of the operational system); and
- absence of planning, i.e. random use of the system by the end user.

A special form of acceptance testing is installation testing. In this the system is installed in the target environment and the goal is the discovery of installation errors. The following conditions must be tested:

- All system parts exist and have the correct installation state, i.e. files or databases and libraries are defined and initialised in their basic state.
- The hardware configuration corresponds with the requirements.

Where 50 to 60 per cent of project cost is due to the test process, goal and result-orientated test planning is absolutely essential. Experience has shown that awareness of this is often not evident or that preconditions are not given. Without a well-structured and methodically supported test process, efficient quality evaluation cannot be achieved.

Test organisation

Test organisation should be independent of the developer organisation. Its task is to test the developed products with the highest possible accuracy, to note deviation from the specified requirements and to test application suitability. If faults are found, the product is not accepted for introduction and use, and is returned to the developer.

A further task of the testing organisation can be software application planning. In larger computing organisations, a separate unit should be established for this task. This company unit can be referred to as the software headquarters. Here the correct use of programs and databases is planned for an application in the production area.

In order to increase the efficiency of test processes, the employment of external testers is recommended. Their role and relationship to the developer organisation should be based on a contract. In most cases this type of test organisation is limited to a stipulated period of time in which test know-how is made available on a short-term basis. In large American military and space projects, the employment of external test companies is common. In addition to there being a basic financial agreement, the success of the testing is further rewarded according to the number of discovered faults.

For smaller and medium-size computing organisations (up to 200 developers), a procedure-orientated model of a test organisation is recommended. This is illustrated in Figure 4.25.

The test management carries the responsibility for planning, organisation and execution of the test process, but not for the quality of the system to be tested.

The functions of test case creation and test evaluation are carried out by the test group together with the respective specialist department (or user representatives). Test preparation and test execution are carried out solely by the test group.

Important success factors for an efficient test organisation are the existence of specially allocated testing equipment (e.g. computer), up-to-date test databases and test tools. As regards test infrastructure tasks which are carried out by the test group itself, requirements must be observed.

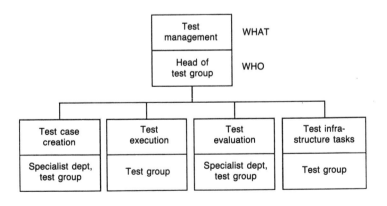

Figure 4.25 Model of a procedure-orientated test organisation

Test documentation

For structure and content of test documents we refer to IEEE Standard 829−1983. The following documents must be used according to this standard (Figure 4.26):

- test plan;
- test design specification;
- test case specification;
- test procedure specification;
- test item transmission report;
- test log;
- test incident report; and
- test summary report.

The test plan plays a central part in testing. It constitutes the prerequisite for the control and direction of test preparation and test execution. At the same time it forms a basis for quality assurance of the test process. The following observations have been made in connection with test plans:

- The test plan must exist, must be used and will be changed.
- The test plan must be created as early as possible (it should be complete and available at the latest at the stage of system design).
- The test plan must be referenced in the project plan.

The test plan contains the following content structure:

- test plan identifier;
- introduction;
- test items;
- features to be tested;
- features not to be tested;
- approach;
- item pass/fail criteria;
- suspension criteria and resumption requirements;
- test deliverables
- testing tasks;
- environmental needs;
- responsibilities;
- staffing and training needs;
- schedule;
- risk and contingencies; and
- approvals.

The test design specification stipulates the test strategy and outlines it in detail. Furthermore, it identifies the functions and features for the test cases. It also contains criteria on the basis of which it is decided whether a test feature is or is not fulfilled.

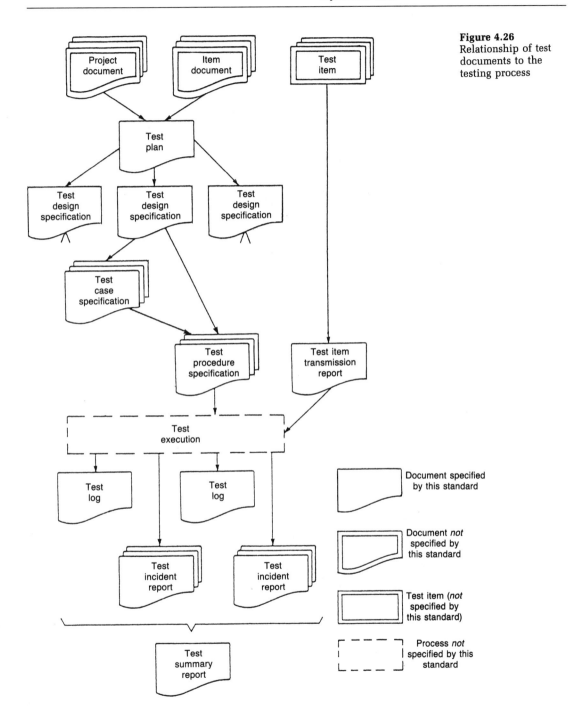

Figure 4.26
Relationship of test
documents to the
testing process

Within the test case specification, test cases are defined which have been identified in the test design specification. It contains mainly a test case identifier, a pointer/reference to the test object, an input/output specification, possible requirements related to the test environment and guidance with regard to the sequence of test cases.

The test procedure specification describes the actual test procedure, and the exact execution of the test procedure is stipulated for each individual test.

The test item transmission report lists the test items in detail, in accordance with the configuration list. This report is particularly important if the development team is not the same as the test team, and if acceptance testing is laid down in a contract.

The test log describes all the relevant details of each executed test in chronological sequence (exact error messages, crashes, operator requirements, etc.).

The test incident report collates deviations which have occurred and provides the connection between test specifications and test log entries. It contains the expected and the actual results, description of the environment, anomalies, attempted repeats of tests and identification of the tester. An appropriate problem classification and problem description with an indication of degree of urgency are important for subsequent efficient error analysis.

The test summary report collates the results of test activities and gives an evaluation of whether the set goals and requirements have been achieved.

Creating and archiving test documentation have so far been neglected in many computing organisations. Samples of test documents are often missing. Without test documentation it is impossible to direct and control the test process. A test plan, the listing of test cases with test results and an index of problems and deviations which occurred should form the minimum of test documentation.

Control of the test process

Testing plays a decisive part in the project procedure in terms of both cost and importance. Through testing and reviews the function of analytical quality assurance is performed. This demands that the test process should be controlled as part of the development process. Without suitable control mechanisms for the test process, the management and the project leader do not have the necessary information to enable them to assess project progress and problems that arise.

The most important elements of effective test control are:

- recording and follow-up of problems, faults and errors;
- error analysis (causes, categories, effects);
- test cost and test progress; and
- up-to-date and complete test documentation.

We shall now comment in more detail on these elements of test control and shall recommend practical aids for their application. We referred to test documentation in detail on pp. 180–2.

Recording and follow-up of problems, faults and errors. Recording and follow-up of reliable information about problems, faults and errors which occur during testing and during system operation is an important control function. This information is analysed, collated and evaluated in order to recognise trends and significant events.

In computing organisations, special forms and reports are used for this purpose. Two documents which support this control function are test logs and the test incident report, which are described in IEEE Standard 829−1983. Experience shows that the function cannot, in the long run, be carried out without computer-supported systems. Examples of such systems are the Electronic Incident Report System (EIR) [SBG88] and the Problem/Change Management System [IBM87a]. They make possible the construction and maintenance of extensive error data banks, which are prerequisites for cause-related error analysis.

Error analysis. Error analyses are widely used. On the one hand, periodic analysis can be undertaken of the frequency of errors/problems per month, per module, etc., and trends spotted in incidents in the test process or difficulties in the handling of application modules. On the other hand, causes of errors and problems in the development and maintenance process can be revealed.

The following simple classification of error types has proved to be useful:

- requirements errors;
- design errors;
- programming errors;
- database errors;
- interface errors;
- errors in job control statements;
- errors in the test environment; and
- others.

For error cause analysis, it is important to know when the error was discovered (in which phase) and when it was generated. For the categorising of causes, the following classification scheme is recommended, [Jone85, Wall88]:

- Absence of information because of missing or inadequate training and further training:
  application related;
  computing knowledge related.
- Lack of communication.
- Inadequacy in implementation and work supervision:
  typing errors;
  negligence;
  lack of control.

In the past, the test process was seen as an error discovery mechanism. Through error analysis and the observation of results, the test process serves increasingly for error prevention, since the sources of potential problems and faults are discovered and eradicated in the development or maintenance process.

Figure 4.27 Test
cost observation

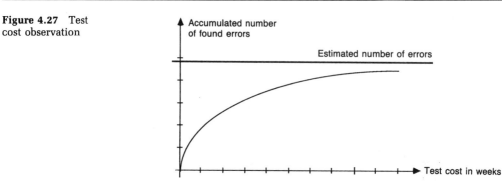

The determination of test cost and test status. Prerequisites for an efficient determination of test cost and test status are good planning and up-to-date test documentation. The following information about test status should be available:

- status of test design work;
- status of work for test case specification;
- number of available test cases;
- what has been tested and what is to be tested;
- which program versions have been tested with which test; and
- test cost outstanding.

Experience shows that this information is neither available nor used as might be desirable. Instead the mythical '90 per cent ready' status is still widespread, while the remaining test time can in no way be estimated.

In extensive projects it has been found effective to observe two factors: the accumulated number of found errors; and test cost (e.g. in weeks) (see Figure 4.27). Together with a rough estimate of potentially existing errors in the application (e.g. 0.5−1 per cent of all lines of the source code contain errors), this constitutes a very practical guide to controlling test cost.

The number of already tested requirements or functions of the software product with respect to the incurred cost also helps in the observation of test cost or test status. However, this requires a function-orientated development methodology.

In conclusion, efficient test control requires detailed test planning and can be realised with discipline and a few aids, such as problem and error logging systems, error databases and trend charts.

5 Software quality assurance in maintenance

In many companies, maintenance activities take up most of the time. The development activities and consequently the development of new applications are put back, thereby creating an application backlog. According to estimates in the USA, more than 80 per cent of the life-cycle cost of a software product comes about through maintenance [Wien84].

In more common usage, the word 'maintenance' means returning a machine or an appliance to a satisfactory state. In most instances, maintenance is caused by natural wear and tear or through alteration. The maintenance of a television set is relatively simple, since the faulty part can be exchanged. The requirements of someone who maintains television sets are low compared to those who design and build them.

In software systems, there is no material wear and tear or ageing process which can lead to maintenance. Software maintenance means improvement of the original state. The requirements of someone who is involved in software maintenance activities are high. On the one hand, he or she needs adequate specialist knowledge about the application in order to understand the software and requirements. On the other hand, sufficient software engineering knowledge is required in order to implement the requirements.

Reasons for maintenance of software systems are:

- corrections for the removal of existing faults (stabilising, corrective maintenance);
- adaptation of the product to a different application environment (adaptive maintenance);
- alteration in order to improve quality features, such as the maintainability or reliability of the product (tuning, perfective maintenance); and
- extensions in order to meet new requirements.

Included within these extensions is often an extensive amount of new development work which is hidden behind the term 'maintenance'. Using suitable incremental release or development planning, this hidden new development work can be avoided. Extension work is then referred to as maintenance only when the cost amounts to less than six person-months.

Therefore we can define software maintenance as planned and systematically executed correction, alteration or extension of a software product.

Practical experience shows that maintenance takes up a large amount of resources in a computing organisation, and causes serious problems. The reasons for this are as follows:

- The development process cannot, as a rule, be retraced.
- Alterations are not documented.
- Alterations reduce the stability of the product.
- Alterations can have a ripple effect on different product parts and influence product behaviour.
- Product development is planned and executed without giving thought to later maintenance.

Maintenance also tends to cause problems these days for a number of additional reasons:

- 75 to 80 per cent of existing software was developed before the general use of structured programming;
- high personnel turnover in computing organisations;
- lack of planning — in particular, the absence of a release plan in product development; and
- no cross-checking of requirements and design decisions with code.

Maintenance is further influenced by the size of a product. Statistics over the last twenty years show a marked increase of LOC values in applications/projects [Boeh87]. This makes not only the localising of alterations but also the estimation of the effects of alterations harder. Large systems include flight reservation systems, highly integrated banking systems, electronic fund transfer systems, operating systems, and military command and control systems.

The term 'software evolution' is a better description of the permanent alteration of existing software than the term 'maintenance', which is less explicit. The main operations of software evolution are:

- understanding existing software and the requirements for altering, extending or correcting;
- modifying existing software; and
- assessing the correctness of modified software through reviews.

Based on their own analyses, Lehman and Belady [Lehm80] noted the following phenomena in connection with the software evolution of large program systems in IBM:

- *Phenomenon of permanent alteration.* A program which is altered frequently during application loses value. The alteration or deterioration process continues until it becomes more cost effective to write a new program.
- *Phenomenon of growing complexity (untidiness).* The complexity of a program, caused by the large number of implemented functions, user interfaces and system interfaces, increases consistently unless work is invested to reduce them.

With reference to the first phenomenon, it should be said that not only are errors eliminated, but improvements and adaptations are carried out continuously because of changing environments and user requirements. In connection with the maintenance of the operating system OS/360, for example, it was noticed that ever more modules had to be altered in order to avoid side effects.

The second phenomenon is one of the most difficult problems for many of those responsible for maintenance. For reasons of time and cost, the loss of structure is not prevented. Instead quick fixes are carried out and other modules are added to the system without checking the effects on existing modules. In many instances, the authors of the original programs are no longer available and maintenance activities are often carried out by inexperienced staff. The integrity of the product is lost through such alteration processes. Furthermore, module coupling increases and module cohesion decreases.

From the point of view of quality assurance, the question arises of which characteristics and features a product must have to be called 'easily maintainable' or 'maintenance-friendly'. In our discussion of quality models, we have already mentioned approaches to the description of maintainability (see Appendices A1 and A2). Detailed information about features for maintenance-friendliness can be found in [Balz88a], [Asam86] and [Mart83].

Computing management is inhibited and limited in the planning and implementation of new applications by increasing maintenance problems and maintenance requirements. Although better design and implementation methods lead to higher quality in new applications, the quality of old systems where numerous alterations have been carried out remains poor. For economic reasons, it is not possible to replace all old products. Therefore a way must be found for the better planning and control of the evolutionary alteration process, for reasons of both economy and quality. In order to effect this, the following measures are recommended:

- reduce maintenance cost;
- guarantee maintainability; and
- regulate maintenance activities.

5.1   Reducing maintenance cost

As experience in the maintenance of large software products (e.g. in an operating system) has shown, software errors do not occur evenly across all modules, but occur more often in modules which are frequently altered. Other studies show that modules which have been frequently altered require further maintenance activities. As already mentioned, maintenance reduces the quality of programs with regard to modularity, structure and readability. The question arises as to how modules which contain a large number of changes can be identified.

This problem can be solved through the following organisational measures. The maintenance personnel record exactly:

- which module was altered;
- what cost/effort was expended on maintenance activity;

- the reason for maintenance; and
- a short description of executed maintenance work.

This cost is recorded not in person-hours, but in terms of the number of altered lines (source code + documentation).

This information makes evident which modules have caused what maintenance cost, and those modules which have caused the highest maintenance cost can be determined. After a certain number of alterations it becomes cheaper to develop these modules anew.

The results of Boehm will help to clarify this problem. Products which are difficult to maintain reduce the productivity of staff who are entrusted with maintenance tasks in the ratio of 40:1 as compared to those who carry out new developments. If the development of a line of code costs $25, then products that are difficult to maintain can incur maintenance costs of up to $1,000 per line of code [Boeh79b].

Information on what maintenance work was carried out and why helps in the decision as to whether a module should be further maintained or reprogrammed. In [Bert84] the following rules are recommended:

- Destroy the module and develop it new if it is small.
- Restore the module if it is large or complicated or heavily coupled with other modules.

In [Schä84] it is reported that these measures can save up to 45 per cent of maintenance cost.

5.2   Guaranteeing maintainability

Typical commercial products have life cycles of about ten to fifteen years. During this time the product goes through an evolutionary process and needs to be maintained. From the point of view of quality assurance, the question arises of how maintainability can be positively influenced as early as the development stage, so that cost in the maintenance phase can be kept as low as possible.

Parnas [Parn79] recommends the following:

- Structure the requirements into components and separate out those requirements which will be subject to later expansion. The components of requirements so produced make the software design easier and promote flexibility.
- Make use of abstraction levels when designing a product. When alterations are made, functions can then be added and removed without side effects.

In order to follow both of Parnas's recommendations, it is advisable to represent requirements and design in the form of models. Analysis and design decisions can then be more easily checked. Methods such as structured analysis (SA) or the Jackson System Development (JSD) method lead the systematic creation of a model.

The first recommendation of Parnas can be put into practice by using product planning in the form of releases. Product functions which are not considered urgent are documented for a subsequent enhanced release. It is, of course, important that further development (evolution) of the product is allowed for during the initial development with regard to budgeting (time and cost plan) of the enhanced release.

The second recommendation leads to a layered architecture of software systems [Thur88, Dene86]. The following example of an interactive software system consists of four layers (see Figure 5.1). The frequency of alteration increases from the lowest layer upwards.

The lowest layer serves for administration of the database, which is realised through files or a database system. The structure of this layer is derived from the conceptual data model. The layer above contains the basic operations of the application, such as operations that prepare data or that make data available in a specific sequence.

The next layer up contains application-specific operations. This is called the user operations layer. If the modularisation is good, these operations exist, for example, in the form of data descriptions. By chaining these operations, the dialogue is determined. The control and resourcing of the dialogue takes place in the highest layer (dialogue control). This layer contains the dialogue monitor (TP Monitor). The user controls the dialogue using menus and commands. This layer structure facilitates faster localisation of alterations.

Martin [Mart83] suggests the following measures for better maintainability:

- Specify quality goals in the form of clear quality features, and determine maintenance requirements when formulating the project contract.
- Use data encapsulation and abstract data types for modularisation, Codd's normal forms for data model description, and structured programming for implementation.
- Establish analytical quality assurance measures such as audits and reviews.
- Check regularly the implementation of maintenance requirements (e.g. through audits).
- Select a maintenance-friendly programming language such as Ada or Modula-2.
- Improve program documentation bearing in mind the readership of the documentation, and make the program self-descriptive.

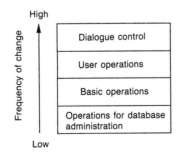

Figure 5.1 Example of layered structure in an interactive software system

In conclusion, by using an engineering approach during development, the maintenance situation can be improved. While the necessity for these measures is generally agreed, the fact that the effects are long-term causes some problems. Software managers today like to make short-term decisions (maximum $1\frac{1}{2}$ years). Such short-term planning tends to lead to short-term use. This often leads to a discrepancy between a long-term software engineering concept and the software solution actually implemented.

5.3   Regulating maintenance activities

Maintenance activities can be carried out either by the developers themselves or by a separate maintenance team. Each approach has advantages and disadvantages.

Developers carry out maintenance themselves

Advantages

- The developers have the best knowledge of their products. Maintenance work can be carried out quickly.
- The users need only communicate with one group of computer specialists who are responsible for an application or a product.
- Decisions ('Who may develop?', 'Who must do maintenance?') are easier, since each developer must also carry out maintenance.
- Maintenance requirements are more likely to be taken into account during development.

Disadvantages

- If a developer has to do too much maintenance work, he or she will probably leave the computing organisation.
- Problems can arise if a developer with excellent product knowledge leaves the computing organisation and no adequate replacement is available.
- The danger exists that the developers spend too much time in perfecting their product.
- When large development projects are implemented, there is the danger of shortening maintenance work, delaying it or transferring it to inexperienced developers.

Maintenance is carried out by a separate maintenance team

Advantages

- Documentation is qualitatively better. Formal transfer guidelines are available when a product demands maintenance.
- Formal guidelines (procedures for maintenance) are established for the implementation of maintenance requirements.

- A specific infrastructure evolves (tools, know-how, etc.) and specialists for maintenance are allocated.

Disadvantages

- In certain maintenance situations, support from the developers is necessary. This leads to an additional communication cost.
- Users have to communicate with two groups of computer specialists.
- In order to maintain a product, one must be conversant with it. This requires training, with its ensuing cost.

In both types of approach, a committee must be formed which examines maintenance requirements and approves, disapproves or alters them. We call this committee the Change Control Board (CCB) (see section 3.6).

The selection of experts for this committee depends on the computing organisation. It would be sensible to include representatives from top management, the developer organisation or the maintenance organisation, the user organisation (either user representatives or specialist organisation), a central computing planning group and software quality assurance. Irrespective of the type of organisation, a simple standard procedure should be used for the development of maintenance activities. The construction and maintenance of this standard is a planning-orientated administrative quality assurance measure. Such a standard procedure could take the following form:

- acceptance of maintenance requirements and estimate of cost;
- analysis of maintenance requirements and construction of a solution concept;
- updating the documentation;
- updating the source and object code;
- acceptance test; and
- terminating the maintenance activity.

In the following this standard procedure for the performing of maintenance activities is described in detail.

Acceptance of maintenance requirements and estimate of cost

The following activities must be carried out:

- Identification of the maintenance case for cost analyses.
- Sorting and classifying of maintenance requirements with respect to the type of requirements (e.g. error correction, adaptation, tuning) and bearing in mind specific products/applications.
- Estimation of maintenance requirements cost, bearing in mind the condition and maintainability of the product:
  cost of localising errors/alterations;
  cost of generating documentation;
  cost of updating code and database;

cost of software tests (testing, reviews);
cost of installation of tested modules into the production environment; and
cost of creating maintenance reports.

The estimate is documented in the form for maintenance requirements, and the actual cost appears in the maintenance report (see Appendix A4).

Analysis of maintenance requirements and construction of a solution concept

In the next step, detailed analysis should follow in order to investigate which form the maintenance should take and what effects the alterations/extensions will have on the existing software elements and their relationships. The better the product is modularised (e.g. through the application of data encapsulation or abstract data types), the smaller are the effects of alterations and extensions. The larger the project and the worse it is modularised, the more costly is this analysis. Support through tools is possible (see section 3.5.1).

On the basis of the rough estimate and of the analysis it is decided whether:

- a recommendation for the release of the product is worked out, so that the maintenance requirements can be satisfied; or
- the maintenance is executed.

In the first case, maintenance requirements lead to the new release of the product. The relevant product release plan has to be altered. This leads to project-overlapping planning processes in order to save time and resources for the project release.

In the second case, it makes sense to decide whether maintenance should be dealt with immediately or whether alterations should begin only when several small, non-urgent maintenance cases have accumulated. The advantage of collecting maintenance components into a single unit is an economical employment of maintenance resources such as time and staff.

One of the main problems in maintenance is the creation of errors through alterations and extensions, and through error correction itself. Colofello and Buck found that the following types of error were caused by maintenance activities [Coll87]:

- 10 per cent of errors came about through the correction of errors;
- 21 per cent of errors occurred in extensions;
- 53 per cent of errors came about through the effects of extensions on existing product parts; and
- 15 per cent of errors were not classifiable.

When the causes and effects of alterations have been assessed, a solution must be constructed which states what must be altered and which building elements must be newly developed. The structure of the altered or extended system must be presented: for example, through graphical means, data flow, hierarchy and procedure call diagrams, or formal aids like attributed grammars. The solution should also contain a description indicating in which sequence alterations and extensions are to be implemented.

Updating the documentation

Before any part of the code is altered, it must be determined on which level of product description alterations are to be carried out. It has proved practical to distinguish between the following product description levels:

- specification level, e.g. requirements definition in the form of data flow and entity-relationship diagrams, user manual;
- design level, e.g. system designs in the form of module dependence graphs, module designs in the form of structure diagrams; and
- code level, e.g. module descriptions in the form of comments.

The application of CASE tools can make localising of documentation alterations considerably easier. There are also aids which support the easy understanding of alterations in the documentation and the code (see also section 3.6.3).

Updating the source and object code

As early as the creation of the maintenance documentation (at the latest, at the time of release/acceptance), a guideline for the updating of the source and object code must be established which can be used in the case of maintenance. It states in which files of the project archive which programs can be found, and which files are necessary for compilation and for linking. As a rule, the code is first altered in a development or maintenance library and not immediately in the product library.

Acceptance test

Acceptance tests are tests as well as reviews of modified products. Of special importance for productivity in maintenance is the repeatability of tests and the archiving of test cases. All altered product parts must be subjected to a review.

Terminating the maintenance activity

Correct termination requires the following activities:

- The program source code and test results must be archived.
- In the module header of each altered module, any maintenance activity must be entered in the alterations entry and the name of the person responsible must be documented.

- The documents maintenance requirements and maintenance report[1] must be completed and archived, and a copy sent to the contractor.

The status of all maintenance activities must be shown periodically in the form of a maintenance report summary. In this report, outstanding and completed maintenance activities are listed. Further measures found to be necessary must also be noted.

Based on maintenance reports, management should create various metrics and statistics in order to promote transparency as well as problem and cost awareness among the decision makers. Some metrics which are widely accepted are:

- number of errors which were caused through maintenance activities in each quarter/1000 NLOC;
- number of person-days used in each maintenance category (e.g. correction) per quarter;
- average number of program alterations per program; and
- average length of time from initial recording up to termination of a maintenance requirement.

These metrics form a basis for decisions on whether improvements in the planning and development process should be made either with regard to staffing or in the project infrastructure. These promote a better understanding of problems and the need for maintenance.

5.4   Importance of quality assurance for maintenance

The main task of quality assurance consists in securing quality within the framework of evolution. Apart from the already described organisational and technical measures, the recycling of old software is gaining increasingly in importance [Snee88b]. Recycling or re-engineering of software means the restructuring of a product with the aim of improving quality features like efficiency, testability and readability.

The first step in re-engineering is static program analysis in order to obtain a model of the program (structure, interfaces, functions). Then an attempt is made to improve the old structure of the product or to redesign it. Thereafter old but still usable and newly described components are added to the product.

Well-known and proven aids and tools of quality assurance for maintenance are (section 3.5.1):

- standards;
- metrics;
- reviews and audits;

---

1. Two documents are recommended for maintenance: a form for recording maintenance requirements; and a form for the final evaluation of executed maintenance activities, the maintenance report (see Appendix A4).

- software information systems;
- analysis tools; and
- education and training.

Standards

Increasing complexity of products and staff turnover make insistence on development standards and standardised maintenance procedures essential. Internationally valid guidelines and standards for maintenance do exist ([McCa85, Osbo83], Appendix A5). These guidelines and standards help to:

- create a software maintenance plan;
- recognise possible improvements of maintainability;
- improve the transparency of maintenance work in computing organisations;
- introduce a bonus system for maintenance staff; and
- improve existing standards.

The key to enforcing these standards lies not only in simplicity and adaptability, but also in tool support. Standards must be maintained and repeatedly checked for their applicability. Applicability can be improved, especially if it is explicitly recorded when the standard is not to be applied. Accepted standards which are used in everyday work can be very useful. An unacceptable standard or insistence on using a useless one can be dangerous and even damaging for a computing organisation (e.g. using outdated computing technology). The maintenance of standards is a traditional task of quality assurance organisations. Keeping and promoting standards, however, needs the support of the management.

Metrics

The construction, maintenance and collection of know-how about maintenance metrics (see also sections 1.3.7 and 1.4 and Appendices A1 and A2) are tasks of the quality assurance group. Some encouraging experiences of the application of metrics within the scope of maintenance activities have been found [Schn87, Arno82].

Kafura and Reddy [Kafu87] examined code and system structure metrics (McCabe's metric, Halstead's cost measure, LOC, Henry and Kafura's information flow measure, McClure's control flow measure, Woodfield's measure, and Yau and Collofello's measure of logical stability) in connection with maintenance of four releases of a relational database system. They found that the metrics show up the growing complexity of a system very well, and were even in the position to identify the badly structured components of the system.

Metrics have become an indispensable instrument for creating more transparency in the maintenance process, and for easier estimation of the effects of maintenance activities on the product.

Reviews and audits

Reviews are set up for assessing the effects of changes and for providing the evidence that a product has been correctly altered.

For the transfer of products from development to maintenance, acceptance and installation audits have proved to be useful. In acceptance audits, it is tested whether the acceptance criteria have been met. In installation audits, it is examined whether all product elements (features of physical completeness) and all product functions (features of functional completeness) exist, and whether all conditions for maintenance (checklists) are met.

In addition, it is recommended that audits be initiated periodically for the analysis of maintainability of those programs which are in the operation phase. Through this kind of audit, potential and actual maintenance problems can quickly be brought to light.

Software information systems

In extensive software systems (i.e. those with thousands of programs, hundreds of databases, etc.), the maintenance organisation needs adequate assistance in order to carry out its activities effectively. Only if structure and overview information about applications, modules, databases, files, etc. can be made available quickly and is complete can maintenance work then be done productively. In many instances, such systems are only just being constructed [Grad87].

Analysis tools

Those responsible for maintenance have increasing difficulties in understanding, testing and handling old code. Consequently, aids and tools are needed for extracting structure and interface information from sizeable software systems. Examples of such tools are information generators (documentation generators on the program and system level) and browsers [Shne85] (see also section 4.1.3). A good overview of these tools is given in [Scot88] and [Abi88].

Education and training

Many managers have been inadequately trained for the handling of technical and organisational maintenance problems. The consequences are not only the absence of cost or investment control, but also chaotic states of new applications and in the development of old products.

University research and development centres hardly occupy themselves with maintenance problems at all because of its low scientific attraction. In computing training, the area of maintenance is likewise dealt with only peripherally.

Quality assurance organisations should provide help with and run courses about maintenance measures. Maintenance metrics should be published regularly and should be discussed with those responsible for maintenance.

Quality assurance is only in its beginnings in the area of software maintenance. Much points to the fact that the solution of quality assurance tasks in maintenance is more likely to be found in a leadership-orientated organisational approach than in a purely technical approach.

6 Organisational aspects of quality assurance — the quality assurance system

In order to be able to carry out constructive and analytical quality assurance measures, certain organisational and personnel requirements arise. We can speak of a quality assurance system (QA system) if the construction and procedure organisation, responsibilities, measures and means for quality assurance have been established.

The project risk (see section 1.2.3) determines the size and the kind of measures and requirements which are selected for guaranteeing product quality and process quality within a quality assurance system.

With increasing project size and increasing risks, the extent of quality assurance measures must expand. For this a suitable organisation dealing with construction and procedures is necessary in order to achieve and maintain specified software quality. The quality assurance system must be brought into line with all factors which influence quality. These factors include:

- applied methods and tools;
- standards applied in development and maintenance;
- process organisation for development and maintenance (process model);
- software production environment (hardware);
- organisation of personnel in software development;
- qualifications of staff;
- motivation and working conditions of staff; and
- quality of deliverables produced by external project subcontractors.

This list is not exhaustive. It shows how multi-faceted is the influence on process quality and product quality. From this we can see the necessity of the application of a quality assurance system.

Recent studies of quality assurance systems are largely based on those companies which produce hardware as well as software products [Lumb82, Dett85]. However, in the future, through international trends towards increased product liability and proof of quality, and the extension of executed quality assurance measures in software products, quality assurance systems are likely to find their way increasingly into the commercial software industry.

6.1   Construction of the organisation of a quality assurance system

At the present time, no generally accepted model for the construction of the organisation of a quality assurance system can be identified. The dependence on company-specific details, product type, project size and the existing infrastructure of software production is too great. The construction of the organisation of a quality assurance system must acknowledge the current organisational structure of a company (line, matrix, project organisation) with regard to its present position and level of resourcing.

Depending on the organisational form of the company, the quality assurance tasks are allocated to different units of the organisation structure. In a line organisation, quality assurance has equal status with other units, such as sales and development. We frequently come across this form of organisation in companies which produce hardware and software systems, such as IBM, AT&T and Siemens [Zill82, Lumb82].

Figure 6.1 shows the organisation structure of a computer producer. The company is divided into different product groups, and these, in turn, are divided into individual product divisions. In a product division, for example, a computer system of a specific performance class with relevant system software is being produced. Quality assurance, which takes on an extensive task in this connection, is responsible for guaranteeing the quality of the system, the software and the hardware. A pertinent problem in such an organisational form consists in the exact delineation of tasks (e.g. to which category does the quality assurance of firmware belong?).

In large companies, we also find information about the organisation of quality assurance in the company guidelines. One example of this is as follows (see [Zill82]):

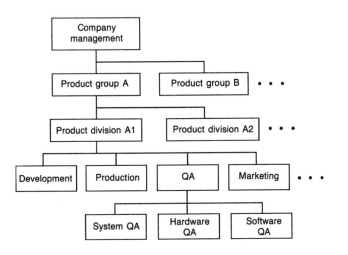

Figure 6.1 Quality assurance in a line organisation

Each product division must have an independent quality assurance office. It consists of a small organisational unit next to the development laboratories and production works. It has the responsibility for adequate testing and analysing of all products so that specifications, performance features, quality goals and duties which the company undertakes are reached and adhered to.

In a matrix organisation, the necessary resources and services are made available for the individual projects or the different product areas via a central organisation unit. In this central organisation unit (e.g. a department or section), quality assurance must be established in the form of a support post (see Figure 6.2).

A matrix organisation is usually found in companies in which products are produced on a contract basis. Those responsible for the project or product in most cases report directly to the company management. In this type of organisation, the product/project control is seen from different positions. The product or project manager 'buys' resources from the numerous support contractors. This causes a potential conflict because of overlapping capabilities. A positive aspect of this form of organisation is the flexible use of resources. This flexibility makes it easier to cope with a high demand on the resources. From the point of view of quality assurance, this form of organisation has the advantage that it favours independent quality testing.

In project organisations which we find not only in software houses but also in suppliers of turnkey solutions, quality assurance has an integrating role. Quality assurance is present under the auspices of project management. Quality tests take place directly in the project and are carried out in conjunction with the developers (see Figure 6.3).

An important precondition for the effectiveness of a quality assurance system is a clear and balanced outline of the tasks, capabilities and responsibilities of

Figure 6.2 Quality assurance in a matrix organisation

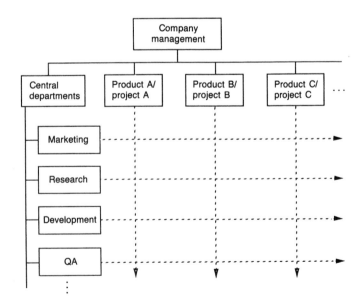

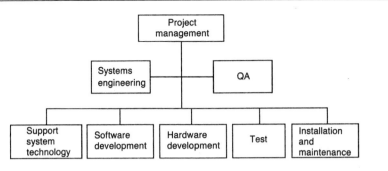

Figure 6.3 Quality assurance in a project organisation

each organisation unit (especially in a decision-making body). Within an organisation constructing a quality assurance system, the tasks, capabilities and responsibilities of the quality assurance section are clearly stipulated [Gast81]. By the term 'capability' we mean the authority which a member of staff with specific assigned tasks is allocated for the completion of his or her tasks. If these stipulations are missing or cannot be formulated clearly, the result is an unbalanced distribution of tasks, capabilities and responsibilities (see Figure 6.4). The result is the decreased performance capability of quality assurance. The consequences are unjustified criticism from outside and waning motivation of staff.

What kind of generally valid experiences are there for the organisation of a quality assurance department? In an American study [Mend83] the following findings on quality assurance organisations were noted:

- Software quality assurance occupies an important place in overall product safety.
- The staff have software engineering experience of between one and five years.
- The manager of a software quality assurance department has more than five years' software engineering experience and belongs to the middle management of the company.

The key to a successful quality assurance department lies in its independence from the development team/organisation. The quality assurance department must report to the same department to which the developer organisation reports.

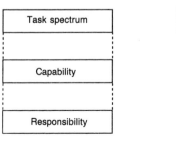

Balanced distribution   Unbalanced distribution

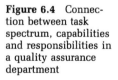

Figure 6.4 Connection between task spectrum, capabilities and responsibilities in a quality assurance department

The qualifications of quality assurers or developers can be considerably increased through job rotation. This can be done in such a way that a quality assurer works for one to two years in the development section and, vice versa, a developer about one to two years in the quality assurance section.

A further aspect concerns product and project responsibility. Any organisational measure involving the distribution of responsibility (e.g. two project managers for one project) cannot be accepted. This also applies to quality assurance. The responsibility for quality cannot be delegated to a quality assurance department. It remains with the person responsible for the product or the project.

The principles which must be observed in building the organisation of a quality assurance department can be summarised as follows:

- Highest possible degree of independence from the developer organisation.
- Direct reporting to top management/company management. This can be achieved through the appropriate position of the quality assurance department in the overall organisation structure.
- Indivisibility of product and project responsibility.

Experience shows that considerable effort by top management is necessary to implement these principles. Lack of management support, and lack of a clear understanding of the development process and of the requirements of quality assurance, frequently cause problems.

6.2 Operational organisation of a quality assurance system

By the operational organisation of a quality assurance system we mean the structuring of its working procedures. These working procedures must be established across projects at the project level and within individual project phases. In these working procedures, project staff as well as quality assurance staff are involved. The most important tasks which must become evident are [DGQ86]:

- quality planning;
- quality control;
- quality testing; and
- quality engineering.

The first three tasks were described in detail in Chapter 1. By quality engineering we mean the preparation and making available of scientific insights for the improvement of methods and means of quality assurance. This function is mostly found under the heading of software engineering and quality assurance in 'organigrams'. It is frequently organised in the form of a team.

An efficient operational organisation for a quality assurance system is marked by purposeful integration of the above tasks into the process model. This integration is documented in the project plans: in particular, in the quality assurance plan.

We assume that before the beginning of each phase certain prerequisites exist, such as the project contract or a preliminary study for the phase requirements analysis and definition or a log book and a requirements definition for the system design phase. Before a phase actually begins, the quality requirements regarding the process and the phase products must be defined. For example, for the requirements definition, features such as completeness, consistency, feasibility, comprehensibility and easy maintainability must be specified. All these requirements must be defined, if possible, in a quantifiable and testable form. This means that methods and resources must be identified in the quality assurance plan in order to guarantee the checking of these criteria.

At the start of the actual development, activities are initiated by the project leader. In parallel, quality assurance tasks can also begin. For example, the project staff responsible for quality assurance tasks or the quality assurance department can carry out release preparations. These include the creation of specifications and procedures for tests within a phase. When the phase results are available, either in part or completely, quality testing can begin. As a rule, phase results are subject to reviews.

Each quality test should be closed with the creation of a quality report (test report). Through these reports the test results are made available to those responsible for the project and to the staff. Quality reports are also an important element of the quality data system and the quality report system. The quality report is then evaluated by those supervising the project. These can include the project management and the quality assurance department. Here it is decided (so-called phase decision) whether the phase can be completed successfully and the phase deliverables can be released, or whether the phase items should be reworked. If it is decided that the phase results are acceptable, phase closure can be announced (see Figure 6.5).

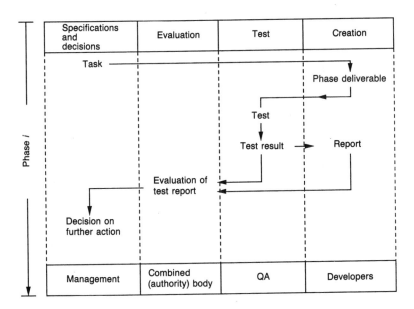

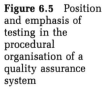

Figure 6.5 Position and emphasis of testing in the procedural organisation of a quality assurance system

The procedure organisation described above can be seen as a possible model for the interplay of quality assurance and development tasks.

Experience shows that in large computing organisations different types of quality assurance application are possible. Dette [Dett85] mentions in this context three possibilities which are used at IBM:

- *Assessment*. The assessment of a product begins after its completion. Since the sale of software to outside customers is becoming increasingly important, this procedure is quite common. Systematic tests are planned on the finished product and executed. The procedure is quite costly and can absorb up to 40 per cent of the development cost.
- *Project consultancy*. This is project support in the form of advice with the aim of achieving the set requirements. Permanent project understanding is not possible here, as it is in the case of assessment. Project consultancy is mostly applied in cases where groups contain inexperienced developers.
- *Project monitoring*. In this procedure, all development plans are evaluated. In doing so, the existence, completeness, executability and adherence to the plans are checked. In addition, partial assessments of milestones are worked out. They contain a description of the actual state of the project (project status), a summary of possible problems in order of urgency, and areas where milestones are still to be reached. The most important steps in this process are: creating a quality assurance plan; creating a milestone plan; and creating a partial assessment.

The three processes listed above are selected according to the situation and requirements of a project. Projects with a high risk and high cost should apply quality assurance project monitoring. Quality assurance achieved with the advice of consultants can help to reduce the risk, but it is no guarantee of project success. The form of assessment should be completed by the issuing of a certificate stating the applied quality assurance measures used in the development.

6.3 Documentation of the quality assurance system

Documentation is important for determining the contents of a quality assurance system (see Figure 6.6). The policy on software quality and software quality assurance within a computing organisation is fixed by directives for which company management is responsible. These directives refer to procedures, aims and responsibilities of company management with regard to software quality and its assurance. The aims can be detailed by means of strategies consisting of a combination of analytical, constructive and organisational quality assurance measures which show ways of achieving the quality goals.

For software quality assurance, a manual, a standard for software quality assurance plans and a standard for a quality model are made available. The software quality assurance manual is a guide through the quality assurance system (construction and process organisation). The manual also describes the

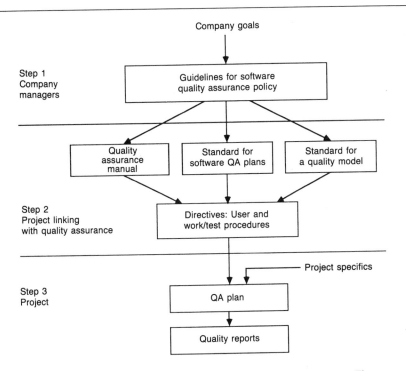

Company goals

Step 1
Company
managers

Guidelines for software
quality assurance policy

Quality
assurance
manual

Standard for
software QA plans

Standard for
a quality model

Step 2
Project linking
with quality assurance

Directives: User and
work/test procedures

Project specifics

Step 3
Project

QA plan

Quality reports

Figure 6.6 Significant documents in a quality assurance system

terminology, principles, responsibilities and processes of the system. The system is based on standards (for example, ISO 9001, 9002 or 9003) to which the manual refers.

This manual must be brought up to date from time to time with regard to the latest requirements or the latest software technology. The problem frequently lies in the size of the manual, which is caused by the inclusion of detailed descriptions of methods and tools which properly belong in separate procedures or project manuals.

In order to make the handling of the quality assurance manual easier, a structured document consisting of manual, directives and working/testing instructions is recommended (see Figure 6.7). The advantage of this document structure lies in its clear target-orientated and user-friendly documentation.

The company-specific standard for a software quality assurance plan must be orientated towards international standards, such as IEEE Std 730-1984 for software quality assurance plans.

A quality model helps in the selection of relevant process and product quality features and metrics. It supports quality planning (see section 1.4 and Appendices A1 and A2).

Directives and work/test instructions facilitate the selection and carrying out of quality assurance measures. The directives should contain details of the quality assurance measures necessary for a project on the basis of risk analysis. In this way, a better selection and a more efficient, project-specific application of quality assurance measures is achieved (see Figure 6.8).

Figure 6.7 Structure of documentation in a quality assurance system

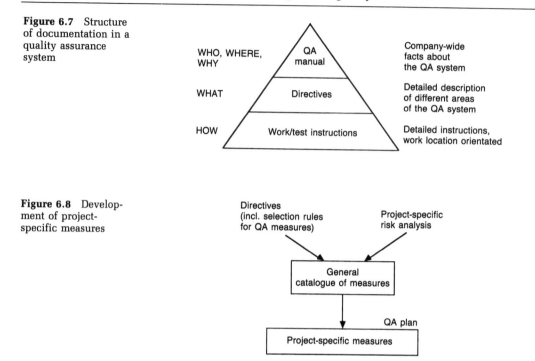

Figure 6.8 Development of project-specific measures

A project requires a software quality assurance plan. This plan must be aligned with other project plans. The plan describes which quality assurance measures apply to each phase. The effects and the efficiency of the selected measures must be recorded for each phase and passed on to project management and the quality assurance group. If necessary, these reports must be followed up with additional audits and correction measures in order to meet the specific requirements of a product or a phase.

There are a number of international and national standards or reference documents for quality assurance systems, such as the Standards IEEE, ISO, NBS, ANSI, DOD and AQAP ([Sanz87, Schu87], see Appendix A5). In Europe the ISO standards series 9000 are gaining in importance in quality assurance. These ISO standards demand a clear, layered and decentralised structure for quality assurance measures. The allocation of responsibilities, competencies and tasks must be made clear. Error prevention is considered much more important in these standards than in earlier standards [SAQ89].

The standardisation process in software engineering and in quality assurance has not been completed at the international or national level. Which international standards will eventually assert themselves for which areas of application will be discernible from specialist literature (standards institutes and specialist organisations, see Appendices A5 and A6).

6.4   Quality reports

Quality reports are of great importance if a quality assurance system is to function well. The purpose of the quality report is to make data available about the quality of the process and product to those who take the final responsibility.

By quality data we mean all data which relates to the quality of a process (e.g. number of milestones in a phase) or of a product (e.g. number of product errors within a period). Project management is particularly interested in the target quality data and deviation from it.

Quality data must be described with the following attributes:

- definition;
- validity;
- interpretation;
- application;
- cost; and
- registration/report.

The quality report provides the data which forms the basis for quality control. The actual collection is done through process audits and through reviews of phase results. An important source of quality data is product application. By means of a suitable report system (e.g. an information system for faults and incidents during product application) or by means of a system of metrics, experience of the product by the user, the customer and the maintenance organisation can be documented and evaluated.

This quality data is relevant for decisions to be undertaken by project management and for the organisation of line management in computing. A well-functioning quality report system guarantees clarity in the development process. It also provides a basis for evaluation, for the assessment of the status of the project, and for product development. On this basis, corrections can be proposed. Further purposes of a report system are the early recognition of higher-risk projects and the continuous reporting of actual values of quality metrics within organisational units that develop or maintain the software.

Examples of quality data in a report system are:

- completion metrics;
- proof of applied quality assurance measures;
- error and problem data;
- productivity metrics; and
- quality cost.

Completion metrics

These metrics give information about adherence to project completion dates. For the collection of data related to completion dates and time factors, data on the deviation from set completion dates and trends must be shown in the form of graphics. Completion metrics also provide information about reliability. Here are some examples:

- Percentage of work units with late completion of a phase. If this value is smaller than some limit (e.g. 20 per cent), we can speak of completion confidence.
- Percentage of work units in a phase where the cost is higher than planned. If this value is smaller than the limit (e.g. 10 per cent), we can also speak of completion confidence.
- Relationship between calendar-days and person-days. This value should, on average, not be smaller than a given limit (e.g. 3).
- Number of milestones passed/total number of milestones in a planned period.

Proof of applied quality assurance measures

In order to show management the volume and effectiveness of quality assurance measures, statistics with application metrics (e.g. how many reviews were carried out in each phase) must be developed. Examples of such proofs are the final test report, the review/management report and audit reports. These proofs give information about which results in a phase were tested according to the stipulations in the quality assurance plan, and whether the release of phase results can be recommended. When software tools are used for quality assurance measures (e.g. static program analysis), computer-supported evaluation can be applied. Examples of this are: how many programs have been analysed and in how many of these programs have anomalies been found (e.g. exceeding of complexity limits, non-conformance to standards)?

Error and problem data

Since errors and problems (e.g. incidents and gaps in the operation of an application) invariably lead to further cost and to loss of image/status, reports about this type of quality data are widely used.

Metrics in the form of the number of errors or the number of incidents per 1000 LOC within a stipulated period of time (e.g. month or quarter) are good indicators of the quality status of an application. Adequate support (e.g. a quality data system in the form of an incident report system) is an essential prerequisite for the recognition and evaluation of this kind of metric in the life cycle of an application.

Productivity metrics

In Chapter 2 the connection between quality and productivity in a system development was discussed. It is useful to observe quality and productivity simultaneously by means of metrics. Important productivity metrics are:

- development and production cost/1000 LOC on delivery of the product;

- maintenance cost per business year/1000 LOC of the previous version of the product; and
- maintenance cost per business year/number of errors in the business year.

The observation of productivity and quality metrics contributes to balanced project control. This method is also useful for the comparison of projects, of development units and of applied quality assurance measures.

Quality cost

The concept of quality cost frequently causes confusion in expert discussion. According to Crosby [Cros79] quality does not cost anything. If this were the case, problems with software quality and increasing maintenance costs would probably not occur. Reality shows that the opposite is true. The problem lies in the definition of quality cost. Often quality cost is thought to be those cost items which appear when development standards are not adhered to ('non-conformity cost'). But this does not deal fully with the problem either.

According to Dobbins and Buck [Dobb87] development and maintenance procedures are liable to shortcomings and errors. These result in the loss of value of a product and non-fulfilment of user and contractor requirements. Quality cost is expressed in monetary units relating to activities which prevent such devaluation (error prevention), increase the price (error removal) and examine whether the requirements are met (tests). Table 6.1 gives examples of these types of activity.

Table 6.1 Types of activity which cause quality cost [Dobb87]

Prevention	Test	Error correction
Training	Inspection	Revision
Planning	Testing	Modification
Simulation	Audit	Service
Modelling	Supervision	Delivery
Advising	Measuring	Recall
Certification	Verification	Correction
	Analysis	Regression test
		Error analysis

Quality data is made available in the form of quality reports. These reports inform the project team as well as the decision-making body external to the project team about quality assurance measures in each phase and about deviations from the project plan, as far as these relate to quality. When and how often quality reports must be produced can be stipulated in the quality assurance plan.

Two widely applied types of quality report are:

- Comments on the results of quality tests. These are also useful for the preparation of decisions about the final phase.
- Regular status reports about project progession, quality problems and quality assurance measures.

Quality reports are made for a project or for a department by the person responsible for quality assurance.

6.5   Tasks of a software quality assurance department

The Swiss Quality Assurance Working Party (Schweizerische Arbeitsgemeinschaft für Qualitätsförderung, SAQ) has defined the tasks of a central software quality assurance department [Jägg88]. They differentiate between two large groups of tasks: external project interface tasks and project development tasks.

The external project interface tasks are as follows:

Construction and maintenance of know-how in the area of quality assurance

- Creation and promotion of quality consciousness.
- Collection of company-specific know-how.
- Further training in the area of software engineering.
- Exchange of experience with other companies and quality assurance institutions.

Dissemination of know-how in the area of quality assurance

- Training courses and workshops.
- Advice on and support for the introduction of new methods and tools, in particular with regard to quality assurance.

Construction and maintenance of a quality assurance system

- Development and maintenance of a quality assurance manual.
- Development and keeping of a data collection and report system for quality data.
- Establishment of directives for quality assessment when purchasing software products.
- Analysis of weaknesses occurring during execution of the project and in the maintenance process of software products.
- Evaluation and introduction of aids and tools for quality assurance.
- Cost analysis of quality assurance.
- Creation and support of certification.

The project development tasks include the following:

Quality assurance planning

- Support in defining quality requirements.
- Support in the creation of the project-specific quality assurance plan and advice on the selection of constructive and analytical measures.
- Support when purchasing software and when subcontracting to other companies.

Quality testing

- Checking of phase results.
- Analysis of applied processes, aids and tools.
- Audit of projects.
- Audit of quality assurance of external contract partners.
- Quality assessment of software products.

Supervision and evaluation of correction measures

- Collection and evaluation of shortcomings which were noted when assessing product quality.
- Following up requests for alterations and correction measures.

The personnel of a quality assurance department must satisfy certain requirements. They must have substantial know-how in software engineering as well as practical experience in creating and maintaining software. A member of staff in quality assurance should also be able to advise and train staff. Many measures suggested by the quality assurance department can only be implemented into the project through advice and training. It is therefore necessary that these people have analytical, didactic and psychological abilities, especially in the areas of communication, motivation and instructing others (natural authority).

Many of the recommended directives can be followed and checked by use of tools. For the testing of directives special quality assurance tools such as static analysers are necessary. The quality assurance department must therefore work hand in hand with a software engineering group, if it exists, for the purpose of provision and maintenance of tools for quality assurance tasks.

6.6 Introductory measures and strategies for quality assurance systems

Experience is still limited in the introduction process for quality assurance systems. Only a few examples of the introduction of such systems are cited in the literature [Gust82, Chow85, Wall87a].

Lumbeck [Lumb82] notes some general steps for the introduction of quality assurance systems:

- *Creation of prerequisites for the introduction of a quality assurance system.* Before one can begin with the introduction of a quality assurance system, it is essential to check whether the existing life cycle matches the requirements or whether it must be revised. Depending on this, processes, methods and aids for the execution of quality assurance tasks must be made available. This means that reviews, for example, must be introduced or the testing method must be improved. Furthermore, documents such as a quality assurance manual, a standard and directives for the application of quality assurance plans must be created. This process must be supported by measures to enhance developers' consciousness of quality and quality assurance.

- *Introduction of a quality report system.* For the assessment of the economic viability of the planned quality assurance activities, measures for the establishment of a quality report system must be established. This enables the cost and usefulness of the selected quality assurance measures to be estimated and controlled.
- *Introduction of a basic system.* A minimum number of quality assurance measures is then stipulated and introduced. For example, a quality assurance manual is created and a review procedure introduced. In [SAQ88b] and [SAQ87], depending on the risk factor, on the accountability and on the degree of complexity of the products, three requirement steps are defined for a quality assurance system. This recommendation is particularly suited to the selection of quality assurance measures for the introductory system, depending on a given situation in an organisation. For the testing of the basic system, pilot projects must be planned and carried out.
- *Extension of the basic system.* If the basic system has proved to be acceptable, it should then be applied to all projects of an organisation. In order to implement this, quality assurance departments with the appropriate capabilities, responsibilities and organisational links must be set up. The extension of software quality assurance depends on the economic viability of the quality assurance system and on the risk profile of the project.
- *Execution of an audit of the quality assurance system.* At regular intervals, such as every two years, the economic viability and effectiveness of the quality assurance system must be tested. This is best done by means of an audit which includes, among other things, the quality assurance organisation. The result of this audit is an analysis of weak points and recommendations for improvements.

In order to speed up and improve the introduction of a quality assurance system, it is advisable to proceed on two levels: at the operative level, members of staff must be convinced that quality assurance is important; and management must be convinced that new features and changes during the introduction of a quality assurance system are necessary.

It is recommended that an organisation should create a working party for software quality assurance which will deal with the following tasks:

- creation of a technological overview within the theme 'Software engineering and software quality assurance';
- activating thought and opinion in connection with this theme, especially with regard to the establishment of a common terminology;
- analysis of weak points in the development process and in organisation structures;
- test runs of changes;
- consensus on concepts and on introductory steps in the quality assurance system; and
- channelling and discussion of propositions and recommendations which were

received either from members of staff or from the software quality assurance department.

The working party should include specialists such as staff from the quality assurance department, from the computing department and from the department responsible for the organisation plus user representatives and external specialists.

Alongside these it would be worthwhile to establish an organisational committee with the title 'Introduction of software quality assurance'. This organisational committee, which is directly answerable to management, should have the following tasks:

- promotion of necessary new initiatives and changes;
- control and avoidance of critical and risky measures; and
- creation of a draft for the introduction.

The members of this committee assert influence as representatives of top and middle management, leaders of quality assurance and important opinion bearers in the company.

In the following, a few measures will be described which proved to be successful during the introduction of a quality assurance system, the SPARDAT project [Wall87a]. The computing organisation where the system was introduced operates in the area of banking. As a first step within the framework of this project, the prerequisites for a quality assurance system were created. A quality assurance department was set up with one member of staff. Then a quality model for the specification of quality requirements (see Appendix A2) was developed. In parallel, the quality assurance manual and the standard for the quality assurance plan were created. In the second step, the basic system was tested in a pilot project called 'Customer self-service'. In the third step, the basic system was applied to a larger pilot project called 'Spar' and a number of extensions to the introductory system were carried out. In the fourth step, training in quality assurance was stipulated for all projects. This was followed by the compulsory introduction of the quality assurance system for all projects. In the fifth step, the effectiveness of the quality assurance system was tested by means of an audit.

It was noted as a positive feature that the central quality assurance department was designed to have an advisory function, and that from the very beginning no attempt was made to establish the quality assurance department as an independent examination and evaluation department. An important factor in the acceptance of the department was the absence of personnel evaluation. However, some members of the management tried to use quality assurance for this purpose. This could not be avoided.

The management and important opinion bearers supported the introduction of quality assurance. The principle that quality should not be neglected in order to gain time and save cost was observed by management and the project leadership. It also proved useful for each project to have a quality representative. During development this was the project leader, and in the maintenance phase it was the person responsible for the product. Particularly critical was the selection of the person to lead the quality assurance department. This selection had to be made with great care.

The entire introduction of the system in the SPARDAT project took approximately three years. The developer organisation had about 180 staff and 6,000 programs with approximately 4.7 MLOC.

During the introduction of the quality assurance system in SPARDAT, the following problems occurred:

- The absence of a practicable set of tools for determining quality requirements (quality model), for the creation of a defined quality (aids and tools for constructive quality assurance) and for proof of quality goals (test procedures and tools for testing).
- The absence of concrete statements with regard to the economic viability of quality assurance measures.
- Insufficient provision for cost/time of quality assurance measures in project calculations. It must be added here that information to this effect was missing at the planning stage, as already mentioned in the previous point.
- Insufficient motivation and lack of quality consciousness among the software developers and management.
- Personnel evaluation through quality assurance measures.
- Excessive expectations by management.

In conclusion, practical experience shows that the introduction and construction of a quality assurance system requires great efforts. The success of the introduction depends on technically competent and experienced staff among the quality assurance personnel. Support by top management in a computing organisation is also critical for the success of the introduction.

6.7   Cost-effectiveness observations

In many computing organisations there is no organised software quality assurance. Much has to be learned about the spreading of knowledge concerning the capabilities of software quality assurance. The capabilities of those responsible for software engineering are limited in many companies, and this, in turn, limits the possibilities of software quality assurance considerably.

Let us once again summarise what can be achieved through quality assurance:

- In the short term an improvement in product quality in all phases can be noted. This, in turn, increases the quality of intermediate and end products and the effectiveness of applied methods. Through the introduction and improvement of test and review procedures, for example, sources of errors in the development process can be considerably reduced.
- In the medium term the test cost can be reduced. Suitable review mechanisms (e.g. a quality report system) can eradicate sources of errors in the development process. In addition, methods and tools are better co-ordinated and this will increase productivity.

- In the long term it is probable that development cost can be reduced and development time in projects can be better planned and adhered to.
- The greatest benefit is a reduction in maintenance costs and an increase in productivity in the entire life cycle.

The problem of proving economic viability is due to the fact that the cost of quality assurance is not easily separated from the total cost of product development. The actual benefit of quality assurance can often be proved only indirectly. A quantitative proof of economic viability is seldom possible for reasons of complexity. Quality assurance must be looked upon as long-term investment. The greatest benefit of software quality assurance does not become evident until the maintenance phase of software products. This means that through quality assurance the maintenance and operational costs can be reduced considerably.

An important prerequisite for cost-effectiveness considerations is a quality report system which takes into account quality cost. The following paragraphs give some published values for the cost and effectiveness of quality assurance.

Ramamoorthy [Rama82] states the following rule: if the cost of quality assurance is doubled, one can assume that the maintenance cost will be reduced by approximately 50 per cent.

In projects with real-time software of more than 20 person-years, quality cost amounted to about 12 per cent of the entire project cost [Gust82]. Of this, 8 per cent was spent on software quality assurance. Experience in the military field showed that quality cost amounted to at least 10 per cent of the entire project cost [Snee88a]. Gustafson reports that development cost approximately doubled during the introduction of a quality assurance system [Gust82]. He explains this by the fact that development documents were created in a complete and consistent form for the first time. He states further that the life-cycle cost was reduced by approximately 70 per cent. Sneed gives a detailed report of the cost of quality assurance for each phase with and without tools [Snee88a]. He estimates that quality assurance in projects for commercial applications increases the project cost by approximately 35 per cent. On application of quality assurance tools, this cost is reduced to a mere 12 per cent.

Sneed, like many others, sees the largest savings and the greatest effectiveness of quality assurance in the maintenance phase. He assumes that today the relationship between maintenance cost and development cost is on average 60:40. With the help of quality assurance measures, approximately 40 per cent of maintenance cost and 30 per cent of life-cycle cost can be saved. He also points to the unquantifiable benefit of introducing of quality assurance.

In conclusion, the establishment of software quality assurance brings the following advantages:

- professional development and maintenance of software products;
- more clarity in the development process;
- early recognition of problems and shortcomings;
- reduction in maintenance and stabilisation of cost;
- reduction in operational cost;

- avoidance of non-production periods;
- improvement of status; and
- increased acceptance of the products among users.

By applying software quality assurance, we have the opportunity to come to terms with the complexity of software. Furthermore, software systems are then better equipped to meet the requirements of, and to satisfy, the user. Management gains more insight into the development and maintenance process through the aids of quality assurance, and also has the opportunity to reduce cost.

7 The future

The software industry is one of the growing markets in the economy. Through the internationalisation of markets, product liability and the increasing importance of software products in the environment, software quality assurance has become an indispensable aid. These trends give quality assurance a new dimension. How, for example, can systems which are knowledge based be tested? How can the quality of databases in different locations or operating systems be guaranteed? These are questions which go beyond the present state of technology in the field of software quality assurance.

In different sections of this book, current weak points and potential development possibilities of software quality assurance have been pointed out. Further development and research work are needed in the following areas:

Planning administrative quality assurance measures

- Software quality assurance systems that are orientated towards an international standard (e.g. ISO 9000–9004).
- Configuration management systems that support the entire life cycle, and which are integrated into a development and maintenance environment.
- Quality planning and control with the aid of quality models.
- Information systems for the development and maintenance of large amounts of software.
- Project cost calculations, which make value- and productivity-orientated project planning possible.

Analytical quality assurance measures

- Static analysers for the support of reviews.
- Test tools for multiple test repeats in the life cycle.
- A comprehensive metrics system for the control of development and maintenance processes and product evaluation in the life cycle.
- Fundamental research in the field of quality features and metrics.
- Application of knowledge-based systems for more effective quality evaluation in the life cycle.

Constructive quality assurance measures

- Software manufacturing in the form of a comprehensive software production environment with a software engineering databank.
- Object-orientated development methods and tools in the entire development cycle.
- Application of knowledge-based information systems for the promotion of quality in the life cycle.

Psychology-orientated quality assurance measures

- The concept of measures for a company culture which is conducive to software quality.
- Measures and technical aids to represent all aspects of non-concrete technical product software.

Despite all the progress that has been made, the software development process will be difficult to plan and to create in the future. This, of course, influences quality assurance. The abilities of qualified software developers and their quality consciousness will in future, as today, be the central element in successful quality assurance.

Appendix A1
McCall's quality model

One of the oldest and most frequently applied models is that of McCall [McCa77]. Other models such as that of Murine [Muri84] or that of NEC [Azum85] are derived from it. McCall's model is used in the United States for very large projects in the military, space and public domain. It was developed in 1976–7 by the US Airforce Electronic System Division (ESD), the Rome Air Development Center (RADC) and General Electric (GE) with the aim of improving the quality of software products. One explicit aim was to make quality measurable.

McCall started with a volume of 55 quality characteristics which have an important influence on quality, and called them 'factors'. For reasons of simplicity, McCall then reduced the number of characteristics to eleven:

- efficiency;
- integrity;
- reliability;
- usability;
- accuracy;
- maintainability;
- testability;
- flexibility;
- interface facility;
- transferability; and
- reusability.

Each of these characteristics is determined by certain criteria, and for each characteristic metrics are given for the purpose of quantitative assessment, although this is difficult if not, in some cases, impossible. In this way, a regression formula is defined for each characteristic:

$$QC = r_1 . m_1 + r_2 . m_2 + \ldots + r_n . m_n$$

where QC is the individual characteristic, r_i are the regression coefficients and m_j the metrics.

Directives for the specification and for measuring the characteristics were created for the application of the model. The structure of this model shows the quality on the top level consisting of eleven characteristics. In my view some of the characteristics make others partially redundant. This impairs the clarity of their labels. For example, maintainability is understood only as the cost/effort involved in localising and removing an error. However, maintainability generally also includes changes which are necessary

219

Figure A1.1 The characteristic 'accuracy' and its features

Figure A1.2 The characteristic 'maintainability' and its features

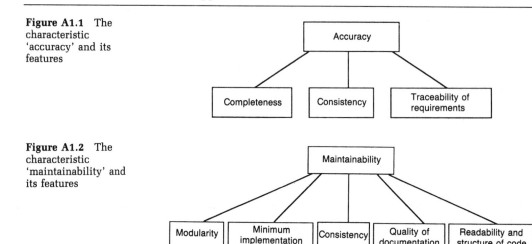

to fit the application environment of a product. This is included in the characteristic 'flexibility'.

At the next level down, the characteristics are separated (see Figures A1.1 and A1.2) into features. One particular feature can be allocated to several characteristics. This means that the separation structure is no longer a tree but a network. For example, the feature 'consistency' can be allocated to the characteristics 'accuracy', 'reliability' and 'maintainability'. The separation hierarchy becomes opaque. Metrics are needed to quantify the level of features.

As an example of the assessment of a metric, the evaluation of the features 'readability' and 'structure' of codes (code simplicity) of a module is shown in Figure A1.3).

Of interest are the varied views of the user of the model elements. McCall differentiates between three user points of view:

- Characteristics are specified from the manager and user points of view.
- Features are specified from the developers' points of view.
- Metrics are specified from the operating point of view. They consist of stipulations which prescribe how the individual metrics should be calculated.

The quality characteristics, following McCall, are separated into application areas as follows:

- product application;
- product revision; and
- changes during product use.

For product application the following characteristics are relevant:

- accuracy (does the product do what I expect it to do?);
- reliability (how satisfactorily does the product fulfil the requirements over a given period of time?);
- efficiency (does the product utilise hardware resources well?);
- integrity (is it safe?); and
- usability (can I easily learn to handle it?).

a) For each module the following 9 metrics are calculated:

(1) Have complicated Boolean expressions (BE) been used?

$$\left(1 - \frac{\text{No. of } BE}{ELOC}\right) \dots\dots\dots\dots\dots\dots\dots\dots\dots\dots\dots \underline{}$$

(2) Are there jumps into/out of loops?

$$\left(\frac{\text{No. of loops with only 1 entry and 1 exit}}{\text{No. of loops}}\right) \dots\dots\dots\dots \underline{}$$

(3) Were loop indices modified?

$$\left(1 - \frac{\text{No. of modified loops}}{\text{No. of loops}}\right) \dots\dots\dots\dots\dots\dots \underline{}$$

(4) How many jump labels (JL) are there?

$$\left(1 - \frac{\text{No. of } JL}{ELOC}\right) \dots\dots\dots\dots\dots\dots\dots\dots \underline{}$$

(5) Were all arguments passed as parameters?

$$(1/0) \dots\dots\dots\dots\dots\dots\dots\dots\dots\dots\dots\dots\dots\dots \underline{}$$

(6) Are all variable names clear? (1/0) $\dots\dots\dots\dots\dots\dots\dots\dots$ $\underline{}$

(7) Have no mixed expressions been used?

$$(1/0) \dots\dots\dots\dots\dots\dots\dots\dots\dots\dots\dots\dots\dots \underline{}$$

(8) How many nesting levels (NL) are there?

$$\left(\frac{1}{\text{Max. } NL}\right) \dots\dots\dots\dots\dots\dots\dots\dots\dots\dots\dots \underline{}$$

(9) How many branches are there?

$$\left(1 - \frac{\text{No. of branches}}{ELOC}\right) \dots\dots\dots\dots\dots\dots\dots \underline{}$$

Total module value $\dots\dots\dots\dots\dots\dots\dots\dots\dots\dots\dots\dots \underline{}$

b) System metrics $\left(\dfrac{\Sigma_i \text{ module value}_i}{\text{No. of modules}}\right) \dots\dots\dots\dots\dots\dots \underline{}$

Figure A1.3 Evaluation of the features 'readability' and 'structure of codes' in a module

For product revision the following characteristics are important:

- maintainability (can I correct a fault easily?);
- flexibility (can I execute a change easily?); and
- testability (can I test the product without additional cost after making changes?).

The following characteristics are important in the case of changes during product use:

- portability (can I use the product on different hardware?);
- reusability (can I use parts of the product for other applications?); and
- interfacing (can I create interfaces to other systems?).

These three areas help to select the relevant characteristics, features and metrics for a specific project environment.

A1.1   Quality characteristics

In the following, a description of the individual quality characteristics listed in McCall's model is given, and a way of evaluating them is also suggested.

Efficiency

Definition
The volume of code or computer resources (e.g. time, external storage requirements) needed for a program so that it can fulfil its function.

We can distinguish between features for execution efficiency and features for storage efficiency. Execution efficiency can be measured relatively simply with the use of comparable code or by carrying out a 'benchmark' test. The storage efficiency of the code can be checked with a checklist which takes into account data packages, paging rates, code density and the like.

Integrity

Definition
The extent to which illegal access to the programs and data of a product can be controlled.

Integrity is concerned with safeguarding against illegal access and with the testability of changes to the product.

Features

- Access control.
- Testability of changes to system elements.

Metrics which are obtained from checklists describe the instrumentation of the product which facilitates access to the system and makes evaluation possible.

Reliability

Definition
The extent to which a program can be maintained so that it can fulfil its specific function.

Features

- Error tolerance.
- Consistency.
- Accuracy.
- Simplicity.

Reliability is related to error-free functioning of a software product during a defined period of time.
    A simple metric is the number of errors per 1,000 LOC which occur within a period

of time (e.g. three months) after the release of the product. Experience shows that between one and three errors occur per 1,000 LOC.

Usability

Definition
The cost/effort to learn and handle a product.

Features

- Retraining.
- User-friendliness.

A system is not usable if it is difficult to handle, or if a large amount of retraining is necessary, or if the trainee has to have special abilities.

Metrics are related to measuring training costs and evaluating ease of product handling.

Usability is one of the most important characteristics. If the end user has difficulties in handling the software product, other characteristics cannot make up for this shortcoming.

Accuracy

Definition
The extent to which a program fulfils its specification.

Features

- Completeness.
- Consistency.
- Easy interpretation of requirements.

The characteristic 'accuracy' is related to the design and implementation of a product. Accuracy is influenced by phase results and by the extent to which these correspond to the project standards and specifications. Accuracy is a function of the features of consistency, completeness and easy interpretation of requirements. Completeness and absence of inconsistency are features which must be observed and checked throughout the development process: for example, in the form of reviews. There are a number of software tools (see sections 3.5.1 and 4.1.3) which especially help us to secure the features of accuracy.

From the scientific point of view, accuracy plays an important part in the life cycle of a product if the maintenance cost is assessed at 60–80 per cent and if one looks at the high cost of error correction. The metrics applied here relate to the evaluation of consistency, testing for completeness, software architecture, comments and the structuring of documentation in the early phases.

Maintainability

Definition
The cost of localising and correcting errors

Features

- Consistency.
- Modularity.
- Minimum effort in implementation.
- Readability and code structure.
- Quality of documentation.

This is a particularly important quality characteristic from the point of view of economic viability. It is essential to bear in mind that the dominant cost in the life cycle of a product is running and maintenance cost. A well-structured and adequately planned development process is a prerequisite for good maintainability.

Consistency is ranked as number five in the hierarchy of importance after modularity, quality of documentation, minimum effort in implementation and readability/code structure. Metrics are related to consistency checklists, the structure and sparsity of designs and minimum implementation, the simplicity of code, the number and quality of comments and the readability of the implementation language.

Testability

Definition

The cost of program testing for the purpose of safeguarding that the specific requirements are met.

Features

- Modularity.
- Simplicity and code structure.
- Instrumentation.
- Quality of documentation.

Testability is that characteristic which is influenced by the relationship between software design and implementation according to product specification. Metrics are related to the structure of the design, the system and module complexity, the simplicity of the code, checklists for testing, the number and quality of comments and the expressiveness of the implementation language.

Flexibility

Definition

The cost of product modification.

Features

- Modularity.
- Simplicity of design and code.
- Quality of documentation.
- General validity.

Flexibility is present if new requirements can be accommodated. Metrics describe internal and external interfaces, the general validity of data and program structures, extendability, the quantity and quality of comments and the expressiveness of the implementation language.

Ease of interfacing

Definition
The cost of connecting two products with one another.

Features

- Modularity.
- Compatibility.

This characteristic is relevant in systems with high interface requirements. It is gaining in importance, since more and more systems are becoming linked with others via local or global communication networks. Quality metrics are related to the module structure, the quality of comments and the use of interface standards.

Portability

Definition
The cost of transferring a product from its hardware or operational environment to another.

Features

- System software and machine independence.
- Modularity.
- Quality of documentation.

This characteristic provides information on the cost of transferring a system from one environment to another or on to a new one. By environment we mean a new machine, a new operating system, etc. Metrics are related to the modularity of implementation, the number and quality of comments, and the independence from machine and operating system details.

Reusability

Definition
The cost of transferring a module or program to another application.

Features

- Simplicity and code structure.
- System software and machine independence.
- Quality and availability of documentation.
- Modularity.
- Independence of application in databases, operating system details, hardware details and specific algorithms.

The difference between this and transferability lies in the use of part of the code in other application systems in the same environment. Metrics of this characteristic relate to the number and the quality of comments, the system software independence and the machine independence.

A1.2   Application of the model

The model is used for:

1. The specification of quality goals through selection and weighting of characteristics, features and metrics.
2. The evaluation of goals, characteristics, features and metrics specified under 1.

The first of these applications should take place as early as possible in the development process, namely when the system and software requirements are being specified. Not all projects require the same characteristics; the category of application and the user environment also play a part.

McCall differentiates between metrics which predict and those which show anomalies. Prediction metrics are important for the evaluation of the development process. If, for example, the assessment value of the data structure were too small, problems could occur during product application if the demands on performance increased.

When the quality characteristics, features and metrics have been selected and their meaning has been determined, these data must be recorded in the requirements specification. The metrics for the entire life cycle are determined through analytical quality assurance methods.

The responsibility for the collection and availability of metrics should be forwarded to a separate locality. If this office is located in the development organisation, it is important to ensure that it retains a high degree of autonomy. The responsibility for this task should be allocated early in the development process.

The structure of code may serve as a simple example of a feature test. The structure of code is tested with the use of a checklist, and is evaluated and recorded on a point scale, e.g. between 0 (code is not structured) and 6 (code is very well structured).

Based on the experience of McCall, it is known that metrics have a indicative character in the phases of requirements analysis and definition, design and coding (part views of the initial product quality are recognisable). In the test process, very good measurable metrics exist already (e.g. number of located errors, test coverage, test costings in hours). The actual product quality comes to light during product application (see Figure A1.4). In the operation phase, for example, the number of operational faults or software errors can be used as a basis for the evaluation of product quality.

It is obvious that the cost of testing and evaluating software quality must be in an economic

Figure A1.4 Characteristics of metrics in a life cycle

Development				Application
Requirements	Design	Code	Test	Operation
↓			↓	↓
Indicative metrics More subjective More objective			Well-measurable test metrics	Actual proven product quality (operation metrics)

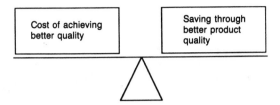

relation to the cost of a product. The cost of the achievement of better quality and the cost of measuring this quality must be in a balanced relation to the savings which are spread over the entire life cycle (see Figure A1.5).

It is possible to draw the following conclusions about McCall's quality model:

- The concepts of some characteristics and features are partly imprecise and overlap.
- The selection of metrics is often faced by subjective influences.
- The relationships between characteristics, features and metrics are based on hypotheses, and their value is, at times, questionable.
- The model is designed for commercial applications.
- The model is based on a practice-orientated procedure for planning and assessment of quality.

The potential use of McCall's model lies in its integrated application within the process. The model provides, among other things, a procedure for quality assurance similar to that of an engineering approach, and a method which takes into account software quality throughout the entire life cycle of the product.

Appendix A2
The SPARDAT quality model

Here a quality model is introduced which was based on the model of Softwaretest e.V. [Schw84].

The aim of the development of this quality model — and, in particular, of the definition of the quality characteristics and features — was to create an evaluation system for quality statements which can be applied in the individual phases of software development. This system was also intended to allow intermittent assessment of developing quality and, if the need arose, the application of measures for quality management (see [Wall87a]).

The structure of the SPARDAT quality model is demonstrated in Figure A2.1. By base characteristic we mean a characteristic which is not based on other characteristics.

For some features, metrics in the form of known measurements can be given (e.g. for the feature 'control flow complexity', the metric of McCabe). With other features, only those metrics are possible which are values based on experience and which are in the form of checklists. The yes/no answers are weighted on a point scale and summed.

Figure A2.2 gives a first overview of the structuring of characteristics which are defined in the model. The three most significant categories of characteristics are applicability, maintainability and adaptability.

A general overview of quality characteristics is given in Figure A2.3. This consists of several possibilities for describing software quality through hierarchically separated quality characteristics.

The model was created for and applied to a commercial software development environment in banking.

Other approaches (e.g. [Pabs85]) restrict quality planning and evaluation to the user interface. This is often justified; external products are often selected and compared where no detailed information about system development is available.

Figure A2.1 Structure of the SPARDAT model

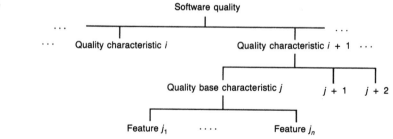

228

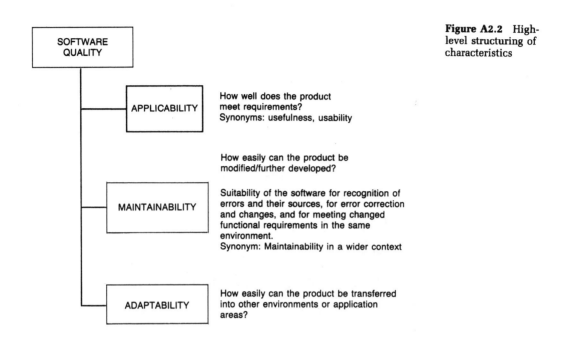

Figure A2.2 High-level structuring of characteristics

SOFTWARE QUALITY

APPLICABILITY — How well does the product meet requirements?
Synonyms: usefulness, usability

MAINTAINABILITY — How easily can the product be modified/further developed?
Suitability of the software for recognition of errors and their sources, for error correction and changes, and for meeting changed functional requirements in the same environment.
Synonym: Maintainability in a wider context

ADAPTABILITY — How easily can the product be transferred into other environments or application areas?

Figure A2.3 Overview of quality characteristics

APPLICABILITY

- Functionality
    - Function coverage
    - Consistency
- Capability
    - Correctness
    - Reliability
    - Security
    - Robustness
    - Executability
    - Efficiency
        - Storage efficiency
        - Execution efficiency
    - Ease of interfacing
- User friendliness
    - Ease of learning
    - Ease of handling
    - Effectiveness
    - Uniformity

MAINTAINABILITY

- Transparency
- Maintainability
    - Changeability
    - Correctability
    - Extendability
- Testability

ADAPTABILITY

- Portability
- Reusability

A2.1 Characteristics and features

This is a detailed overview, relating in particular to features of the SPARDAT model. In the following, the basic characteristics with their determining features are described in some detail.

Function coverage

Definition
Completeness of product functions in relation to functional requirements.

Function coverage tells us whether all stipulated requirement functions are present.

Features
1. *Functional completeness*

Object	Testing point
Requirements definition	Specification review
Design documentation (draft)	Design review
Operational system	Program test
User manual	Final test, project review

Checklist questions:

- Does the software design conform to the requirements?
- Has each function been tested with at least one black-box test case?
- Have missing product functions been documented and justified?

Metrics:

- Metrics for ranking the product functions against requirements

$$FKZ = \frac{\text{Number of actual functions in the product}}{\text{Number of specified functional requirements}} \cdot 100$$

- Test coverage metrics
  Percentage of tested functions relative to all functions.

2. *Completeness of documentation*
The central point of enquiry here is whether all functions have been documented in accordance with a specified standard.

Object	Testing point
Operational system/help system	Program test, final test
User documentation	Final test, project review
Project documentation	Project review
System documentation	Final test

Checklist questions:
- Is each function documented?
- Does the document show company names, type of document, project, version and originator?
- Is the documentation up to date?
- Does an index with page numbering exist?
- Is the documentation laid out clearly?
- Are instructions given in simple language?
- Are instructions made attractive (with graphics, examples)?
- Are instructions realistic?

Functional consistency

Definition

Functional consistency means that two or more functions should not cancel each other out, either at the specification level, or at the implementation level.

Features

1. *Inconsistency between functions*

Checklist questions

- Do inconsistencies exist between functions at the specification level?
- Do inconsistencies exist between functions at the implementation level?

Examples:

- Function: Customer debt in excess of credit limit leads to bar on supply for this customer.
- Function: Customer debt in excess of credit limit in the case of a regular customer has no effect on supply of goods to this customer.

This example shows an inconsistency of specification, since a regular customer is also a customer.

2. *Inconsistency between the operational system and documentation*

Object	Testing point
Specification	Specification review
Design	Design review
User documentation	Specification review, final test
Operational system	Program test, system test

Checklist questions:
- Are there inconsistencies between the dynamic product behaviour and the product descriptions (the help texts, the user documentation)?

Correctness

Definition

By correctness we mean that characteristic of a product which satisfies its specification [DGQ86].

Object	Testing point
Specification	Specification review
Design	Design review
Source code	Program review
Test documentation	Program review
Operational system	Program test, integration/system test

Basically, we can only observe whether a characteristic exists (1) or not (0). In large software systems, proof can be obtained by means of validation and verification activities (analytical quality assurance measures). We estimate the volume and effectiveness of these activities by noting features.

Features

1. *Current review level*: relationship between the number of elements which have been reviewed and total number of elements from the development plan.

2. *Current test level*: test coverage metrics such as C_0 or C_1.

3. *Module-related consistency*

Checklist questions:

*   Do all module designs conform with the program directives?
*   Have standard routines been used in each module (e.g. for input/output)?
*   Are all used variables initialised or calculated in the program, or do they come via an external interface?

Reliability

Definition

Reliability is that characteristic of a product which ensures that it meets the requirements specification during a given application time [DGQ86, Boeh78].

Object	Testing point
Operating statistics	Period of operating

Features
Evaluation of reliability in an applied situation, assessed by the number of product faults or crises.

1. *Product faults*

$$PF = \frac{\text{Number of faults}}{1000 \ LOC} \quad \text{per time unit and application}$$

2. *Power*
Object: error analysis reports

$$P = \frac{\text{Number of error analysis reports}}{1000 \ LOC} \quad \text{per time unit and application}$$

3. *Complaint metrics*
Object: error statistics, complaint statistics
A customer complaint is the existence of an error and/or customer enquiries

$$CM = \frac{\text{Number of complaints}}{1000 \ LOC} \quad \text{per time unit and application}$$

4. *Application*
A = Number of errors per 1000 LOC within 3 months after product application (e.g. at $NEC \leq 1$).

5. *Availability*
Object: on-line statistics
Availability is the period of time in which the system is available related to the target time.

$$AV = \frac{\text{Target time} - \text{Down time}}{\text{Target time}} \quad \text{(target time, e.g. 9 hours per day)}$$

Security

Definition
Security is the characteristic which prevents interference and illegal use from external sources [DGQ86].

Object	Testing point
Specification	Specification review
Design	Design review
Operating system	Program review
Organisation documentation	Project review

The individual objects are being tested for security precautions and their application.

Features

1. *Security control/access protection*

Checklist questions:

- Which kinds of control mechanism exist?
- Do protection/access systems (ID, Password) exist for data (files, input/output data); programs; program functions; tools?
- Do sensible organisational measures exist for the protection of the system from illegal access?

2. *Special security measures built into the system*

Checklist questions:

- How is legality determined for new users?
- Do policing functions exist (e.g. software, hardware monitors)?
- Do detection functions exist which recognise incorrect functions/faults and activate correction measures (e.g. error-handling module)?
- Are critical data stored more than once (generations, deletion after a determined time period)?
- Is legality of access tested (protected transactions)?
- Is database access control guaranteed (authorising table, privacy locks)?
- Is an access log and report function installed?
- Are functions installed which register illegal access?
- Are functions installed which record data present?
- Is the user encouraged to change his/her password from time to time?

3. *Safety measures*

Checklist questions:

- Is data storage safe from the risk of fire and theft?
- Are duplicates kept in different buildings?
- Is an emergency electricity supply available?
- Does an alternative (reserve) computer centre exist?
- Does a time-monitored catalogue for tapes exist?
- Are standby computers installed (e.g. dual processor system, duplicate peripherals)?
- Does a hierarchical archiving system for disks and tapes exist?
- Are disks and tapes periodically saved by duplicating stored data?
- Is a data back-up method installed with transaction logging?
- Is data transmission made reliable and secured through parity checks, self-correcting codes, multiple transmission with comparison, acknowledgements of arrival and recording of message count?
- Has a safety measure been installed against data corruption (checksums, identification)?

4. *Data protection measures*

Checklist questions:

- Have all data protection laws been observed, e.g. access control, distribution, internal control, input accuracy control, supplier control, program transfer control?

Robustness

Definition

Robustness is that characteristic of a system which guarantees that its functionality is maintained even if specified operational and utilisation requirements are violated.

Object	Testing point
Source code	Program review
Operational system	Program review, program test

Features

Acceptability checks and error treatment

Metric:

$$R = \frac{\text{Number of checked input items}}{\text{Total number of input items}}$$

Checklist questions:

- Is there a format check on input values?
- Are check digits used?
- Are error reports identified in accordance with company-specific standards for error reports?

Executability

Definition

Executability is that characteristic of a product which guarantees its functioning in the product environment.

The application of these characteristics is here restricted to organisations which use their products in computer centres.

Object	Testing point
Computer centre documentation	Final test
Operational system	Final test

Features

Completeness, clarity of layout, of instructions and of computer centre documentation

Checklist questions:

- Does each program have at least one operator/user instruction?
- Is computer centre documentation available?

Efficiency

Definition
Efficiency is that characteristic of a product which ensures good resource usage.

For measurements, time behaviour (e.g. response times) and the use of resources such as storage would be relevant.

Object	Testing point
Standard configuration	Program test
Terminal protocol	Program test
Computer centre documentation	Final test

The following comments on efficiency features relate to third-generation languages (e.g. COBOL, FORTRAN, PL/1).

Features

1. *Storage efficiency*
The storage efficiency of programs is determined by those features which influence the data storage requirements (DGQ86).
Object: object code in main storage

$$E_s = \text{maximum main storage in bytes at run-time}$$

Checklist questions:

* Is storage space optimised?
* Are as few parts of the object code as possible in the main storage at run-time?
* How much is in the working storage?

2. *Execution efficiency*
The execution efficiency of programs is determined by those features which influence execution time (e.g. computation time, input/output time).
   Metrics are in general run-times and response times.

Checklist questions:

* Has execution efficiency been tested against requirements?
* Are run-time optimised algorithms being used for run-time critical functions?
* Are as many data items as possible held in storage?
* Has attention been paid to minimum reloading when overlay structures are being used?
* Has the use of external storage been minimised (e.g. through optimum blocking)?
* Are the response times satisfactory with respect to selected user functions?

Execution efficiency and storage efficiency are competing features. The optimisation of one feature causes a reduced performance in the another.
   It is also useful to differentiate between the efficiency of the selected algorithm and the efficiency of its implementation. In the former case, an attempt is made to evaluate the efficiency of the selected algorithm with the aid of algorithm analysis and of complexity

theory. In the latter case, the behaviour of the program in the specified hardware and software system is examined.

Linkability

Definition
Linkability is the characteristic of a product which allows interfacing with other products.

An example is where a newly inserted transaction reduces the performance of the entire system.

Object	Testing point
Operational system	System test
Test documentation	System test

Features

1. *System test in a simulated product environment*

Checklist questions:

• Have all programs of the network used been run without obvious problems?

2. *Interface test*
Objects in this case are the quantitative data flow across interfaces and the compatibility of interfaces.

Checklist questions:

• Have volume tests ben carried out which check the amounts given in the requirement definitions?
• Have data formats and communication protocols (especially in computer networks) been standardised?

Learnability

Definition
Learnability is the characteristic of a product which enables the user to learn how to handle it easily.

Object	Testing point
Prototype	Specifications review
Operational system	Final test
Training materials	Final test
Operation training system	Final test

The measurable object in this instance is the time needed to learn how to handle a product.

Features

1. *Learning time*

LT = average time needed to learn the handling of a product in application examples. For the measuring of learning time the following procedure is recommended:

*   Selection of two standard application cases and two special application cases (exceptional situations in the use of the product).
*   Measuring of the time needed for the learning of the two standard applications and the two special applications.

2. *Prerequisites of learnability*

Checklist questions:

*   Are training materials available?

3. *Evaluation of quality of training materials*

Checklist questions:

*   Does a comprehensive and relevant training example exist?
*   Are the materials: easy to understand; detailed; well presented; clear; unambiguous; self-explanatory?

4. *Help/tutorial system*

Checklist questions:

*   Is a computer-supported help system available?
*   Is a computer-supported tutorial system available?

Ease of handling

Definition

Ease of handling is that characteristic of a product which determines how easily it can be used, how it behaves when errors and faults occur, and whether it contains appropriate help functions and manageable person—machine interfaces.

Object	Testing point
Specification/prototype	Specification review
Operational system	Final test
User documentation	Final test

Features

1. *Input and output*
(a) *Reader-friendly text presentation*

Checklist questions:

- In western cultures we read from left to right; therefore the cursor is situated in front of the input field. Is this always the case?
- People always read from the top down; therefore instructions are at the top and the menu and input fields below. Is this always the case?
- People start counting from 1; therefore selection codes should begin with 1 and count on without gaps. Is this always the case?
- Are capital letters and small letters available?
- Is the readability of figures supported by columns and grouping?

(b) *Dialogue model*

Answers to the following checklist questions should be easily found:

- Where am I? (Is the program situation identifiable, e.g. via status messages?)
- Can the sequence of selection and processing steps be reconstructed?
- Have the next selection and processing steps (in particular, the orderly exit from the program) been made clear?

2. *Rationalisation*

Checklist questions:

- Are tasks clearly ordered for the user?
- To what extent is the information clear enough for the user to carry out his or her tasks quickly and appropriately?
- Does the software enhance the execution of the task?

Effectiveness

Definition
Effectiveness is that characteristic of a product which gives the user utmost support for the completion of his or her task.

Object	Testing point
Specification/prototype	Specification review
Operational system	Final test
User documentation	Final test
User questionnaire	Introduction/location

Features

Location-orientated task completion

Checklist questions:

- Can information be made available fast enough?
- Is the information sufficiently relevant?
- Is the information accurate enough?
- Is the product adaptable to change in the organisation, and can it cope with changes in data volume in special cases?
- Can errors be corrected at low cost?

Uniformity

Definition
Uniformity is that characteristic of the product which guarantees consistency for all functions and takes into account all defined standards.

Object	Testing point
Specification/prototype	Specification review
Design	Design review
Source code	Program review
Operational system	Final test

Features

1. *Standards*

Checklist questions:

- Have company-specific standards been adhered to?
- Were international standards taken into account?

2. *Uniform system behaviour*

Checklist questions:

- Is the construction of screen templates and output reports uniform?
- Do terminal keys have the same function throughout an application?

Transparency

Definition
Transparency is that characteristic of a product which enables the maintenance programmer quickly to recognise and understand the structure and construction of the product.
  Synonyms: Understandability, analysability.

Features

1. *Quality of documentation*

Checklist questions:

*   Is maintenance documentation available?
*   Is a product overview available?
*   Is the structure of the product presented in a diagram?

2. *Complexity of the software*
(a) *Complexity on system level*

The following metrics should be given:

*   Number of programs (on-line, batch) in an application.
*   Number of interfaces to related applications.

(b) *Complexity of source code*

The control flow complexity based on McCabe is established for each program.

$$SC = 1 - \frac{\text{Number of binary decision instructions}}{\text{Number of non-comment instructions}}$$

Object	Testing point
Source code	Program review/code inspection

Changeability

Definition
Changeability is that characteristic of a product which facilitates a recognised and limited alteration correctly and quickly.

Object	Testing point
Design	Design review
Source code	Program review

Features
Modularisation
Metric: Module size in NLOC
    Experience shows that a manageable module size (MS) is an important prerequisite for changeability [DGQ86, Asam86]. The problem lies in the defining of sensible limits of size, which in turn depends on the programming language and the problem structure. A recommended value in LOC is speculative, but in an evaluation situation a recommended

value is always desirable. The recommended value for COBOL 74 programs is $MS \leq 500$ NLOC.

Checklist questions:

- Is access to databases, files, tables and other central data structures encapsulated (data abstraction)?
- How many and which predictions and known facts about the module environment led to the current program procedure?
- How many and which calling relations does the test object have?

Correctability

Definition
Correctability is that characteristic of a product which facilitates error search and error correction.

Object	Testing point
Design	Design review
Source code	Program review
Error statistic	Company

Features

1. *Error finding*

Checklist questions:

- How many and which error reports can be attributed to a known error situation?
- Is additional information available which can be used for analyses in the case of an error (traces, analysis protocol?)
- Are aids for temporary error correction available?
- Are aids available for compilation which test possible syntax, datatype and interface errors?
- Does a test harness (test environment) exist to facilitate the testing of a module in isolation?

2. *Removal of defects*

Checklist questions:

- Has the program been subjected to risk evaluation?
- Are measures for the removal of defects defined?

Otherwise the features for changeability apply.

Extendability

Definition
Extendability is that characteristic of a product which facilitates the extension of the product without high cost.

Object	Testing point
Design	Design review
Source code	Program review

Features

Structure flexibility

Checklist questions:

- Do the requirements imply possible extensions?
- Is the product structure still recognisable despite maintenance activities?
- Were possible extensions included in the design?
- Which and how many interfaces can be altered without affecting the product structure?
- Have possible special circumstances been catered for?

Otherwise the features for changeability apply.

Testability

Definition
Testability is that characteristic of a product which facilitates testing of the accuracy of an alteration, of the correction of an error, or of an extension.

Features

Accessibility

Object	Testing point
User documentation	Final test
Computer centre documentation	Final test
Organisation documentation	Final test

Checklist questions:

- Does a product description exist?
- Is the product clearly labelled with version numbers?
- Have all operating instructions been given (hardware, operating system, help programs, etc.)?

- Is a condensed description of all user functions available?
- Are all interfaces to other systems described?
- Are operating instructions given?
- Does a list of all available documentation exist?
- Are instructions for the installation of the product available?
- Does maintenance documentation exist?
- Does the maintenance documentation comply with the company standard?

Portability

Definition
Portability of a program system is the characteristic of the system which allows it to be transferred to different computer systems.

Object	Testing point
Design	Design review
Source code	Program review

Metric
Gilb's portability metric [Gilb77]

$$PM = 1 - \frac{ET}{ER}$$

where *PM* is the simple conversion of a system from one configuration into another
ET is the resources (manpower, time, engineering time) necessary to port a system from the original environment into the target environment
ER is the resources (manpower, time, engineering time) necessary to implement a system in the original environment.

Features

Dependence on engineering and company systems

Checklist questions:

- Have hardware-dependent details been encapsulated in individual modules?
- Does the code refer to service programs of the company system; can routines from the system library be used?
- Will direct access to the company system be necessary within the modules?

Reusability

Definition
Reusability is the suitability of a product or individual parts of a product for transfer into another field of application in an unchanged system environment.

Object	Testing point
Design	Design review
Source code	Program review

Features

General validity

General validity is the ability of a building block to be used in its present form in different applications. This depends to a high degree on the generality of the task. Examples of such tasks can be found in company module libraries (index of general modules).

Metric

$$GV = \frac{\text{Number of modules used in other applications}}{\text{Total number of modules in an application}}$$

Checklist questions

- Have data structures or abstract datatypes been used during the design stage?
- Have input/output functions been implemented in specific modules?
- Have application- and hardware-related functions been implemented in separate independent modules?

Further features used are accessibility and quality of documentation as well as modularisation.

A2.2   Application and evaluation of the model

The model has been successfully applied in SPARDAT since 1986. Its application starts in the specification phase of the project procedure.

The application of the model can be summarised as follows:

- Determining of the three most important characteristics for a product (target definition and requirements specification to be used as a template).
- Selection of features, defining and, if necessary, extending them.
- Determining of target features (target qualities).
- Agreement on the above points between contractor, developer and management.
- Selection of quality assurance measures to reach quality goals. These are listed in the quality assurance plan.
- Quality goals and quality assurance measures to be improved and adapted before each phase; to implement quality assurance plan.

The quality model serves as an aid for the optimisation of quality goals and quality requirements in the selection process and for their precise and complete specification.

In SPARDAT a separate one-day course has been arranged. The quality assurance department gives project guidance and demonstrates the model on concrete projects.

The quality model is an active aid for the implementation of quality assurance tasks with the use of the quality assurance plan. The model should be continually extended and modified in response to requirements and changing development processes. The characteristics of maintainability and adaptability show some overlapping features. Improvements can be made by combining both characteristics into one, or by applying new distinguishing features.

Appendix A3
Review forms

Review profile

System: _____   Release: _____
Date: _____   Unit:_____

Review for the testing of:

☐ requirements definition   ☐ detailed design   ☐ test plan
☐ high-level design   ☐ code   ☐ test cases

Size of test objects: [LOC, pages of documentation]: _____
                      [$V(g)$, number of files/DB]: _____

Review repeat: ☐ yes   ☐ no
Goals:

Commentary:

Review preparation

System: _____   Release: _____

Date: _____   Unit: _____

Review participants: _____

Role: ☐ Author   ☐ Moderator   ☐ Participant

Pre-review meeting: ☐ yes   ☐ no

Test object received on: _____

Preparation time in hours: _____

Discovered faults/problems

Position [page/line]   Description

_____   _____
_____   _____
_____   _____
_____   _____
_____   _____
_____   _____
_____   _____
_____   _____
_____   _____
_____   _____
_____   _____
_____   _____
_____   _____
_____   _____
_____   _____
_____   _____
_____   _____
_____   _____
_____   _____
_____   _____
_____   _____
_____   _____
_____   _____
_____   _____
_____   _____
_____   _____

Review fault list

System: _____   Release: _____
Date: _____   Unit: _____
Moderator: _____

Review for testing of:

☐ requirements definition   ☐ detailed design   ☐ test plan
☐ architectural design   ☐ code   ☐ test cases

Document	Position	Description of faults	Fault Type	Class
_____	_____	_____	___	___
_____	_____	_____	___	___
_____	_____	_____	___	___
_____	_____	_____	___	___
_____	_____	_____	___	___
_____	_____	_____	___	___
_____	_____	_____	___	___
_____	_____	_____	___	___
_____	_____	_____	___	___
_____	_____	_____	___	___
_____	_____	_____	___	___
_____	_____	_____	___	___
_____	_____	_____	___	___
_____	_____	_____	___	___
_____	_____	_____	___	___
_____	_____	_____	___	___
_____	_____	_____	___	___
_____	_____	_____	___	___
_____	_____	_____	___	___
_____	_____	_____	___	___
_____	_____	_____	___	___
_____	_____	_____	___	___
_____	_____	_____	___	___
_____	_____	_____	___	___
_____	_____	_____	___	___
_____	_____	_____	___	___
_____	_____	_____	___	___
_____	_____	_____	___	___
_____	_____	_____	___	___

Types of fault: interface (IF), data (DA), logic (LO), input/output (IO), performance (PE), human factors (HF), standard (ST), documentation (DO), syntax (SY), test environment (TE), test coverage (TC), other (O)

Fault class: incomplete (IC), wrong (WR), obsolete (OB)

Summarising fault report

System: _____   Release: _____
Date: _____   Unit: _____
Moderator: _____

Review for testing of:
☐ requirements definition   ☐ detailed design   ☐ test plan
☐ architectural design   ☐ code   ☐ test cases

Type of fault	Fault class			Total
	IC	WR	OB	
Interface (IF)				
Data (DA)				
Logic (LO)				
Input/output (IO)				
Performance (PE)				
Human factors (HF)				
Standard (ST)				
Documentation (DO)				
Syntax (SY)				
Test environment (TE)				
Test coverage (TC)				
Other (O)				
Total				

Management report

System: _____   Release: _____
Date: _____   Unit: _____
Moderator: _____

Review participants: _____
_____

Review for the testing of:
☐ requirements definition   ☐ detailed design   ☐ test plan
☐ architectural design   ☐ code   ☐ test cases
Pre-review meeting: ☐ yes   ☐ no
Duration: _____   Number of participants: _____

Number of review meetings: _____
Total time of review meetings: _____
Total number of review participants: _____
Total preparation time: _____
State of test object: ☐ released
                       ☐ in revision
                       ☐ review repeat necessary

Estimated review time [days]: _____
Review ready by: _____
Actual review work: _____
Review repeat planned for: _____
Commentary:

Signature of Moderator: _____

Appendix A4
Maintenance documents

Maintenance requirements

Initiator of maintenance requirement: _____

Application: _____

Module/program name: _____

to be completed by: _____

Urgency: ☐ emergency   ☐ high   ☐ medium   ☐ low

Description of problems/requirements:

Identification of maintenance case: _____

Identification of maintenance action: _____

Estimated cost: _____

Start of maintenance work: _____

Estimated end of maintenance work: _____

Accumulated cost: _____

Effects on the product/affected module/commentary:

Accepted/rejected: _____

Maintenace work finished on: _____

Date/signature: _____

Maintenance report

Identification of the maintenance case: _____

Identification of the maintenance executive: _____

Type of maintenace requirement:

☐ correction   ☐ adaptation   ☐ tuning   ☐ extension

Causes and effects of maintenance requirements:

Where was the maintenance problem caused, and which effects do the solving of the problem have?

	Cause	Effect on
Requirements definition		
Design		
Code		
Software environment		
Hardware environment		
Optimising		
Other		

Identification of all modules/systems which were maintained and information about the cost/effort involved in change:

Module identification	Number of maintained lines			Effort in person-hours
	source code	documentation	total	
Total				

Commentary on maintenance work done:

Date/signature: _____

Appendix A5
Important international standards institutes and their software engineering standards

Institute of Electrical & Electronics Engineers (IEEE)
1730 Massachusetts Ave. NW
Washington, DC 20036-1903
Tel.: 202/371-0101

American National Standards Institute (ANSI)
1430 Broadway St.
New York, NY 10018
Tel.: 212/354-3300

Software Engineering Standards and Guides (ANSI/IEEE):

729-1983	Standard Glossary of Software Engineering Terminology
730-1984	Standard for Software Quality Assurance Plans
828-1984	Standard for Software Configuration Management Plans
829-1983	Standard for Software Test Documentation
830-1984	Guide to Software Requirements Specifications
983-1986	Guide for Software Quality Assurance Planning
990-1987	Guide for the Use of Ada as a Program Design Language
1002-1987	Standard Taxonomy for Software Engineering Standards
1008-1987	Standard for Software Unit Testing
1012-1986	Standard for Software Verification and Validation Plans
1016-1987	Recommended Practice for Software Design Descriptions
1042-1987	Guide for Software Configuration Management
1058.1-1987	Standard for Software Project Management Plans
1063-1987	Standard for Software User Documentation

International Standards Organization (ISO)
1 rue de Varembé
CH-1211 Genève 20
Tel.: 022/734 12 40

The following committees and working groups are of interest to software engineering and quality assurance:

- TC97   Information Processing Systems
- SC7   Software Development and System Documentation
- TC176   Quality Assurance
- SC2/WG5   Software Quality Assurance

On the basis of Standards ISO 9000–9004 a pre-standard for quality assurance (N33, Quality Systems — Guidelines for Software Quality Assurance) is being developed in group ISO/TC176/SC2/WG5.

Standards Administration Office
Institute for Computer Science and Technology
U.S. Department of Commerce
Springfield, VA 22161

FIPSPUB.38   Guidelines for Documentation of Computer Programs and
               Automated Data Systems
FIPSPUB.64   Guidelines for Documentation of Computer Programs and
               Automated Data Systems for the Initiation Phase
FIPSPUB.99   A Framework for the Evaluation and Comparison of Software
               Development Tools
FIPSPUB.101   Guideline for Life Cycle Validation, Verification and Testing of
               Computer Software
FIPSPUB.105   Guideline for Software Documentation Management
FIPSPUB.106   Guideline for Software Maintenance

Military Software Engineering Standards:
- United States

  DOD-STD-2167A   Defense Systems Software Development
  DOD-STD-2168   Defense Systems Software Quality Program
  DOD-STD-480B   Configuration Control — Engineering Changes, Deviations
                   and Waivers
  DOD-STD-1838   Military Standard Common Ada Programming Support
                   Environment (APSE) Interface Set (CAIS)
  MIL-STD-1815A   Ada Programming Language
  MIL-S-52779A   Software Quality Assurance Program Requirements
  MIL-STD-1679   Weapons Systems Software Development
  MIL-Q-9858A   Quality Program Requirements
  MIL-STD-109B   Quality Assurance Terms and Definitions
  MIL-STD-499A   Engineering Management
  MIL-STD-1456   Contractor Configuration Management Plans
  MIL-STD-490A   Specification Practices
  MIL-STD-1521B   Technical Reviews and Audits for System Equipment and
                   Computer Programs
  MIL-STD-847B   Format Requirements for Scientific and Technical Reports
  MIL-STD-483A   Configuration Management Practices for Systems,
                   Equipment, Munitions, and Computer Programs
  MIL-HDBK-334   Evaluation of a Contractor's Software Quality Assurance
                   Program

- Europe (NATO)

AQAP-13	NATO Software Quality Control System Requirements
AQAP-14	Guide for the Evaluation of a Contractor's Software Quality Control System for Compliance with AQAP-13
AQAP-15	Glossary of Terms Used in QA-STANAG and AQAP

Appendix A6
Specialist organisations for quality assurance

(a) In German-speaking countries

- Germany
  Deutsche Gesellschaft für Qualität (DGQ)
  Kurhessenstr. 95
  60431 Frankfurt am Main

- Austria
  Österreichische Vereinigung für Qualität (ÖVQ)
  Wiedner Hauptstr. 63
  A-1045 Wien

- Switzerland
  Schweizerische Arbeitsgemeinschaft für Qualitätsförderung (SAQ)
  Postfach 2613
  CH-3001 Bern

(b) In European countries
European Organization for Quality Control (EOQC)
This is the umbrella organisation of all European specialist quality organisations: The addresses of committees and sections can be obtained via the national standards organisations.

(c) International

International Academy for Quality (IAQ)
IAQ-Administrative Office
c/o Deutsche Gesellschaft für Qualität
Kurhessenstr. 95
60431 Frankfurt am Main

Appendix A7
Quality testing of software

Gütegemeinschaft Software e.V. (GGS)
Lyoner Str. 18
Postfach 71 08 64
60528 Frankfurt am Main
Tel.: 069/6603-534
The quality and test regulations of software are documented in:

- Software Gütesicherung RAL-GZ901
  Güte- und Prüfbestimmungen Software
  Berlin, Beuth Verlag, Nov. 1985

- DIN V66285
  Anwendungssoftware, Prüfgrundsätze
  Berlin/Köln, Beuth Verlag, Okt. 1985

Procedure for obtaining the 'Quality Label Software'

The applicant, usually a member of the quality association, has developed a software product which fulfils the quality and testing regulations set by the quality association. This 'Quality Label Software' is proof of a high performance standard for the software user.

The applicant, therefore, has to submit his or her software product to an authorised test station for testing.

The conditions for testing are:

- Program: tested for completeness of functions, accuracy, user-related robustness, uniformity and clarity of error messages, uniformity of dialogue behaviour, consistency.
- Product description: checked for completeness and testability.
- User documentation: tested for completeness, consistency, clear presentation.

After a positive outcome of testing, the quality committee issues the applicant with a certificate. The certificate contains the exact title of the software product and allows the applicant to label his or her product with the label 'Quality Label Software' (in German: 'Gütezeichen Software').

Appendix A8
Glossary

Audit

An activity to determine through investigation the adequacy of, and adherence to, established procedures, instructions, specifications, codes and standards or other applicable contractual and licensing requirements and the effectiveness of the implementation.

Baseline

A configuration which is selected and released at a particular time in the development process.

Certification

Certification follows testing and evaluation of a software product or of a quality assurance system and consists of a written acknowledgement of conformance of the product with stipulated requirements.

Company culture

The totality of thinking (ideas, standards, philosophy), of feeling (values, ethics) and of actions (attitudes, strategies, working practices) which are initiated and adopted by a company.

Computer Aided Software Engineering (CASE)

The production and development of software with computer-based tools, resulting in a high degree of automation.

Constructive Quality Assurance

The application of technical, organisational or psychological means and aids with the aim of developing or maintaining a product with specific attributes by minimising the number of faults and errors during the development and maintenance process.

Debugging

The process of locating, analysing and correcting faults and errors.

Defect

A deviation from the expected behaviour of a feature.

Efficiency

Fast response times and high utilisation of storage capacity.

Equivalence class

In the context of testing, a set of items/values each of which is 'equivalent' to other members of the same class (same effect, discover same error types and produce output of the same nature).

Error	A discrepancy between the computed, observed or measured value or condition and the true, specified or theoretically correct value or condition (ANSI).
Estimating	The evaluation of an expected feature whereby the product which is being developed or finished is used in an actual application.
Failure	Where the unit under consideration ceases to function correctly.
Fault	The inability of an entity to perform its function.
Feature	An attribute/property of a product, activity or a characteristic which allows quantitative and qualitative comparison and measurements.
Formalism	A well-defined textual or graphical notation.
Hypertext system	A system for storing, connecting and performing selective searches on graphical and textual data. The base text is structured in the form of information nodes and dynamically activated links.
Measuring	The collecting of values with the aid of tools in the development/maintenance process or in a software product.
Method	A detailed approach to the achieving of prescribed goals.
Metric	A quantitative characteristic/feature which describes the requirements (e.g. implementation requirements) which are assigned to a characteristic/feature.
Predictions	The expected behaviour of a feature. The evaluation is achieved with the help of a model description of the product or its application area.
Principle	A fundamental notion on which our actions are based.
Procedure	A practical solution to a problem.
Process metric	A metric which can be used to measure the characteristics of the methods, techniques and tools employed in acquiring, developing, verifying and operating the software.
Process model	An idealised and abstract description of a development and maintenance process. The transformations of process results are implemented through activities. A minimal description of a process comprises all types of activities and results as well as their interconnections.
Product metric	A metric which can be used to measure the characteristics of the delivered documents and software.
Quality	The totality of characteristics and features of a product or service which bear on its ability to satisfy given needs.

Quality assurance	Procedures, techniques and tools applied by professionals to ensure that a product meets or exceeds prescribed standards during a product's development cycle. Without specific prescribed standards, quality assurance entails checking that a product meets a minimum level of excellence acceptable to industry and/or commerce.
Quality assurance plan	An aid for the planning and control of quality assurance for a software project. It contains all planned and achieved quality assurance measures, and therefore provides evidence that the software product has been developed with quality in mind.
Quality data	All the data encountered in the development process of a software product which has been subjected to a formal approach to achieving quality in the product (e.g. number of milestones passed in a phase, number of errors in a product discovered within a period of the product's use).
Quality feature	An attribute which contributes to the quality of an entity under consideration.
Quality management	The control, management and correction of the implementation of a deliverable with the aim of fulfilling the prescribed requirements.
Quality model	An aid for planning and specifying quality requirements.
Quality planning	The determining of requirements related to the development process and the product, taking into account implementation possibilities. In practice, features and their goals or contraints are selected, classified and evaluated.
Quality policy	The intentions and aims of an organisation with regard to quality, as declared by its management.
Quality testing	The determining of the extent to which a unit meets the prescribed requirements.
Re-engineering	The restructuring of a software product with the aim of improving quality features such as efficiency, testability, readability.
Review	A more or less formally planned and structured analysis and evaluation process, in which project results are presented to a team of evaluators who will comment on them and/or approve them.
Software configuration	The collection of software items which are, at some point in their life-cycle, related to each other. A software element or software configuration item is either the smallest indivisible part in a system or a collection of items which make up a configuration.
Software configuration management	The deliberate use of a combination of methods, tools and aids which support and control the

	development and maintenance of a software product as it goes through different phases during development and new versions and releases during maintenance.
Software engineering	A discipline which provides the developer with engineering methods and economic procedures, enabling him/her to generate and maintain high-quality software (Bauer).
	It is the development of a software product under at least one of the following conditions:
	1. More than one person develops and uses the software product.
	2. More than one generation of the software product is created (Parnas).
Software maintenance	The planned and systematic correction, modification or extension of a software product.
Software product	This consists of source code, object code and documentation.
Statistical analysis	The testing and evaluation of quality features of a product using software tools — especially its form, structure, contents or documentation.
Symbolic program execution	This is achieved with the use of program paths whereby expressions are mathematically verified against predefined conditions and requirements.
Technique	A combination of principles, methods, formalisms or tools.
Testing	The process of exercising or evaluating a system or system component by manual or automated means to verify that it satisfies specified requirements, or to identify differences between expected and actual results (IEEE Std 729-1983).
Tool	A computer-supported aid with which a software product or its components are created, tested, generated and managed, or with which the development and maintenance processes are planned and controlled.
Validation	The testing and evaluation of a software product at the end of the development process in order to show that the product meets its requirements.
Verification	Tests and evaluations by which agreement between intermediate and end results of a phase in the life cycle are shown.
Version	A collection of software elements which are related by 'variant of' and 'revision of'.

References

[Abi88]   Abi, R., 'Software Maintenance: Tools and Techniques', *System Development*, August 1988, pp. 3−6.

[Abra87]   Abramowics, K., *et al.*, 'DAMOKLES: Entwurf und Implementierung eines Datenbanksystems für den Einsatz in Software-Produktionsumgebungen', *GI-Softwaretechnik-Trends*, Vol. 7, No. 2, 1987, pp. 2−21.

[Albr79]   Albrecht, A., 'Measuring Application Development Productivity', *Proc. of IBM Application Development Symposium*, Oct. 1979, pp. 83−92.

[Albr83]   Albrecht, A., Gaffrey, I., 'Software Function, Source Lines of Code and Development Effort Predication: A Software Science Validation', *IEEE Transactions on Software Engineering*, Nov. 1983, pp. 639−48.

[Alfo77]   Alford, M., 'A Requirements Engineering Methodology for Real-Time Processing Requirements', *IEEE Transactions on Software Engineering*, SE-3, No. 1, 1977, pp. 60−9.

[Alfo85]   Alford, M., 'SREM at the Age of Eight', *IEEE Computer*, Vol. 18, No. 4, 1985, pp. 36−46.

[Arno82]   Arnold, R., Parker, D., 'The Dimensions of Healthy Maintenance', *Proc. of 6th Int. Conf. on Software Engineering*, Sept. 1982, pp. 10−27.

[Arth85]   Arthur, L.J., *Measuring Programmer Productivity and Software Quality*, Wiley & Sons, 1985.

[Asam86]   Asam, R., Drenkard, N., Maier, H.-H. *Qualitätsprüfung von Softwareprodukten*, Siemens AG, 1986.

[Azum85]   Azuma, M., Sunazuka, T., Yamagishi, N., 'Software Quality Assessment Technology', *Proc. of 8th Int. Conf. on Software Engineering*, 1985, pp. 142−8.

[Azum87]   Azuma, M., 'Software Quality Assurance', *Vortragsmanuskript zum Vortrag*, Vol. 12, No. 6, 1987 an der ETH Zürich.

[Bake75]   Baker, F., 'Structured Programming in a Production Programming Environment', *IEEE Transactions on Software Engineering*, SE-1, No. 2, 1975.

[Balz82]   Balzert, H., *Die Entwicklung von Software-Systemen*, BI, 1982.

[Balz83]   Balzert, H. (ed.), *Software-Ergonomie*, Teubner, 1983.

[Balz85]   Balzert, H., 'Phasenspezifische Prinzipien des Software Engineering', *Angewandte Informatik*, Vol. 3, 1985, pp. 101−10.

[Balz88a]   Balzert, H., Wix, B. (eds), *Softwarewartung*, BI, 1988.

[Balz88b]   Balzert, H., 'Aspekte der Qualitätssicherung in einer integrierten Entwicklungsumgebung', Softlab Congress '88, 'Strategien der Software-Entwicklung', Tagungsunterlagen, 1988.

[Barn82]   Barnes, J., *Programming in Ada*, Addison-Wesley, 1982.

[Bart84]   Bartsch-Spörl, B., 'Wie fördert man die Entstehung von projektbegleitender Dokumentation?', *Proc. of. COMPAS'84*, 1984, pp. 61–9.

[Basi83]   Basili, V., Selby, R., Phillips, T., 'Metric Analysis and Data Validation Across FORTRAN Projects', *IEEE Transactions on Software Engineering*, SE-9, No. 6, 1983, pp. 652–63.

[Basi84]   Basili, V., 'Presentation to IEEE Working Group for Software Productivity Metrics', Nashua, NH, Sept. 1984.

[Basi87]   Basili, V., Baker, F., Selby, R., 'Cleanroom Software Development: An Empirical Evaluation', *IEEE Transactions on Software Engineering*, Vol. 13, 1987, pp. 1027–37.

[Baze85]   Bazelmans, R., 'Evolution of Configuration Management', *ACM SIGSOFT Software Engineering Notes*, Vol. 10, No. 5, 1985, pp. 20–9.

[Beie88]   Beierle, D., Olthoff, W., Voss, A., 'Qualitätssicherung durch Programmverifikation und algebraische Methoden in der Softwareentwicklung', *Informatik-Spektrum*, Vol. 11, No. 6, 1988, pp. 292–302.

[Bers79]   Bersoff, E., Henderson, V., Siegel, S., 'Software Configuration Management: A Tutorial', *IEEE Computer*, Jan. 1979, pp. 6–14.

[Bers80]   Bersoff, E., Henderson, V., Siegel, S., *Software Configuration Management*, Prentice Hall, 1980.

[Bers84]   Bersoff, E., 'Elements of Software Configuration Management', *IEEE Transactions on Software Engineering*, SE-10, No. 1, 1984, pp. 79–87.

[Bert84]   Bertelsmann Datenverarbeitung, *Workshop zum Bertelsmann DV-Modell*, Seminarunterlagen, May 1984.

[Bige88]   Bigelow, J., 'Hypertext and CASE', *IEEE Software*, March 1988, pp. 23–7.

[Birk82]   Birkenbihl, V., *Kommunikationstraining*, Goldmann, 1982.

[Biro85]   Birolini, A., *Qualität und Zuverlässigkeit technischer Systeme*, Springer, 1985.

[Bisc89]   Bischofberger, W.R., Pomberger, G., 'SCT: A Tool for Hybrid Execution of Hybrid Software Systems', *Proc. of the 1st Conference on Modula-2*, Bled, Oct. 1989.

[Blac77]   Black, R., *Effects of Modern Programming Practices on Software Development Costs*, IEEE Compcon, Fall, 1977.

[Blas85]   Blaschek, G., 'Statische Programmanalyse', *Elektronische Rechenanlagen*, Vol. 2, 1985.

[Boeh73]   Boehm, B., 'Software and its Impact: A Quantitative Assessment', *Datamation*, Vol. 19, No. 5, 1973, pp. 48–59.

[Boeh76a]   Boehm, B., Brown, J.R., Lipow, M., 'Quantitative Evaluation of Software Quality', *Proc. of 2nd Int. Conf. on Software Engineering*, 1976, pp. 592–605.

[Boeh76b]   Boehm, B., 'Software Engineering', *IEEE Transactions on Computers*, Dec. 1976, pp. 1226–41.

[Boeh78]   Boehm, B., *Characteristics of Software Quality*, North-Holland, 1978.

[Boeh79a]   Boehm, B., *Guidelines for Verifying and Validating Software Requirements and Design Specification*, Euro IFIP, 1979, pp. 711–19.

[Boeh79b]   Boehm, B., 'Software Engineering: R&D Trends and Defense Needs', in *Research Directions in Software Technology*, P. Wegner (ed.), MIT Press, 1979, pp. 44–86.

[Boeh81]   Boehm, B., *Software Engineering Economics*, Prentice Hall, 1981.

[Boeh84]   Boehm, B., *et al.*, 'A Software Development Environment for Improving

Productivity', *IEEE Computer*, June 1984, pp. 30–43.

[Boeh86]   Boehm, B., 'A Spiral Model of Software Development and Enhancement', *ACM SIGSOFT Software Engineering Notes*, Vol. 11, No. 4, 1986, pp. 22–42.

[Boeh87]   Boehm, B., 'Improving Software Productivity', *IEEE Computer*, Sept. 1987, pp. 43–57.

[Boeh88]   Boehm, B., 'A Spiral Model of Software Development and Enhancement', *IEEE Computer*, May 1988, pp. 61–72.

[Boeh89]   Boehm, B., 'Project Management Principles and Practice', in *Taking CASE into the 1990s*, DEC-Tagung, Tagungsband, C. Gerelle (ed.), Genf, 1989.

[Boud88]   Boudier, G., *et al.*, 'An Overview of PCTE and PCTE(+)', *ACM SIGSOFT*, Vol. 13, 1988, pp. 248–57.

[Brer88]   Brereton, P., *Software Engineering Environments*, Wiley & Sons, 1988.

[Broo75]   Brooks, F., *The Mythical Man-Month*, Addison-Wesley, 1975.

[Brya87]   Bryan, W.E., Siegel, S.G., 'Software Configuration Management: A Practical Look', in *Handbook of Software Quality Assurance*, G. Schulmeyer, J. McManus (eds), Van Nostrand Reinhold, 1987.

[Buck81]   Buck, F., *Indicators of Quality Inspections*, IBM Tech. Rep. 21.802, Sept. 1981.

[Budd86]   Budde, R., Kuhlenkamp, K., Züllighoven, H., 'Prototypenbau bei der Systemkonstruktion: Konzepte der Systementwicklung', *Angewandte Informatik*, Vol. 5, 1986.

[CAIS88]   KIT, *Common APSE Interface Set (CAIS)*, proposed DOD-STD-1838A, 1988.

[Camp87]   Campbell, I., 'Standardization, Availability and Use of PCTE', *Information and Software Technology*, Vol. 29, No. 8, 1987, pp. 411–14.

[Case85]   Case, A., 'Computer Aided Software Engineering (CASE): Technology for Improving Software Development Productivity', *Database*, Fall, 1985, pp. 35–43.

[Char86]   Charette, R., *Software Engineering Environments*, McGraw-Hill, 1986.

[Chow85]   Chow, T.S., 'Implementation of Software Quality Assurance Programs', in *Tutorial: Software Quality Assurance — A Practical Approach*, T.S. Chow (ed.), IEEE Computer Society Press, 1985, pp. 443–7.

[Chro86]   Chroust, G., *et al.*, 'Modellierungsprobleme bei der maschinellen Unterstützung eines Vorgehensmodells', in *Die Zukunft der Informationssysteme: Lehren der 80er Jahre*, A. Schulz (ed.), Springer, 1986.

[Chro89]   Chroust, G., 'Application Development Project Support (ADPS)', *ACM SIGSOFT Software Engineering Notes*, Vol. 14, No. 5, 1989.

[Chry78]   Chrysler, E., 'Some Basic Determinants of Computer Programming Productivity', *Comm. of the ACM*, Vol. 21, No. 6, 1978, pp. 472–83.

[Clar81]   Clarke, L.A., Richardson, D.J., 'Symbolic Evaluation Methods: Implementations and Applications', in *Computer Program Testing*, B. Chandrasekaran (ed.), North-Holland, 1981.

[Clar84]   Clarke, L.A., Richardson, D.J., 'Symbolic Evaluation: An Aid to Testing and Verification', in *Software Validation*, H.-L. Hausen (ed.), North-Holland, 1984, pp. 141–66.

[Coll87]   Collofello, J., Buck, J., 'Software Quality Assurance for Maintenance', *IEEE Software*, Sept. 1987, pp. 46–51.

[Conn88]   Connors, T., Lyngbake, P., 'Providing Uniform Access to Heterogeneous Information Bases', in *Advances in Object Oriented Database Systems*,

Springer LCNCS 334, Sept. 1988.

[Cont86]   Conte, S.D., Dunsmore, H.E., Shen, V.Y., *Software Engineering Metrics and Models*, Benjamin/Cummings, 1986.

[Craw85]   Crawford, G., Fallah, M., 'Software Development Process Audits: A General Procedure', *Proc. of 8th Int. Conf. on Software Engineering*, 1985, pp. 137–41.

[Cros79]   Crosby, P., *Quality is Free*, New American Library, 1979.

[Curt81]   Curtis, B., 'Substantial Programming Variability', *Proc. of IEEE*, Vol. 69, No. 7, 1981.

[Daen78]   Daenzer, W.F., *Systems Engineering*, (2nd edn), P. Hanstein, 1978.

[DeMa78]   DeMarco, T., *Structured Analysis and System Specification*, Prentice Hall, 1978.

[DeMa82]   DeMarco, T., *Controlling Software Projects*, Yourdon, 1982.

[Dene80]   Denert, E., Hesse, W., Projektmodell und Projektbibliothek: Grundlagen zuverlässiger Software-Entwicklung und -Dokumentation; *Informatik-Spektrum*, Vol. 3, 1980, pp. 215–28.

[Dene86]   Denert, E., 'Software Engineering in der Praxis', Vorlesungsskript, TU München, 1986.

[Dett85]   Dette, W., 'Qualitätssicherung', in *Methoden und Werkzeuge zur Entwicklung von Programmsystemen*, W.E. Proebster, *et al.* (eds), Oldenbourg, 1985.

[Deut82]   Deutsch, M.S., *Software Verification and Validation*, Prentice Hall, 1982.

[Deym84]   Deym, A., *et al.*, *Planung durch Kooperation*, Siemens, 1984.

[DGQ86]   DGQ/NTG, *Software-Qualitätssicherung*, Beuth, 1986.

[Diek83]   Diekow, S., *DV-Anwendungsprojekte*, (2nd edn), Oldenbourg, 1983.

[Dies81]   Diesteldorf, H., Bons, H., van Megen, R., 'Strukturierte Gruppengespräche bei der Software-Entwicklung in der Praxis', *Informatik Fachberichte* 2/81, Univ. of Köln, 1981.

[Dijk75]   Dijkstra, E., 'Correctness Concerns', in 'SIGPLAN Notices', *Proc. of Int. Conf. on Reliable Software*, Vol. 10, 1975, pp. 546–50.

[Diss86]   Dissmann, S., Zurwehn, V., Vorschlag für ein sichtenorientiertes Qualitätsmodel', *Forschungsbericht*, No. 11, Lehrstuhl Software-Technologie, Universität Dortmund, May 1986.

[Dobb87]   Dobbins, J.H., Buck, R.D., 'The Cost of Software Quality', in *Handbook of Software Quality Assurance*, G. Schulmeyer, J. McManus (eds), Van Nostrand Reinhold, 1987.

[DOD86]   United States Department of Defense, *Military Standard Common Ada Programming Support Environment (APSE) Interface Set (CAIS)*, DOD-STD-1838, 9 Oct. 1986.

[Dunn84]   Dunn, R.H., *Software Defect Removal*, McGraw-Hill, 1984.

[End86]   End, Gotthardt, Winkelmann, *Softwareentwicklung*, Siemens AG, 1986.

[Endr88]   Endres, A., 'Software-Wiederverwendung: Ziele, Wege und Erfahrungen', *Informatik-Spektrum*, Vol. 11, No. 2, 1988, pp. 85–95.

[ESF89]   ESF, 'ESF/OSS Requirements Specification', draft, March 1989.

[Evan87]   Evans, M.W., Marciniak, J.J., *Software Quality Assurance and Management*, Wiley & Sons, 1987.

[Faga76]   Fagan, M., 'Design and Code Inspections to Reduce Errors in Program Development', *IBM Systems Journal*, Vol. 15, No. 3, 1976.

[Faga86]   Fagan, M., 'Advances in Software Inspections', *IEEE Transactions on Software Engineering*, SE-12, No. 7, 1986.

[Fair85] Fairley, R., *Software Engineering Concepts*, McGraw-Hill, 1985.

[Färb86] Färberböck, H., 'LITOR-A, ein interaktives Werkzeug für die Methode LITOS-A', Diplomarbeit, Institut für Informatik, J. Kepler Universität Linz, 1986.

[Färb87a] Färberböck, H., Wallmüller, E., 'LITOR-A, ein Werkzeug zur Anforderungs-définition und seine Auswirkungen auf die Software-Qualitätssicherung', in *Requirements Engineering '87*, Schmitz, Timm, Windfuhr (eds), GMD-Studie No. 121, 1987.

[Färb87b] Färberböck, H., Ludewig, J., Lichter, H., Matheis, H., Wallmüller, E., *Software-Entwicklung durch schrittweise Komplettierung*, RE' 87, Fachtagung der GI/GMD, 1987.

[Fish80] Fisher, D., *'Stoneman': Requirements for Ada Programming Support Environment*, US-DOD, 1980.

[Floy67] Floyd, R., 'Assigning Meanings to Programs', *Proc. of Symp. Appl. Math.*, Vol. 19, Am. Math. Soc., 1967, pp. 19−32.

[Floy84] Floyd, C., 'A Systematic Look at Prototyping', in *Approaches to Prototyping*, Springer, 1984.

[Fole84] Foley, J., Wallace, V., Chan, P., 'The Human Factors of Computer Graphics Interaction Techniques', *IEEE Computer Graphics Applications*, Nov. 1984, pp. 13−48.

[Fris88] Frisse, M., 'From Text to Hypertext', *Byte*, Oct. 1988, pp. 247−53.

[Früh87a] Frühauf, K., Ludewig, J., Sandmayr, H., *Software-Projektmanagement und -Qualitätssicherung*, vdf, Zürich, 1987.

[Früh87b] Frühauf, K., 'Konstruktive Maßnahmen in der Software-Qualitätssicherung', in *Software-Qualitätssicherung*, 1987, Tagungsband, SAQ, pp. 43−60.

[Gane82] Gane, T., Sarson, C., *System Analysis*, Prentice Hall, 1982.

[Garm85] Garmand, J., 'Data Systems for the Space Station and Beyond', AIAA Conference on Computers in Aerospace, 1985.

[Garv84] Garvin, D.A., 'What does Product Quality Really Mean?', *Sloan Management Review*, Fall, 1984, pp. 25−43.

[Gast81] Gast, D., Rommerskirch, W., Seitscheck, V., *Rahmenempfehlungen für die Qualitätssicherungs-Organisation*, Beuth, 1981.

[Geha86] Gehani, N., 'Tutorial: Unix Document Formatting and Typesetting', *IEEE Software*, Sept. 86, pp. 15−23.

[Gilb77] Gilb, T., *Software Metrics*, Whintrop, 1977.

[GMD84] Höcker, H., *et al.*, *Comparative Descriptions of Software Quality Measures*, GMD-Studie No. 81, 1984.

[GMO87] GMO, GUIDE: Dialog-Vorgehens- und -Methodensystem', *Einführunghandbuch*, June 1987.

[Gold83] Goldberg, A., Robson, D., *Smalltalk-80, the Language and its Implementation*, Addison-Wesley, 1983.

[Grad87] Grady, R.B., Caswell, D.L., *Software Metrics: Establishing a Company-Wide Program*, Prentice Hall, 1987.

[Grun80] Grunwald, W., Lilge, H., *Partizipative Führung*, UTB, 1980.

[Gust82] Gustafson, G., Kerr, R., 'Some Practical Experience with a Software Quality Assurance Program', *Comm. of the ACM*, Vol. 25, No. 1, 1982, pp. 4−12.

[Gutt77] Guttage, J., 'Abstract Data Types and the Development of Data Structures', *Comm. of the ACM*, Vol. 20, No. 6, 1977, pp. 396−405.

[Habe86] Habermann, A.N., Notkin, D., 'Gandalf: Software Development

Environments', *IEEE Transactions on Software Engineering*, SE-12, No. 12, 1986, pp. 1117–26.

[Hals77]   Halstead, M.H., *Elements of Software Science*, North-Holland, 1977.

[Hant76]   Hantler, S., King, J., 'An Introduction to Proving the Correctness of Programs', *Computing Surveys*, Vol. 8, No. 3, 1976, pp. 331–51.

[Haus84]   Hausen, Müllerbug, Sneed: *Software-Produktionsumgebungen*, R. Müller, 1984.

[Heid84]   Heidrich, W., 'Qualitätsplanung und -bewertung von Anwerdersoftware', *Proc. of COMPAS'84*, 1984, pp. 429–39.

[Hein76]   Heinrich, L.J., *Systemplanung*, Vols 1 and 2, Walter de Gruyter, 1976.

[Hein88]   Heinrich, L.J., 'Aufgaben und Methoden des Informationsmanagements: Einführung und Grundlagen', *HMD*, Vol. 142, 1988, pp. 3–26.

[Hell74]   Heller, K., Rosemann, B., *Planung und Auswertung empirischer Untersuchungen: Eine Einführung für Pädagogen, Psychologen und Soziologen*, Klett, 1974.

[Hoar69]   Hoare, C., 'An Axiomatic Basis for Computer Programming', *Comm. of the ACM*, Vol. 12, No. 10, 1969, pp. 576–84.

[Höft85]   Höft, D., Schaller, H., 'Software-Konfigurationsmanagement in großen Softwareprojekten', *Informatik-Spektrum*, Vol. 8, 1985, pp. 138–52.

[Hort88]   Horton, L., 'Tools are an Alternative to "Playing Computer"', *Software Magazine*, January 1988, pp. 58–67.

[Howa81]   Howar, J., 'What is Good Documentation?', *Byte*, March 1981, pp. 132–50.

[Howd77]   Howden, W.E., 'Symbolic Testing and the DISSECT Symbolic Evaluation System', *IEEE Transactions on Software Engineering*, SE-3, No. 4, 1977, pp. 266–78.

[Howd82]   Howden, W.E., 'Contemporary Software Development Environments', *Comm. of the ACM*, Vol. 25, No. 5, 1982, pp. 318–29.

[Huan81]   Huang, J., 'Experience with Use of Instrumentation Techniques in Software Testing', *Proc. of NSIA Nat. Conf. Software Tech. and Mgmt*, Oct. 1981, pp. D1–D10.

[Hüls75]   Hülst, D., *Erfahrung — Gültigkeit — Erkenntnis: Zum Verhältnis von soziologischer Empirie und Theorie*, Campus, 1975.

[IBM85]   IBM, *VIDOC: Einführungsbroschüre*, GE12-1632-0, 1985.

[IBM87a]   IBM, *Problem/Change Management Reference Card*, GC34-4045, 1987.

[IBM87b]   IBM-Laboratories Böblingen, *ASCOT: A Software Complexity Analysis Tool*, Product Assurance Dept 5787, June 1987.

[IEEE83]   IEEE Std 729-1983, *Glossary of Software Engineering Terminology*.

[IEEE86]   ANSI/IEEE Std 1012-1986, *Standard for Software Verification and Validation Plans*.

[IEEE88]   IEEE, *Guide to Software Configuration Management*, 1988.

[Itzf84]   Itzfeld, W., Schmidt, M., Timm, M., 'Spezifikation von Verfahren zur Validierung von Software-Qualitätsmaßen', *Angewandte Informatik*, Vol. 1, 1984, pp. 12–21.

[Itzf87]   Itzfeld, W., 'Einsatz von Software-Qualitätsmaßen in der Praxis und Konsequenzen für Forschung', in *Software-Metriken, Arbeitsgespräch der GI-Fachgruppe Software-Engineering*, March 1987, pp. 73–97.

[Ivie77]   Ivie, E., 'The Programmer's Workbench: A Machine for Software Development', *Comm. of the ACM*, Vol. 20, No. 10, 1977, pp. 746–53.

[Jack83]   Jackson, M.A., *System Development*, Prentice Hall, 1983.

[Jack85]   Jackson, M.A., *Principles of Program Design* (6th edn), Academic Press, 1985.

[Jägg88]   Jäggin, R., *et al.*, 'Aufgaben einer unabhängigen Software-Qualitässicherungsstelle', *SAQ-Bulletin-ASPQ*, Vol. 1, 1988, pp. 18−19.

[Jone85]   Jones, C., 'A Process-Integrated Approach to Defect Prevention', *IBM Systems Journal*, Vol. 24, No. 2, 1985, pp. 150−67.

[Jone86]   Jones, C., *Programming Productivity*, McGraw-Hill, 1986.

[Kafu87]   Kafura, D., Reddy, G., 'The Use of Software Complexity Metrics in Software Maintenance', *IEEE Transactions on Software Engineering*, SE-13, No. 3, 1987, pp. 335−43.

[Kell89]   Keller, R., *Prototypingorientierte Systemspezifikation: Konzepte, Methoden, Werkzeuge und Konsequenzen*, Verlag Dr Kovac, 1989.

[Kinc81]   Kincaid, J., *et al.*, 'Computer Readability Editing System', *IEEE Transactions on Professional Communication*, PC-24, No. 1, 1981, pp. 38−41.

[Knut84]   Knuth, D., 'Literate Programming', *The Computer Journal*, Vol. 27, No. 2, 1984, pp. 97−111.

[Kupp81]   Kupper, H., *Zur Kunst der Projektsteuerung*, Oldenbourg, 1981.

[Lai84]   Lai, H., 'Empfehlungen zur Konzeption einer Software-Entwicklungs-Produktivitäts-Strategie', in *Effizienzverbesserung in der Software-Entwicklung, Proc. of CW/CSE*, Fachtagung, München, 1984.

[Lans86]   Lansman, G., *Systems Development Productivity Improvement Methodology, Part 1: System Development*, May 1986, pp. 4−7.

[Lars75]   Larson, R., *Testplan and Testcase Inspection Specification*, IBM Tech. Rep. 21.585, 1975.

[Lebl84]   Leblang, D., Chase, R., 'Computer Aided Software Engineering in a Distributed Workstation Environment', in *SIGPLAN/SIGSOFT Symposium on Practical Software Development Environment ACM*, April 1984.

[Lehm80]   Lehman, M., 'Life Cycles and Laws of Software Evolution', *IEEE Proc.*, Vol. 68, 1980, pp. 1060−76.

[Lins89]   Lins, C., 'An Introduction to Literate Programming', *Structured Programming*, Vol. 2, 1989, pp. 5−10.

[Lumb82]   Lumbeck, H., Schubert, K.P., 'Qualitätssicherungssysteme für Software', in *Software-Qualitätssicherung*, H.M. Sneed, H.R. Wiehle (eds), Teubner 1982, pp. 67−86.

[Lyon87]   Lyons, T., Tedd, M., 'Recent Development in Tool Support Environments: CAIS and PCTE', *Ada User*, Vol. 8, 1987, pp. 65−78.

[Mart83]   Martin, J., McClure, C., *Software Maintenance*, Prentice Hall, 1983.

[Mart87]   Marty, R., Gamma, E., Weinand, A., *Objektorientierte Softwareentwicklung*, Tagungsband, Institut für Informatik, Universität Zürich, Oct. 1987.

[Masi88]   Masing, W. (ed.), *Handbuch der Qualitätssicherung* (2nd edn), Carl Hanser, 1988.

[Math87]   Matheis, H., *Software Engineering Datenbanken*, Techn. Bericht No. 71, ETH Zürich, Institut für Informatik, Jan. 1987.

[Mats87]   Matsumoto, Y., 'A Software Factory: An Overall Approach to Software Production', in *Software Reusability*, P. Freeman (ed.), IEEE, 1987.

[McCa76]   McCabe, T., 'A Complexity Measure', *IEEE Transactions on Software Engineering*, SE-2, No. 4, 1976, pp. 308−20.

[McCa77]   McCall, J.A., Richards, P.K., Walters, G.F., *Factors in Software Quality*, Vols I−III, Rome Air Development Centre, 1977.

[McCa85]   McCall, J.A., Herdon, M., Osborne, M., *Software Maintenance Management*, Nat. Bureau of Standards, NBS Publ. No. 500–129, Oct. 1985.

[McCl88]   McClure, C., 'The CASE for Structured Development', *PC Tech. Journal*, Aug. 1988, pp. 51–67.

[McGu79]   McGuffing, R., *et al.*, 'CADES: Software Engineering in Practice', *Proc. of 4th Int. Conf. on Software Engineering*, 1979, pp. 136–44.

[Mend83]   Mendis, K., 'Software Quality Assurance Staffing Problems', *ASQC Technical Conference Transactions*, 1983, pp. 108–12.

[Metz77]   Metzger, P., *Software-Projekte*, Carl Hanser, 1977.

[Mill72]   Mills, H., *On the Statistical Validation of Computer Programs*, IBM Report FSC72-6015, FSDI, 1972.

[Mill87]   Mills, H., Dyer, M., Linger, R., 'Cleanroom Software Engineering', *IEEE Software*, Sept. 1987, pp. 19–25.

[Mizu83]   Mizumo, Y., 'Software Quality Improvement', *IEEE Computer*, March 1983, pp. 66–72.

[MSP88]   MSP, "ManagerView", *Einführungshandbuch*, 1988.

[Müll82]   Müller, W., Köster, R., Trunk, M., *Duden: Fremdwörterbuch*, BI Dudenverlag, 1982.

[Müll89]   Müllerburg, M., 'Programmier- und Produktionsumgebungen: Grundlegende Konzepte', in *Online '89*, Tagungsband, K., Fähnrich (ed.), 1989.

[Muri84]   Murine, G., Carpenter, C., 'Measuring Software Product Quality', *Quality Progress*, Vol. 17, No. 5, 1984, pp. 16–20.

[Myer79]   Myers, G.J., *The Art of Software Testing*, Wiley & Sons, 1979.

[Myer87]   Myers, G.J., *Methodisches Testen von Programmen* (2nd edn), Oldenbourg 1987.

[Naur69]   Naur, P., Randell, B. (eds), *Software Engineering: A Report on a Conference sponsored by the NATO Science Committee*, NATO, 1969.

[Nenz83]   Nenz, H., 'Management der Software-Qualitätssicherung', *Softwaretechnik-Trends*, Vol. 3–1, 1983, pp. 19–37.

[Niev81]   Nievergelt, J., 'Der computergesteuerte Bildschirm: Mensch und Maschine im Dialog', *Output*, Vol. 9, 1981, pp. 31–6.

[Oldh83]   Oldham, G.R., Rotchford, N.L., 'Relationships Between Office Characteristics and Employee Reactions: A Study of the Physical Environment', *Administrative Science Quarterly*, Vol. 28, 1983, pp. 542–56.

[Osbo83]   Osborne, M., Martin, R., *Guidance of Software Maintenance*, Nat. Bureau of Standards, NBS Publ. No. 500-106, Dec. 1983.

[Öste88]   Österle, H., Gutzwiller, T., (eds), *Anleitung zu einer praxisorientierten Entwicklungsumgebung*, Vols. 1 and 2, AIT, 1988.

[Oste81]   Osterweil, L., 'Software Environment Research: Directions for the Next Five Years', *IEEE Computer*, April 1981, pp. 35–43.

[Pabs85]   Pabst, R., 'Die Zugänglichkeit von Software: Voraussetzung für Softwareprüfungen', in *Wirtschaftsgut Software*, R. Kölsch *et al.* (eds), Teubner, 1985, pp. 95–105.

[Parn79]   Parnas, D., 'Designing Software for Ease of Extension and Contraction', *IEEE Transactions on Software Engineering*, Vol. 2, 1979.

[Parn85]   Parnas, D., 'Active Design Reviews: Principles and Practices', *Proc. of 8th Int. Conf. on Software Engineering*, 1985.

[Paul80]   Paulus, P.B., 'Crowding', in *Psychology of Group Influence*, P.B. Paulus (ed.), Erlbaum, 1980, pp. 245–89.

[PCTE86]   PCTE, *A Basic for a Portable Common Tool Environment Functional Specification*, Vol. 1 (4th edn), 1986.

[Pirs74]   Pirsig, R., *Zen and the Art of Motorcycle Maintenance*, William Morrow & Co., 1974.

[Pomb87a]   Pomberger, G., *Softwaretechnik und Modula-2* (2nd edn), Hanser, 1987.

[Pomb87b]   Pomberger, G., Wallmüller, E., 'Ada und Modula-2: ein Vergleich', *Informatik-Spektrum*, Vol. 10, No. 4, 1987.

[Pomb88]   Pomberger, G., 'Integration von prototyping in Software-Entwicklungsumgebungen', in *Anleitung zur einer praxisorientierten Software-Entwicklungsumgebung*, Vol. 1, H. Österle (ed.), AIT, 1988, pp. 101−16.

[Pomb89]   Pomberger, G., 'Methodik der Software-Entwicklung', in *Handbuch der Wirtschaftsinformatik*, Kurbel, Strunz (eds), Pöschl-Verlag, 1989.

[Pres87]   Pressman, R., *Software Engineering: A Practioner's Approach*, McGraw-Hill, 1987.

[Pres88]   Pressman, R., *Making Software Engineering Happen*, Prentice Hall, 1988.

[Radi85]   Radice, R., Roth, N., O'Hara, A., Ciarfella, W., 'A Programming Process Architecture', *IBM Systems Journal*, Vol. 24, No. 2, 1985, pp. 79−90.

[Rama82]   Ramamoorthy, C.V., Dong, S.T., Ganesch, S.L., Jen, C.-H., Tsai, W.-T., 'Techniques in Software Quality Assurance', in *Software-Qualitätssicherung*, H.M. Sneed, H.R. Wiehle (eds), Teubner, 1982, pp. 11−34.

[Rech86]   Rechenberg, P., 'Ein neues Maß für die softwaretechnische Komplexität von Programmen', *Informatik in Forschung und Entwicklung*, Vol. 1, No. 1, 1986.

[Reif85]   Reifer, D., *State of the Art in Software Quality Management*, Seminarunterlagen, Reifer Consultants, NY, 1985.

[Remm87]   Remmele, W., Pomberger, G., 'Prototyping-orientierte Software-Entwicklung', *Information Management*, Vol. 2, 1987, pp. 28−35.

[Remu82]   Remus, H., *Productivity in System Programming*, IBM Tech. Rep. 03.191, May 1982.

[Roch75]   Rochkind, M., 'The Source Code Control System', *IEEE Transactions on Software Engineering*, Dec. 1975.

[Rock89]   Rock-Evans, R., *CASE Analyst Workbenches: A Detailed Product Evaluation*, Ovum Ltd, 1989.

[Ross75]   Ross, D., 'Software Engineering: Process, Principles and Goals', *IEEE Computer*, Vol. 8, No. 5, 1975, pp. 17−27.

[Ross77]   Ross, D., 'Structured Analysis (SA): A Language for Communication Ideas', *IEEE Transactions on Software Engineering*, SE-3, No. 1, 1977, pp. 16−34.

[Roth87]   Roth, C., 'Ein Verfahren zur Quantifizierung der Strukturiertheit von Software', in *'Software-Metriken': Arbeitsgespräch der Fachgruppe Software Engineering*, H. Fromm, A. Steinhoff (eds), GI, 1987, pp. 56−72.

[Royc70]   Royce, W., 'Managing the Development of Large Software Systems: Concepts and Techniques', *Proc. of WESCON*, 1970.

[Rube68]   Rubey, R., Hartwick, R., 'Quantitative measurement of program quality', *Proc. of the ACM National Conference*, 1968, pp. 671−7.

[Sanz87]   Sanz, I., 'Standards for Quality and Quality Assurance in Software Industry Today', in *European Quality Control*, Tagungsband, München, June 1987.

[SAQ87]   Schweizerische Arbeitsgemeinschaft für Qualitätsförderung, *SAQ-Empfehlung für Anforderungen an Qualitätssicherungssysteme von Software-Erstellern*, SAQ 222, 1987.

[SAQ88a]   'SAQ — Arbeitsteam 2 Checkliste für Anforderungsspezifikationen', Internes

Arbeitspapier, Oct. 1988.

[SAQ88b]   SAQ, 'Leitfaden zur SAQ-Empfehlung 222 für Anforderungen an Qualitätssicherungssysteme von Software-Erstellern', SAQ/AT-2, Arbeitspapier, 1988.

[SAQ89]   SAQ, 'Leitfaden zur SN-ISO-Normenreihe 9000', 1989.

[SBG88]   SBG Incident Reporting, *Benutzerhandbuch*, June 1988.

[Schä84]   Schäfer, H., 'Metrics for Maintenance Management', *Proc. of COMPAS'84*, 1984.

[Schm82]   Schmitz, P., Bons, H., van Megen, R., *Software-Qualitätssicherung: Testen im Software-Lebenszyklus*, Vieweg, 1982.

[Schm84]   Schmid, W., 'Die Güte- und Prüfbestimmungen der Gütegemeinschaft Software', *Proc. of COMPAS'84*, 1984, pp. 489−506.

[Schm85]   Schmidt, M., 'Ein Komplexitätsmaß basierend auf Entscheidung und Verschachtelung', in *Technische Zuverlässigkeit*, Vol. 13, Fachtagung, Nürnberg, VDE-Verlag, 1985, pp. 194−9.

[Schm87]   Schmidt, M., 'Über das Messen und Bewerten von Software-Qualität Maß und Metrik', in *'Software-Metriken': Arbeitsgespräch der Fachgruppe Software Engineering*, H. Fromm, A. Steinhoff (eds), GI, 1987.

[Schn87]   Schneidewind, N., 'The State of Software Maintenance', *IEEE Transactions on Software Engineering*, SE-13, No. 3, 1987, pp. 303−10.

[Schn88]   Schnurer, K., 'Programminspektionen', *Informatik-Spektrum*, Vol. 11, 1988, pp. 312−22.

[Schö87]   Schönpflug, W., Wittstock, M. (eds), *Software-Ergonomie '87*, Teubner, 1987.

[Schu87]   Schulmeyer, G., 'Standardization of Software Quality Assurance', in *Handbook of Software Quality Assurance*, G. Schulmeyer, J. McManus (eds), Van Nostrand Reinhold, 1987.

[Schw84]   Schweiggert, F., *Software-Qualitätsmerkmale*, Softwaretest e.V., Aug. 1984.

[Schw85]   Schweiggert, F., Schoitsch, E., *Qualitätssicherung in der Software*, OCG-Computerakademie, Seminarunterlagen, 1985.

[Scot88]   Scott, T., Farley, D., 'Slashing Software Maintenance Costs', *Business Software Review*, March 1988, pp. 35−43.

[Seew82]   Seewg, *A Software Engineering Environment for the Navy*, Report of the NAVMAT Software Engineering Environment Working Group. 31.3.1982.

[Shne85]   Shneiderman, B., et al., 'Display Strategies for Program Browsing', in *Conference on Software Maintenance*, N. Zvegintzov (ed.), IEEE, 1985, pp. 136−43.

[Sieg84]   Siegmund, A., 'Die richtige Einführungsstrategie: der Schlüssel zum erfolgreichen Einsatz neuer Methoden und Werkzeuge', *Proc. of COMPAS'84*, 1984, pp. 161−90.

[Siev85]   Sievert, G., Mizell, T., 'Specification-Based Software Engineeering with TAGS', *IEEE Computer*, Vol. 18, No. 4, 1985, pp. 41−8.

[Smit70]   Smith, E., Kincaid, J., 'Derivation and Validation of the Automated Readability Index for Use with Technical Materials', *Human Factors*, Vol. 12, No. 5, 1970, pp. 457−64.

[Smith80] Smith, C.P., *A Software Science Analysis of IBM Programming Products*, IBM Tech. Rep. 03.081, Jan. 1980.

[Snee83]   Sneed, H.M., 'Sinn, Zweck und Mittel der dynamischen Analyse', *Angewandte Informatik*, Vol. 8, 1983, pp. 321−7.

[Snee88a]   Sneed, H.M., *Software-Qualitätssicherung*, R. Müller, 1988.

[Snee88b]   Sneed, H.M., 'Software-Sanierung', in [Balz88].

[Soft84]   Softlab, *Benutzerhandbuch des MAESTRO-Systems*, 1984.

[Somm85]   Sommerville, I., *Software Engineering* (2nd edn), Addison-Wesley, 1985.

[Stad88]   Stadler, J., 'Qualität und Betriebskultur: Erfahrungen aus einem Forschungsprojekt', *SAQ-Bulletin*, ASPQ 1, 1988, pp. 5–7.

[STAR86]   *DOD Preliminary Systems Specification*, Department of Defense STARS Joint Project Office, Jan. 1986.

[Stro86]   Stroustrup, B., *The C++ Programming Language*, Addison-Wesley, 1986.

[Sund78]   Sundstrom, E., 'Crowding as a Sequential Process: Review of Research on the Effects of Population Density on Humans', in *Human Responses to Crowding*, A. Baum, Y. Epstein (eds), Erlbaum, pp. 31–116.

[Sund80]   Sundstrom, E., Burt, R.E., Kamp, D., 'Privacy at Work: Architectural Correlates of Job Satisfaction and Job Performance', *Academy of Management Journal*, Vol. 23, 1980, pp. 101–17.

[Taus77]   Tausworthe, R., *Standardized Development of Computer Software*, Jet Propulsion Laboratory, Pasadena, 1977.

[Teic77]   Teichrow, D., Hershey, E., PSL/PSA, 'A Computer Aided Technique for Structured Documentation and Analysis of Information Processing Systems', *IEEE Transactions on Software Engineering*, SE-3, No. 1, 1977, pp. 41–8.

[Thay81]   Thayer, R.H., *et al.*, 'Major Issues in Software Engineering Project Management', *IEEE Transactions on Software Engineering*, SE-7, No. 4, 1981, pp. 333–42.

[Thur88]   Thurner, R., *Technologie der Software-Wartung*, in [Balz88].

[Tich82]   Tichy, W., 'Design, Implementation, Evaluation of a Revision Control System', in *Proc. of 6th Int. Conf. on Software Engineering*, Sept. 1982, pp. 58–67.

[Tich88]   Tichy, W., 'Tools for Software Configuration Management', *Softwaretechnik-Trends*, Vol. 8–1, 1988, pp. 51–70.

[Vosb84]   Vosburgh, J., *et al.*, 'Productivity factors and programming environments', *Proc. of Int. Conf. on Software Engineering*, 1984, pp. 143–52.

[Wald81]   Walden, T.A., Forsyth, D.R., 'Close Encounters of the Stressful Kind: Affective, Physiological, and Behavioral Reactions to the Experience of Crowding', *Journal of Nonverbal Behavior*, Vol. 6, 1981, pp. 46–64.

[Wall84]   Wallmüller, E., 'Erfahrungen mit einem softwaretechnischen Verfahrens- und Methodenmix bei einem universitären Projektpraktikum', *Angewandte Informatik*, Vol. 1, 1984, pp. 22–6.

[Wall85]   Wallmüller, E., Färberböck, H., 'LITOS-A und LITOR-A: eine Methode und ein Werkzeug für die Analyse- und Definitionsphase von Software-Projekten', in *Tagungsband GI/OCG/ÖGI-Jahrestagung 1985*, Springer, 1985, pp. 182–92.

[Wall87a]   Wallmüller, E., 'Aufbau einer Software-Qualitätssicherung in einer industriellen Umgebung', *Informationstechnik*, Vol. 2, 1987, pp. 103–7.

[Wall87b]   Wallmüller, E., 'Beeinflussung der Software-Qualität durch Einsatz eines Werkzeugs zur Anforderungsdefinition' in *'Software-Metriken': Arbeitsgespräch der Fachgruppe Software Engineering*, H. Fromm, A. Steinhoff (eds.), GI, 1987, pp. 163–75.

[Wall88]   Wallmüller, E., 'Fehler- und Ursachenanalyse mit EIR', SBG, Interne technische Mitteilung, March 1988.

[Wals77]   Walston, C., Felix, C., 'A Method of Programming Measurement and Estimation', *IBM Systems Journal*, Vol. 16, No. 1, 1977.

[Wehr88]   Wehrum, R., 'Ada-Entwicklungsumgebung: Stand, Entwicklung und Relevanz', in [Öste88].

[Wein74]   Weinberg, G.M., Schulman, E.L., 'Goals and Performance in Computer Programming', *Human Factors*, Vol. 16, No. 1, 1974, pp. 70–7.

[Wein84]   Weinberg, G.M., Freedman, D.P., 'Reviews, Walkthroughs, and Inspections', *IEEE Transactions on Software Engineering*, SE-10, No. 1, 1984, pp. 68–72.

[Wien84]   Wiener, R., Sincovec, R., *Software Engineering with Modula-2 and Ada*, Wiley & Sons, 1984.

[Will85]   Willmer, H., *Systematische Software-Qualitätssicherung anhand von Qualitäts- und Produktmodellen*, Springer, 1985.

[Wirt80]   Wirth, N., *Modula-2*; Bericht No. 36, Institut für Informatik, ETH Zürich, 1980.

[Wolf85]   Wolf, P.F., Schmid, H.A., 'Zur Wiederverwendbarkeit von Software', in *Methoden und Werkzeuge zur Entwicklung von Programmsystemen*, W.E. Proebster *et al.*, (eds.), Oldenbourg, 1985.

[Yau85]   Yau, S., Colofello, J., 'Design Stability Measures for Software Maintenance', *IEEE Transactions on Software Engineering*, SE-11, 1985, pp. 849–56.

[Your78]   Yourdon, E., Constantine, L., *Structured Design* (2nd edn), Yourdon Press, 1978.

[Zill74]   Zilles, S., *Algebraic Specification of Data Types*, Project MAC, Progress Report 11, MIT, 1974.

[Zill82]   Zilliken, P., *Qualitätssicherung eines Software-Produktes*, VDI-Bericht No. 460, 1982, pp. 91–6.

[Zinc84]   Zincke, G., 'CAS System LITOR: Konzept und Realisierung einer Arbeitsumgebung für den interaktiven graphisch unterstützten Software-Entwurf', in *Programmierumgebungen und Compiler*, H. Morgenbrod, W., Sammer (eds), Teubner Berichte No. 18, 1984, pp. 225–47.

[Zopf88]   Zopf, S., 'Praktisches Vorgehen zur Sicherung definierter Software-Qualitätsziele', *Tagungsband zur 3. Softwaretest-Fachtagung*, 1988.

[Zuse85]   Zuse, H., 'Meßtheoretische Analyse von statischen Softwarekomplexitätsmaßen', Dissertation, TU Berlin, 1985.

Index